P9-APM-881

The Festive State

The Festive State

RACE, ETHNICITY, AND
NATIONALISM AS CULTURAL
PERFORMANCE

DAVID M. GUSS

UNIVERSITY OF CALIFORNIA PRESS
Berkeley   Los Angeles   London

Frontispiece: Logo from the Festival of Tradition program, 1948.
Courtesy of the FUNDEF Archives.

University of California Press
Berkeley and Los Angeles, California
University of California Press, Ltd.
London, England
© 2000 by the Regents of the University of California
Library of Congress Cataloging-in-Publication Data

Guss, David M.
The festive state : race, ethnicity, and nationalism as cultural performance / David M. Guss.
    p.   cm.
Includes bibliographical references and index.
ISBN 0-520-20289-9 (cloth : alk. paper) — ISBN 0-520-22331-4 (pbk. :
alk. paper)
1. Venezuela—Social conditions.   2. Popular culture—Venezuela.
3. Festivals—Latin America—Venezuela.   4. Cultural performance—
Latin America—Venezuela.   5. Mestizos—Venezuela.   I. Title.
HN363.5.G87   2000
306′.0987—dc21   99-056890
                                                                        CIP

Manufactured in Canada
9 8 7 6 5 4 3 2 1 0
10 9 8 7 6 5 4 3 2 1
The paper used in this publication meets the minimum requirements of
ANSI / NISO Z39 0.48-1992 (R 1997) (Permanence of Paper). ∞

To those before and after—
To my father, Harry A. Guss, 1915–1991,
& to my daughter, Chloe Indigo

Contents

Illustrations

Acknowledgments

Benito Yrady led me into this project by introducing me to the village of Curiepe between visits to the Yekuana in the early 1980s. It was with him as well that I first attended the Day of the Monkey, met Chilo Rojas, and got splattered with blue paint. Few guides to popular culture are as able and knowledgeable as Benito, and I have been fortunate to have him as a friend throughout. Curiepe is a town that defines hospitality, and there are many in it who not only aided my work but also opened their homes to me. I am grateful to each of them but above all to Angel Lucci, Tomás and Norris Ponce, Isabel Cobos, and Javier Rodríguez. Jesús "Chucho" García, Fernando Yvoski, and Alfredo Chacón also helped navigate the rich world of Barloventeño culture.

In Caracas, Carlos García, among others, helped introduce me to another world, that of urban popular culture. He also encouraged me to begin investigating the Bigott Foundation. Members of the Clavija, Tulio Hernández, María Teresa López, and Bigott director Antonio López

Ortega all contributed to making this study possible. I am especially indebted to José Pérez of the Popular Culture Workshops, a wonderful teacher, friend, and musician. He shared with me not only his work at the *talleres* but also his great insight into the life of *Tamunangue*.

But my real introduction to Tamunangue, as well as to the community of Sanare, was through my dear friend Norma González. In addition to sharing her enormous experience, she also aided in the transcription of various tapes, particularly those of José Humberto Castillo, "El Caiman," that inimitable storyteller to whom I am also very grateful. While in Sanare, I also worked with Lotte Darsø of Denmark. Her many insights and years of support have been invaluable.

My work in different communities over a number of years has been possible only through the generous support of various foundations and institutes. They have included the Wenner-Gren Foundation for Anthropological Research, the Mellon Foundation, the National Endowment for the Humanities, the Social Science Research Council, the Rockefeller Foundation for the Humanities, the Latin American Studies Center at the University of Maryland, the Center for the Study of World Religions and the Committee on Folklore and Mythology at Harvard University, and, finally, Tufts University, from which I received two Faculty Research Awards.

I am also grateful to the *American Ethnologist, Public Culture,* and the Latin American Studies Center Series at the University of Maryland, where versions of three chapters of this book previously appeared. One of them was awarded the Joseph T. Criscenti Best Article Prize for 1996; another, Honorable Mention, the Joseph T. Criscenti Best Article Prize for 1994. I am grateful to the New England Council of Latin American Studies for both of these honors.

Grateful acknowledgment is also made to Miguel Betancourt of Quito, who so generously provided his painting *Fiesta 1989–1990* for the cover; to the archives of the Foundation for Ethnomusicology and Folklore (FUNDEF) for graphic materials from the 1948 Festival of Tradition; to the Bigott Foundation for concert and workshop photographs as well as the image of its train logo; and to María Magdalena Colmenárez for Tamunangue photographs from her private collection. I am equally grateful to John Sposato for his wonderful design suggestions and for his help in producing the map. My many thanks, too, to Peg Bruno, who so carefully oversaw the final preparation of the manuscript.

Numerous friends and colleagues read various drafts of this book and contributed valuable suggestions and ideas throughout. I am particularly grateful to Jean-Paul Dumont, Ken George, Richard Handler, Catherine Howard, Peter Hulme, Lisa Markowitz, David Roche, Rosalind Shaw, Charles Stewart, Lawrence Sullivan, Kate Wheeler, and Norm Whitten. It was Yolanda Salas, however, who made the greatest contribution. Her insight, wisdom, and wit concerning every aspect of Venezuelan culture have enriched this entire book, and without her endless cheer and generosity, it might not have been written.

Chapter 1 Variations on a Venezuelan Quartet

Cuando hay santo nuevo
los viejos no hacen milagros.

When there's a new saint
old ones don't make miracles.

VENEZUELAN SAYING

Catuaro is a village in the eastern hills of Venezuela, not far from the Gulf of Cariaco. It is so small that for many years its ancient church was shuttered and there was not even a priest to hold mass. For much of this time an Indian woman, referred to as "La Padra," instead of "Padre" or "Father," conducted services. Only for Holy Week was the church opened and the various saints taken out and carried in long processions through the town. People would come from all over then, descending from their isolated homes in the mountains to pay *promesas* made to individual saints during the year. For the men, these "promises" meant hoisting onto their shoulders huge platforms with the figure of a saint on top. Powerful attachments formed between the bearers and the saints, attachments filled with deep love and emotion. But the greatest devotion was claimed to be that of the men who carried La Dolorosa, the

munity's reality regardless of how isolated it appeared to be. Whether it was the arrival of tourists, the transmission of television and radio, the demands of party politics, or the discovery of oil, what were once called "local traditions" were now embroiled in a much greater flow of national and global interests. At its worst, as in San Francisco de Guarapiche, these concerns could lead to a town's complete destruction. But in most instances the consequences have been less severe, and, as in Catuaro, people have found ways to negotiate and discuss them. For the anthropologist, the challenge has been to discover new strategies with which to present this increasing collision between the local, the national, and the global, between the many forms of cultural difference that now seem to converge at every point. It is this challenge of finding a way in which to write about these transformed cultural landscapes that is at the very heart of this book. And it is festive behavior, the point of greatest convergence and resistance, that I take as my point of departure.

THE POPULAR TERRAIN

Until recently, anthropologists and folklorists have ignored the pluralistic nature of festive forms, preferring to characterize them as the uniform expression of a collective consciousness.[1] The origins of this tendency can be traced to the work of Durkheim, along with that of the functionalists upon whom he had so much influence. But this only provides a partial explanation. For although functionalists such as Malinowski and Radcliffe-Brown were determined to deny the importance of historical consciousness among the peoples they studied, the fact remains that very little historical information has been provided in the analyses of most ritual and festive traditions. With the absence of such time depth (often the consequence of single viewings), it has been difficult to present alternatives to the belief that such rites are simply mechanisms for the maintenance of "social solidarity" (Radcliffe-Brown 1965: 164). And yet, the introduction of history has not automatically reversed such tendencies. Traditions said to have been molded by the demands of small, bounded communities, where orality and an imaginary lack of contact were believed to dominate, were often seen as victims of increased literacy and other technological innovations. In fact, it was the need to rescue these "disappearing worlds" from the onslaught of history that gave anthropology its initial sense of urgency and mission. Coexistence simply did not seem possible. And if modernization permitted any vestiges of this premarket form of behavior to exist, it would be that relegated to the museum, or to state-sponsored performances orchestrated to reinforce a new national solidarity.

Fortunately, alternatives to this moribund vision of a contaminated primitive paradise are now starting to appear. In concepts such as "hybridity" (García Canclini 1990, 1995), "creolization" (Hannerz 1992), and "public culture" (Appadurai and Breckenridge 1988, 1992), forms of behavior previously condemned to immediate extinction once released from the airtight environments said to have produced them are now being granted new and even more complex lives. Instead of simply dissolving into a market-driven global culturescape, these forms may actually enlarge their semantic fields. The expanded audiences and contexts created by such forces as urbanization, tourism, and new technology, to name but three, may multiply rather than reduce the range of meanings suggested by these events. As James Clifford writes:

> New dimensions of authenticity (cultural, personal, artistic) are making themselves felt, definitions no longer centered on a salvaged past. Rather, authenticity is reconceived as hybrid, creative activity in a local present-becoming-future. Non-western cultural and artistic works are implicated by an interconnected world cultural system without necessarily being swamped by it. Local structures produce *histories* rather than simply yielding to *History*. (1987: 126)

In Latin America, various scholars have addressed this particular process of modernization, in which the traditional or popular has not been eliminated but rather reformulated into new social and structural relations. William Rowe and Vivian Schelling even write of an "alternative modernity, where modern industrial technology comes together with magic" (1991: 105). Whether or not this is always the case, a "rearticulation of tradition" (Yúdice 1992: 18) has certainly been observed, in which expressive forms once thought to be limited to small rural, subsistence communities are both adapting and thriving in radically different circumstances. Rowe and Schelling locate the beginning of this process with the arrival of the Spaniards, claiming that "the concepts of reconversion, resignification and resemanticization are particularly appropriate to popular culture as ways of handling the constant refashioning of cultural signs which keeps alive the sites of the popular and prevents them from being wholly absorbed into the dominant power structures" (1991: 11). But it is in the work of Néstor García Canclini that this process is most carefully examined.

An Argentine trained in philosophy who now works as an anthropologist in Mexico, García Canclini has attempted to answer in his numerous works why it is that traditional forms of expressive behavior have expanded rather than disappeared under the pressures of modernization in Latin America. His preoccupation began with a recognition that such forms, whether artisanal or festive, were consistently defined "in opposition to modernity" and hence were incompatible with the economic forms of organization it imposes (1988: 484). And yet, evidence demonstrates that traditional production did not collapse in the face of widespread social and economic change but inserted itself into new market and communication systems. While García Canclini offers various market-inspired explanations for this seemingly contradictory phenomenon, he nevertheless insists that it is not a one-way street but rather a space of contestation in which local and global continue to struggle for dominance.[2] As a result, García Canclini claims, they are "doubly enrolled" in two systems of cultural production: *historical* (a process that gives identity to ethnic groups) and *structural* (within the present logic of dependent capitalism)" (1988: 486; 1993: 45).

In order to make sense of the various contradictions caused by such "double enrollment," García Canclini develops an analysis that does not define popular culture by either its origin or its content but as "a system of production" (1993: 11). Recalling the work of Raymond Williams (1977, 1980) and Janet Wolff (1984), among others, he demonstrates how this system consists of production, circulation, and consumption and shows how changes in any one of these three elements may lead to a significant shift in both reception and meaning.

The brilliance of García Canclini's analysis is that it undermines the Western preoccupation with issues of authenticity and tradition, preferring instead to see them as part of a continually changing interplay of political, economic, and historical forces. While traditional forms characteristically find themselves in an asymmetrical relation to the new structures of power created by these changes, their expressive importance is not necessarily diminished. In fact, as both the state and private media solidify their control over official forms of communication, that of the popular may actually become more important. This does not mean, however, that the popular should be seen as the exclusive domain of resistance and protest. As the examples in this book illustrate, these forms will always be threatened with appropriation and commodification. Nevertheless, the more that special corporate and political interests dominate the means of cultural production, the more that popular forms will be relied upon to express what otherwise has no outlet.[3] And yet, the very popularity of these forms—the fact that they mobilize so many potential voters, consumers, and protesters—makes them too valuable to be left to the people alone. Instead they will become increasingly contested or, as Stuart Hall claimed, cultural "battlefields" (1981: 237).

This view of the popular, particularly as it is constellated in festivals, is far different from the one I expected to find when I began to seriously observe them in 1989. Like many, I believed that popular culture, and its corollary folklore, were being rapidly devoured by a market hungry for new products and consumers and a central government in need of unifying symbols. My first visits during the years prior had led me to this conclusion as I saw evidence of commercial paraphernalia displayed everywhere—the drummers wearing official T-shirts inscribed with the names of beers, the streets hung with banners advertising cigarettes and rum, the busloads of tourists, the postfestival parties featuring imported salsa and rock bands. Then there was the presence of the government and the various political parties, which regularly used such events to promote causes or gain support. But as I began to observe more closely, I realized that beneath these dissonant intrusions were many new local forms struggling to emerge. The process was not simply a one-way street in which the center inevitably consumed the periphery. Rather, it was filled with ambiguity and contradiction, with the popular and the elite constantly shifting places. Meaning, it became clear, was not something that simply resided in an ideal model (or "text") waiting to be released. It was something that was created with each performance, and to understand it meant comprehending the entire context in which it was produced. It also meant recognizing that this context was continually changing and that festivals were being readily deployed to meet these changes.

CULTURAL PERFORMANCE
AND THE PRODUCTION OF MEANING

An important strategy for relocating festive practice in the sociopolitical reality in which it occurs has been to view it as cultural performance. The term, which Milton Singer introduced while working in India in the 1950s, was applied to a range of clearly framed occasions, such as weddings, festivals, dances, concerts, recitations, and even devotional movies. Employing this category was a way for Singer to organize the overwhelming diversity of Indian experience while revealing how Indians themselves conceptualized it. As Singer explained:

> Indians, and perhaps all peoples, think of their culture as encapsulated in such discrete performances, which they can exhibit to outsiders as well as to themselves. For the outsider these can conveniently be taken as the most concrete observable units of the cultural structure, for each performance has a definitely limited time span, a beginning and end, an organized program of activity, a set of performers, an audience, and a place and occasion of performance. (1959: xiii)

Equally important to Singer was the way in which these cultural performances allowed him to grapple with the complex relation between the innumerable local, indigenous forms, or "Little Traditions," and an elusive, overarching national one, "the Great Tradition" (1959, 1972).

Although sensitive to the way in which these traditions interacted and co-opted one another, Singer was aware of the need to historicize his analysis even more.

A study that did succeed in exploring the full historical contingency of cultural performance was the pioneering work of Abner Cohen (1980, 1993). By looking at the development of London's Notting Hill Carnival from its inception in 1965, Cohen was able to overcome the limited time depth that has plagued most studies of ritual behavior. Identifying his approach as a "dramaturgical" one, he shows how the carnival has responded to various socioeconomic changes, taking on new meanings with each performance. Although the celebration, like all symbolic systems, is relentlessly multivocal and therefore "irreducible" to any one interpretation, he nevertheless argues that certain motivations and ideas emerge to dominate different phases.[4] As a result, there is no single analysis that will apply to all performances of the carnival. As Cohen states: "It raise[s] the question of whether popular culture is an 'opium of the masses', inspired by the ruling classes as part of the dominant culture, whether it is a counter culture, an ideology of resistance and opposition, or whether it is a contested ideological terrain" (1993: 134).

In the end, it is all of these things at different times. Yet to understand exactly which it is at any given moment demands that the carnival be understood as an historical creation performed by actors who often have competing interests. By applying a "dramaturgical approach," Cohen avoided identifying the Notting Hill Carnival as the manifestation of a set of transcendental values and instead focused on the way meaning was produced through individual performance.

From studies such as those of Singer and Cohen, an outline of what cultural performance is quickly starts to emerge, and it might be useful before going any further to consider what at least four key elements of it are. The first, as noted by Singer, is that the performances are clearly framed events set off from what might be considered normative, everyday reality. While Erving Goffman has provided invaluable insights into how these performances are "framed," "keyed," and "bracketed" (1974), it is in the work of Victor Turner that the limits of this terrain are most thoroughly mapped.[5] Through his discussions of ritual process and social drama, Turner has shown how both "separation" and "breach" establish a space in which intense social transformation can occur (1969, 1974). One should not, however, mistake this spatial and temporal bounding for an exclusive, hermetically sealed world, particularly as new forms of mediation continue to redefine its borders. In fact, it is the very porousness of these frames that has made such cultural performances, whether they be festivals, fairs, or other forms, so attractive as sites of investigation. As Turner himself recognized: "What was once considered 'contaminated,' 'promiscuous,' 'impure' is becoming the focus of postmodern analytical attention" (1986: 77; see also Manning 1983: 4).

In addition to being set apart and framed, cultural performances are important dramatizations that enable participants to understand, criticize, and even change the worlds in which they live. And it is without doubt this reflexive quality that has been the most appreciated aspect of cultural performance. The fact that these public displays provide forums in which communities can reflect upon their own realities has meant that both anthropologists and participants attend to them with special interest: "They are cultural forms about culture, social forms about society, in which the central meanings and values of a group are embodied, acted out, and laid open to examination and interpretation in symbolic form, both by members of that group and by the ethnographer" (Bauman 1986: 133).

And yet, as the question of "group" becomes more problematized, so too will the issue of interpretation. Or put another way, whose reality is it that is being reflected? As such, cultural performances will remain both contentious and ambiguous, and while the basic structure of an event may be repeated, enough changes will be implemented so that its meaning is redirected. The same form, therefore, may be used to articulate a number of different ideas and over time can easily oscillate between religious devotion, ethnic solidarity, political resistance, national identity, and even commercial spectacle.

This is precisely what David Cahill (1996) and others have found in their exhaustive studies of the history of Corpus Christi in Peru. Falling as it did close to both the solstice (Inti Raymi) and a native harvest festival, this holiday proved a useful tool in the Spanish co-optation of local religions. Yet indigenous peoples found it equally useful for the subversive display of ethnic identity and repressed beliefs, particularly once all other native forms of dance were outlawed. And even though both church and Crown tried to eradicate any signs of apostasy, indigenous peoples eventually subsumed the festival into the newly created Qoyllur Rit'i celebration, which in time became Peru's greatest expression of native devotion.[6] Today, more than 400 years after its first appearance in the Andes, Corpus Christi is still a semiotic battlefield where, as Cahill notes, there is "so much overlap that it is often unclear what is 'popular' and what is 'elite' and who is appropriating whom" (1996: 101).

Similar examples could also be summoned from other sources, many closer to home, in which festive forms have become part of local histories, reflecting both their antagonisms and their contradictions. Nevertheless, while the massive colonization of one people by another is by no means a necessary ingredient, the example of Corpus Christi clearly illustrates what might be identified as cultural performance's third essential feature—the fact that it is a profoundly discursive form of behavior. Actors use these events to argue and debate, to challenge and negotiate. Thus, rather than thinking of cultural performances as simply "texts," to be read and interpreted, a discursive approach recognizes that they are dialogical and even polyphonic. They are fields of action in which both dominant and oppressed are able to dramatize competing claims or, as Jeremy Boissevain states, "duel with rituals" (1992: 3).

This discursiveness has only increased as local forms become more entangled within national and global debates. Suddenly, television and other forms of media have the potential of making every citizen a participant if not an "authority." To understand this "crosstalk" (Kelly 1990: 65) now demands a certain binocularity as each tradition leads a double life, that within its own community and that beyond. But separating them may be impossible, as the recent example of the Saint Patrick's Day Parade in South Boston demonstrates. After gay and lesbian activists were refused permission to march in the 1992 New York version of this event, a support group formed in Boston and applied for the right to participate, which was rejected by parade organizers. But a state court reversed this decision, claiming that their First Amendment rights of expression were being violated. Although only twenty-five members of the gay and lesbian coalition (GLIB) were permitted to march, the parade was covered by media from around the world. Eventually, in 1995, after several trials, a parade cancellation, and a veterans' protest, the U.S. Supreme Court overturned the Massachusetts decision and permitted the organizers to ban their participation. The parade belonged to the sponsors, the Court held, and it was a violation of their freedom of speech to force them to express something they did not wish to. For the Allied War Veterans who ran the parade, this meant expressing "traditional Catholic family values," along with pride in their Irish heritage and community (Guss 1996a; Walkowski and Connolly 1996). GLIB, on the other hand, had wished to redefine that community as well as to expand the rights of homosexuals. The choice of the parade as a medium to do so was a brilliant strategy that had enabled them to communicate not only with the participants in the event but also with the millions of viewers and readers throughout the world who followed them as they wound their way through the streets of Boston to the Supreme Court.

The example of the Saint Patrick's Day Parade illustrates how public celebrations may serve as discursive events challenging notions of family, community, and ethnicity. By insisting on their inclusion, Irish American gays and lesbians were forcing other marchers to recognize that they too were part of the civic body being celebrated. The fact, however, that the event was mediated by so many additional forms of communication, including the courts, television, and newsprint, permitted many beyond the immediate community to also participate in this discourse. Yet for most the question was not the enchoric one of who belonged in South Boston but a growing national one over issues of sexuality and civil rights. In both instances, whether experiencing the event directly or as mediated through another source, the parade demonstrates cultural performance's fourth key element—the ability to produce new meanings and relations. Although this idea is obviously related to notions of reflexivity and discursiveness, it underlines the important fact that these performances are actively engaged in cultural production. As John MacAloon notes, "Performance is constitutive of social experience and not something merely additive or instrumental" (1984: 2). The expressiveness and creativity that are part of all performative behaviors therefore must be understood in their truest sense; that is, as *poiesis,* the making or producing of something.

As already noted, festive forms have often been dismissed as mere instruments of social control. Even when they exhibited transgressive or inverted behavior, they were still perceived as being convenient safety valves through which the ruling class could dissipate revolutionary energy and thus maintain the status quo (Gluckman 1954). And while there is no doubt that many celebratory forms have served dominant interests, there are also many examples in which they exploded into rebellion (Burke 1978: 199–204). But the idea of cultural production (as opposed to simple reproduction) is not contingent on the permanent overturning of the social order, for oppositional practices may take many other forms as well. In addition, there is the possibility (as chapter 4 illustrates) that what is produced may only shift allegiances from one dominant force to another. What is important is that cultural performances be recognized as sites of social action where identities and relations are continually being reconfigured. Often this process is imperceptible, with the event appearing as a mere affirmation of the relations that already exist. At other moments, however, groups will use a festive form to shift the way in which history is told, to rethink the boundaries of a community, or to reconsider issues of race and ethnicity or, as in the case of the Saint Patrick's Day Parade, sexuality. In each instance, the festive form will remain what Mikhail Bakhtin claimed it was: "a powerful means of grasping reality . . . not the naturalistic, fleeting, meaningless, scattered aspect of reality but the very process of becoming, its meaning and direction" (1984: 211).

TRADITIONALIZING THE TRADITIONAL
AND THE IDEOLOGY OF FOLKLORE

The notion that festivals could serve as powerful vehicles for the forging of new identities has long been recognized by social architects on both the right and the left. One of the earliest of these was Jean-Jacques Rousseau, who even before the French Revolution suggested the use of festivals as a type of "social dramaturgy" that would both instruct and uplift a newly liberated human being (Duvignaud 1976: 16). Later, when the Revolution did occur, festivals were immediately set in place. As their names—Festival of the Federation, Festival of Reason, Festival of the Supreme Being—suggest, these were meant to effect a "transfer of sacrality from the Old Regime to the new" (Beezley, Martin, and French 1994: xix; Ozouf 1988). Similar experiments also occurred in the aftermath of the Russian and Mexican Revolutions, with newly created festivals serving as secular analogues instilling faith in an infant state. The extensive use of festivals by Hitler and his National Socialists, on the other hand, combined folkloric exhumations with new patriotic holidays (Day of the Martyrs) as the "new" German was to be a mythic incarnation of the old. And more recently, when Cuba sought a way to commemorate the beginning of the July Revolution and Antigua its emancipation, they simply rescheduled carnival to coincide with them. Such examples, which continue to proliferate with the emergence of new nations and the rebirth of old ones, remind us that states too have always recognized the incomparable power of festivals to produce new social imaginaries.[7]

The manner in which states have appropriated these forms, however, has had consequences far different from those of other interventions, particularly when the festival in question is uprooted from the specificities of its local environment. Events that were not only structured by local histories and conflicts but that also celebrated them now become symbols for a nation at large, a purpose for which they were never intended. To accomplish this has required that the hallmark of festive behavior, its superabundance of symbols and meanings, be shrunk as much as possible to a handful of quickly and easily understood ideas. At its most reduced, a festival is transformed into an icon of "national tradition," a borrowed image of difference made to stand for the nation as a whole.[8] With the audience magnified many times over, the subtle ambiguities of local performance, the layerings of history and context, must be all but eliminated. In analyzing this process, García Canclini claimed that popular forms suffer a type of "double reduction": from the rich ethnic diversity of the regional to the unified national and from the flux of social process to that of codified object (1988: 479).

Although it is tempting to dismiss the results of such reductions as mere representations, like paintings or tableaux based on live models, these performances have to be understood as parts of the same discursive traditions from which they have come. Like Richard Handler's insightful example of rural Quebecois taking a break from their Christmas *réveillon* dance in order to watch themselves perform it on English-language television, these variations are continually fed back in a circular loop (1988: 55–56). The effect of this expanded discourse, or what Handler calls the process of "cultural objectification," is twofold: aesthetic and ideological. The first of these will be dealt with extensively in the discussion of *Tamunangue,* a suite of dances, in chapter 5. Still, the aesthetic makeover required in order to translate these forms into national spectacles shares many features cross-culturally. The privileging of the visual, accomplished through colorful costumes and dramatic choreography, combines with technical excellence and virtuosity to present a cheerful, unceasingly optimistic world. This increased theatricalization abjures any mention of true historical conditions and replaces them with the staged creation of a mythic, detemporalized past.

Of course the fact that this aestheticization is driven by the need to erase any signs of conflict, poverty, or oppression (common elements of all popular forms) underscores the impossibility of disconnecting the aesthetic from other issues of ideology. For at the heart of all traditionalizing processes is the desire to mask over real issues of power and domination. By classifying popular forms as "traditions," they are effectively neutralized and removed from real time—or at least that is the hope of ruling elites who wish to manipulate them as part of a much larger legitimizing enterprise. Promoted as natural entities with ties to both land and origin, they become important supports for broader claims to national authority. It is in relation to these claims that questions of "authenticity" suddenly become important as well. For if "traditions" are to be commodified like valuable family jewels (national patrimony), then they must also be subject to some means of verification. In this sense, authenticity and tradition are coconspirators in ensuring that the socially constructed and contingent nature of festive practice will continue to be misrecognized.

Equally important to the ideology of folklore is the selection process by which particular forms are canonized as official traditions. As Williams has effectively argued, all traditions are by their very nature selective and must be viewed as part of the hegemonic work of naturalizing asymmetric relations of power (1977: 115–120). Choices are guided, therefore, by the desire of certain dominant groups to impose specific versions of history and the past. The success of this hegemonic process is evidenced by the tenacity with which local groups have incorporated this authenticating discourse into their own festive vocabularies. Part of this is an economic strategy, as such valorization often leads to the procurement of government support and the attraction of tourists. But it is just as internalized in the way that competing village groups debate among themselves. As Jane Cowan reports, as soon as the carnival in the community of Sohos in northern Greece was "discovered" for its unique folkloric and touristic qualities, local factions began to struggle over control. The language of their rival claims was primarily that of the newly imported discourse of tradition:

> The Sohoians' subsequently heightened awareness of the uniqueness of the local celebration and of the fame, prestige, and resources it potentially brings to the town has not enhanced feelings of solidarity and community. Rather, opposing communal factions—by and large, party-political factions acting under the auspices of ostensibly non-political "education, cultural, and folkloric associations"—struggle for control over the celebratory proceedings. For a variety of reasons, the discourse of "tradition" has emerged as the dominant—though not the only—legitimating discourse in local controversies over how Carnival should be celebrated. Appropriating political party rhetoric, folkloric texts, and various scholars' "authoritative" opinions, each faction attempts to characterize its own initiatives as "traditional," "authentic," and "pure," while castigating those of its enemies. (1992: 174–175)

A similar example of this internalizing process is to be found in chapter 3. When disputes over the origins of Caicara's December 28 celebration surfaced, those supporting claims for the indigenous-inspired Day of the Monkey invoked the authority of official government recognition. They subsequently began to refer to the event as "a national folkloric dance" and "the folkloric festival of the Monkey." And when the local church instituted an annual mass to commemorate past cele-brants, it was called *Misa de los Folkloristas Difuntas* (Mass for the De-ceased Folklorists). The implications of this are quite startling: It is as if a group of Native American performers decided to call themselves an-thropologists in order to legitimate a certain interpretation. It is also ironic that the role of scholar and practitioner should be symbolically reversed at a moment when various non-Western peoples are resisting attempts by contemporary anthropologists to undo their discipline's past cultural "inventions."[9]

But such inversions are not uncommon, as recent debates at the Smith-sonian's annual Festival of American Folklife demonstrate. Here it has been folklorists who have insisted on an "ascetic approach to staging," discouraging costumes and other dramatic modes of representation (Kirshenblatt-Gimblett 1998: 72–74). The "folk," on the other hand, hav-ing incorporated these presentational strategies into their repertoires, now argue for their inclusion. These dizzying reversals confirm once again that what defines the popular is its relation to the dominant order and not some inherent quality or content. For, as Hall cautions, "Almost every fixed inventory will betray us [and] this year's radical symbol or slogan will be neutralized into next year's fashion" (1981: 235)—and, one might also say, the reverse. One only has to consider the current symbol of indigenous women's resistance in Bolivia—the *pollera,* a style of native dress closely patterned on the clothing of the country's former colonial elite.

The instability of these symbols demonstrates once again that no he-gemony is ever total and that even within the most folklorized traditions new emergent forms will continue to appear (Williams 1977: 123). At the same time, it is important to recognize that there has been a long history of resistance to these appropriations throughout Latin America. As early as 1927, the great Peruvian theorist José Carlos Mariátegui warned:

Contrary to what the nationalists would like, tradition is alive and changing. Those who would forbid it to renew and enrich itself are only fabricating it. They are killing it if they want it to be fixed and dead, a projection of the past into a spiritless present. . . . I am speaking here of that tradition which is called patrimony and historical continuity. . . . Tradition is made up of heterogeneous and contradictory elements. To try to reduce it to a single concept, to be satisfied with its so-called essence, is to renounce its many crystallizations. (1970 [1927]: 117)[10]

Some in Latin America have insisted that the solution is to ban the use of the term "folklore" altogether and to replace it with either "popular culture" or "popular arts" (de Carvalho 1991; de Carvalho-Neto 1990).[11] The mere application of this term, they theorize, creates a type of double bind. On the one hand, it stigmatizes whatever it is applied to, causing it to be viewed as marginal and backward. To be labeled "folkloric" is to be premodern, preliterate, preindustrial, and, just as important, non-European. Yet this second-class citizenship is maintained by the desire to "preserve" the integrity and authenticity of these forms. The situation becomes even more perilous when traditions are elevated to the status of national patrimony, for any alterations may now be viewed as acts of disrespect or, even worse, treason. The policing of these forms is commonly attributed to professional folklorists who vigilantly guard against any innovation or change.

In Venezuela, Jesús García and other activists have begun calling for "the de-folklorization of traditional culture," arguing that it is the first step in regaining control of the means of cultural production (1992: 135). He tells of a time in the 1940s when the Afro-Venezuelan communities of Barlovento were filled with musical experimentation and innovation. Trombones, trumpets, and saxophones were being introduced to the famous drum ensembles, and new rhythms and lyrics were being developed. He equates this with the type of creative explosion that was bringing salsa and merengue to other parts of the Caribbean. But in 1946 the Servicio de Investigaciones Folklóricas Nacionales (the National Folklore Investigations Service) was created, and overnight all of this came to an end. Rural black culture was suddenly put under glass, and a "do not disturb" sign was hung on it. Yet this loss of control may actually have stimulated rather than silenced creativity, and what were perceived as primarily religious forms may have entered into a much larger discourse, where these very issues of oppression could be articulated.

THE VENEZUELAN QUARTET

Although the National Folklore Service was legally established by the Ministry of Education in October 1946, it was not actually inaugurated until February of the following year. The occasion was an exhibition of photographs documenting the San Juan festival and drum dances of the black communities of Barlovento. Like so many early anthropological exhibits, it was held at a natural science museum. Then, several months later, when Rómulo Gallegos was selected as president in Venezuela's first democratic elections, the service was enlisted to organize the main inaugural event. This "Festival of Tradition," as it was called, would be a great celebration of a new nation's unique heritage. After years of dictatorship, it would symbolically announce that the government now belonged to the people and, at the same time, would attempt to define who they were. As the service's director, Juan Liscano, said in his opening remarks, "In organizing this festival, this government recognized three fundamental things: that in order to govern democratically you need popular support; that in order to develop a sense of one's own nationality, one needs to understand one's own Tradition; that Tradition, in the final instance, is Folklore" (1950: 217).[12]

The event, which was held in a Caracas bull ring, began on February 17 and ran for five consecutive evenings. The crowds of up to 15,000 were both delighted and amazed. For few had ever imagined that such things existed in Venezuela, a fact that many still recounted to me nearly fifty years after they attended the festival. The sixteen groups that Liscano assembled had been brought from small rural communities from throughout the country. None had ever performed onstage, nor had they ever considered their music and dances anything other than acts of religious devotion (Fig. 1). Their audience was usually that of a saint

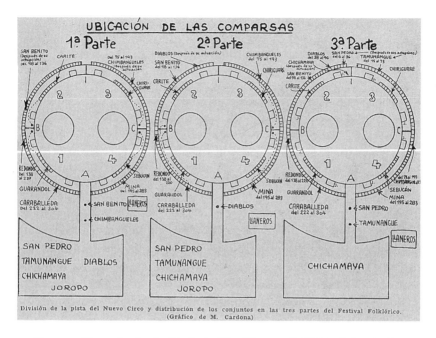

Figure 1. Floor plan for the Festival of Tradition, 1948. (Original drawing by Miguel Cardona, courtesy of the FUNDEF Archives)

who was being honored or repaid for a particular favor. But it was a challenge to find a unique popular culture in Venezuela that was not already attached to the church. This contradiction, however, would be only one of many as these forms now gained new meanings as symbols of national identity and pride.

While the Festival of Tradition had a tremendous impact on the way that urban populations subsequently viewed Venezuela, it also transformed the worlds of the rural actors who had participated in it. Liscano was particularly aware of this, and, in an article published the following year, he commented on the sudden self-consciousness that the performers experienced as they realized they were now parts of a "tradition." But the real payoff for Liscano was in the way these individual forms all blended together to create a new national synthesis:

> Nothing could match the emotion we felt when, at the first of five rehearsals, we saw the astonishment that the dances and music of certain

Venezuelans aroused in other Venezuelans. When, for example, the plainsman applauded the mountaineer, the man of the coast praised the farmer from the central valleys, or the Indian of Goajira beheld the Black of Barlovento. This meeting produced an immediate stimulation, an awareness of tradition itself, that exalted the dancers to heights of aesthetic perfection. Each group yearned to surpass the others in fair fight and win new prestige for its own region. Moreover, putting this variety of traditional expressions of the people in contact gave rise to cultural exchange, to the perfection of techniques and enrichment of tones. This is the very process of culture: the cross-breeding of expressions and of peoples to attain a perfect synthesis. (1949: 35)[13]

For those participating in the Festival of Tradition, the folklorization process had begun. Permanently suspended between the worlds of ritual obligation and national spectacle, these festive forms now began to negotiate a new and complex reality.

Like the lives of those who animated them, they too existed in increasingly different environments. As the tensions between these realities—be they local and national, secular and religious, or household and market—continued to develop, it would be through such cultural performances that these conflicts were dramatized. This is not to say that festivals had not already served as important vehicles for articulating new and oppositional views in Venezuela. The Caracas Carnival, in particular, had long been a site of active, and even violent, contestation. In fact, it was there that the first student protests were mounted against the Gómez regime in 1928, events that only culminated twenty years later with the election of Gallegos.[14] But the Festival of Tradition marked a special turning point. For the first time festivals were being transported from one location to another and their performances expanded to include national and even global significance.[15]

For the investigator interested in historicizing the way in which festive practices have been understood, the freshness of these events offers a rare opportunity. Yet there is also a paradox: No sooner does one pick up the trail, when suddenly it explodes in a maze of different directions. If in their isolated communities these forms seemed to submit to a totalizing analysis, their newly situated circumstances resist it at every level. With the competition of local factions, political parties, commercial interests, government, church, media, and tourism all tearing at the meaning of these events, there is no longer any possibility of reducing them to a single model. And yet, although the luxury of such a totalizing vision may have vanished, a more realistic view has replaced it. Instead of speaking about what festivals mean, the focus has shifted to how their multiple meanings are produced.

In selecting the quartet of examples for this study, I was concerned not only with exploring how celebratory practices create meaning but also with using them to address the greater problem of how anthropologists can represent the realities of culture today. In particular, I was concerned with Venezuela, a country I had come to know well since first going to work there in 1976. Although it was clear that no number of examples could ever exhaust the infinite possibilities that Venezuelans had for describing themselves and their world, I selected four cases that might at least touch on the cardinal points. In addition to reflecting the great ethnic and geographical diversity of this nation of 23 million people, the examples also suggest the range of ways in which festive behaviors can be deployed. And yet, none of these should be seen as being completely independent from any other. Like spokes in a wheel, they all intersect in the center and share an equal preoccupation with their relation to the state. But if the dialogues in which they are engaged share many of the same referents, what they do with them is determined by radically different histories.

In the case of Curiepe's San Juan Festival, the celebration itself has been an important form of historical remembering. Manipulated at various times by both national and commercial interests, the festival has most recently served to reconsolidate the community in a time of tremendous social turmoil. Equally important, it has created a space in which the history of its Afro-Venezuelan participants can be recalled and celebrated. The fact that this history has been erased from all official accounts has transformed the event into an important site of oppositional practice. It has also provided its participants with a way in which to speak about the commonly avoided issue of race and how it is both constructed and denied.

The Day of the Monkey, which takes place in the eastern village of Caicara, is concerned with recalling another history, that of Venezuela's pre-Columbian population. However, some members of the community challenge this indigenous interpretation and question whether it is not a recent invention. This conflict reveals the importance of the festival to those members who have been forced to migrate to the cities in order to find work. Its invented ethnicity provides them with a new form of solidarity in a respatialized world. It also creates a new ambiguity in relation to the state as members try to enlist official support for their claims of authenticity.

The popular culture campaign instituted by British American Tobacco's Bigott Foundation introduces another key actor in the massification of these festive forms: the multinational corporation. With headquarters in Caracas, this foundation has been active in almost every area of cultural production since 1981. Not only have its school, publications, and television programs multiplied the audiences for these forms, they have also helped redefine the way they are interpreted and performed. At the same time, they have provided British American Tobacco with a new "*criollo*" identity. An analysis of the Bigott Foundation's work demonstrates that the "discourse of tradition" is now more deterritorialized than ever and must take into account both urban and transnational voices.

The Tamunangue celebration danced in the western state of Lara to honor San Antonio de Padua has also been affected by this deterritorializing process. Often referred to as Venezuela's most beautiful folkloric dance, Tamunangue has been staged in numerous performative contexts, including museums, festivals, television, and even the national opera house. Part of its attraction has been its association with the Venezuelan racial ideal of *mestizaje,* or "mestizoness." Yet many also contest this, claiming that it is an African dance. As its choreography has changed to accommodate new performative demands, so too has the relationship of the dancers. Of particular importance has been the way in which gendered roles have been redefined, paralleling in many ways the emerging status of Venezuelan women. By tracing this movement along with the directorial decisions involved, the important place of aesthetics in the politics of performance can be identified.

In each instance, the festive forms are viewed not as static, "authoritative texts" but rather as unique performances responding to contemporary historical and social realities. All four are saturated with multiple and contested meanings. Whether they are indigenous, African, or mestizo, urban or rural, they are the sites of continual struggle, public stages on which competing interests converge to both challenge and negotiate identity. And yet, as these examples demonstrate, the location of these stages, along with the actors, are continually shifting. By presenting a multisite ethnography of four intersecting cases, the flux and dynamism of present-day Venezuela will hopefully be captured. For it is only in this intersection of forms and meanings that we can perceive identity as a performed reality, a layering of metaphors and symbols drawn from the full range of human experience. And it is in the festive state, above all, that these identities are imagined and created.

Chapter 2 The Selling of San Juan

THE PERFORMANCE OF HISTORY
IN AN AFRO-VENEZUELAN COMMUNITY

Si Dios fuera negro

todo cambiaría.

Sería nuestra raza

la que mandaría.

If God were black

all would change.

It would be our race

that held the reins.

"SI DIOS FUERA NEGRO,"

SALSA COMPOSITION

BY ROBERTO ANGLERÓ

Even the most casual perusal of anthropological literature over the last fifteen years will reveal an increasing, if not obsessive, preoccupation with what some have called "the selective uses of the past" (Chapman, McDonald, and Tonkin 1989).[1] The growing awareness that histories (and not merely History, writ large) are more than simply static traditions inherited from a neutral past parallels an equally significant realization that the most common subjects of anthropological study (that is, oral-based tribal cultures) actually possess historical consciousness. The erosion, therefore, of functionalism's long-dominant view of Primitive Man as an ahistoric, mythic being has gradually given way to one of contested realities in which any purported absence of history becomes suspect as part of a privileged construction of it. In this sense, the acknowledgment of history or, inversely, its denial is not about the accuracy of memory; it is about the relationship to power. Although Arjun Appadurai, in a 1981 article, attempted to rein in what he called the "widespread assumption that the past is a limitless and plastic symbolic resource," he nevertheless insisted that it is through the "inherent debatability of the past" that cultures find a way not only to "talk about themselves" but also to change (1981: 201, 218).

This view, that history is primarily about the contemporary social relations of those who tell it, has important repercussions for the way in which any group defines itself in relation to another. It is for this reason, Raymond Williams writes, that "much of the most accessible and influential work of the counter-hegemony is historical: the recovery of discarded areas or the redress of selective and reductive interpretations" (1977: 116). Nowhere, perhaps, is this observation more true than in the experience of the African-descended populations of the Americas. Brought to the New World under brutal conditions that quickly severed them from all ethnic, linguistic, and familial ties, these populations have been systematically denied the histories that others accept as a birthright. Yet many of these groups have shown, through often brilliant and resourceful strategies, that the past *is* recuperable and that proud and autonomous histories may be hidden within it. One such group that has demonstrated this is the Afro-Venezuelan community of Curiepe, a village located just two hours east of Caracas (see map). For the people of Curiepe the dramatic vehicle with which to tell this history has been the performance of a three-day drum festival dedicated to San Juan.

SAN JUAN BAUTISTA

The Fiesta de San Juan, known in English as either Saint John's Day or Midsummer Eve, is considered one of the oldest of all church festivals (James 1963: 226). Strategically placed six months before Christmas, it celebrates the birth of Saint John the Baptist, herald of the New Era and, as Jesus said, "the greatest prophet among those born of women" (Luke

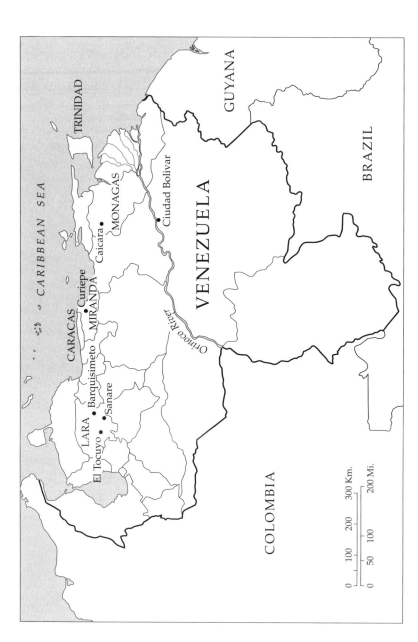

Map of Venezuela showing festival locations

7: 28). But San Juan, falling as it does on the 24th of June, also celebrates the summer solstice and thus has led many to speculate that it predates the Christian era by many centuries. Saint Augustine, writing in the fifth century, saw the advantage of locating this holiday on a date already widely celebrated throughout Europe. He discouraged the church from attempting to prohibit the inclusion of pagan elements, foreseeing that their appropriation could accelerate Christianity's growth (Fuentes and Hernández 1988: 6). This openness resulted in not merely one of the most widely diffused holidays but also one of the most syncretic. Dominated by rituals of fire and water, typical San Juan celebrations also included divination, fertility rites, matchmaking, harvest ceremonies, and even carnivalesque inversion (Burke 1978: 194–195; Frazer 1953 [1922]: 720–732).[2]

With such a wealth of associations, San Juan was easily transported to the New World. In each country throughout Latin America, it was adapted to the particular character of the population that developed there. In Argentina, for example, with its principally European population, descended mainly from Spaniards and Italians, the festival was celebrated with little variation. Bonfires were lit for couples and individuals to jump over and eventually, when the flames died, to walk through. The forms of divination were also the same: eggs dropped in glasses, mirrors read in the dark, cloves of garlic placed under beds, hair cut at midnight, gunpowder and melted tin sifted into water (Coluccio 1978: 74–76).

In the Andes, with its predominantly Indian population, however, San Juan took a decidedly different turn. In Bolivia the saint was known as Tata, or Father San Juan, and was revered as the protector of cattle, llamas, and sheep. Although San Juan also served this function in Peru, his identification with the Inca solstitial celebration of Inti Raymi provided the Catholic Church with an expedient mode of appropriation (Morote Best 1955: 169–170). In Ecuador the festival developed in still another direction. Seen as an opportunity to momentarily reverse both economic and social oppression, it became the occasion for a carnivalesque satire in which all members of the community participated. Indians dressed and performed as whites, while the latter assumed the subservient role of those they normally dominated. So important was this counterhegemonic performance of political subversion that Muriel Crespi refers to San Juan as "the Indian Saint" and to the zone surrounding Cayambe-Imbabura in northern Ecuador as a "St. John culture area" (1981: 488, 501).[3]

In Venezuela it was neither the mestizo population nor the indigenous one that adopted San Juan. Rather, it was the large black population inhabiting the many coastal plantations stretching west of Caracas to Yaracuy and east to an area commonly known as Barlovento. However, it was with the latter region, settled in the seventeenth century by cacao growers and slaves, that San Juan became most closely associated. A pie-shaped piece of land bounded by the Caribbean on the north and mountains on the south and east, Barlovento is less a political or geographical entity than a cultural one. Although it covers nearly 2,000 square miles, its name, derived from a Spanish nautical term meaning "whence the wind comes," rarely appears on any map or legal document. Nevertheless, its population, descended principally from the African slaves brought there in the seventeenth and eighteenth centuries, reveals a striking uniformity both economically and culturally. Despite the improved access to Caracas, which can now be reached in less than two hours, and the dramatic rise in beach-front speculation, Barlovento is still an agricultural area dominated by small landholders.[4] And although each community has its own patron saint and local celebrations, the region as a whole shares a cultural heritage, as witnessed in the performance of such seasonal rites as the Easter Week processions, the Cruz de Mayo, and the Parrandas de Navidad. But of all of these, none has become so thoroughly identified with Barlovento as has that of San Juan. In fact, so widespread and passionate is the cult among these coastal communities that San Juan has become commonly known as "the saint of the blacks" (Monasterio Vásquez 1989: 107).

Unlike the northern Ecuadorean celebrations of San Juan, which joined landowner and Indian in a parody of quotidian life, the celebrations in Barlovento have always been performed solely by the blacks. This does not mean, however, that the festival was not also converted into an important expression of resistance. The time allotted for San Juan was the only free time allowed the slaves, who were compelled to work six and a half days a week, 362 days a year. It was a time when they were permitted to gather freely, not only to dance and play drums but also to conspire and plan revolts. As the only moment of freedom given them during the year, the festival could not help but become associated with the reversal of an oppressive social order. As Bernardo Sanz, a leading drummer in the community of Curiepe, recently observed:

> The Festival of San Juan isn't just a festival. The Festival of San Juan has its meaning. It was the three days given the slaves. And you know why the 25th of June is so popular? For the following. . . . As they were about to end the days given them to celebrate freely, they cried and jumped all over. That was the most joyous day of all . . . because they thought, "Caramba, let's take advantage of this, because from now till the end of next year. . . . Look, let's go. We're not going to serve that man or that one or that one over there any more."
>
> And I'd flee. I'd go up to one of those mountains there, and then the next year I'd come down just for those days. Because on those days no one was put in jail. They were free.
>
> And that's the way people would run off, taking advantage of that chance. And that would be the day to enjoy and let loose. And some would cry because it was the last day of freedom they gave us.[5]

Recognizing these dangers, colonial authorities tried to prohibit the mingling of slaves and free blacks during the festival. Yet as threatening as these occasions may have been to the slaveholders, outlawing them altogether was considered even more dangerous. It was seen as essential to give the slaves some "illusion" of freedom, some release from their insufferable social condition, some connection to an African past of dignity and meaning (Acosta Saignes 1967: 201, 205).

But why was San Juan chosen as the saint with whom to express this? Was it, as Norman Whitten suggests, that, as the prophet of a new era, San Juan symbolized "the transformation from savage (sinner) to civilized (absolved Christian)" (editor's note in Crespi 1981: 502; see also Monasterio Vásquez 1989: 108)? Or was it that his festival evoked the memory of an African solstitial ritual in a climate not unlike that of Venezuela? Certainly the cacao harvest and the initiation of the rainy season encouraged the celebration of a holiday at this time. And as some have suggested, "along with Carnival, San Juan is the most plebeian festival on the ecclesiastical calendar" (Liscano 1973: 66). Its use of divination, amulets, baths, and fires was easily absorbed into a preexistent African tradition. It was also, as Saint Augustine had observed centuries earlier, a convenient means by which the church could sanction and hence incorporate behavior that would otherwise be repellent. For San Juan, in keeping with his syncretic and adaptive history, appears to have been added to this celebration like a new frame through which to experience it (Fig. 2). Isabel Cobos, a teacher and organizer in Curiepe, explained it this way: "The twenty-third, fourth, and fifth is San Juan. And they gave them to the slaves to celebrate their saint. They played their drums and sang *malembe*.[6] The whites, they had no idea what saint that was. And so they said, 'You want a saint? Okay, here, take this.' And they set down San Juan."

Some have suggested that San Juan may actually be Shango, the Yoruba god of thunder, whose color, like that of San Juan, is red.[7] But the importation of slaves to Venezuela ended long before the Yoruba began arriving in the New World. This greater separation from Africa, and the fact that Venezuela's slave population was much more heterogeneous than was that of countries like Cuba and Brazil, makes it difficult to ascribe any prior native identity to this saint (Brandt 1978: 7–9; García 1990: 87; Liscano 1973: 69). What is not difficult to ascribe is the African origin of most of the festival's performative elements. For although certain features, such as bathing, divination, church liturgy, and propitiation of the saint, do recall its Spanish heritage, the principal elements remain those imported from Africa.

Beginning at noon on the 23rd of June and continuing almost nonstop through the night of the 25th, the festival's activity focuses on two different sets of drums. The first, called the *mina*, in memory, perhaps, of the area in Ghana from which it came, is composed of two different drums, the mina proper and the *curbata*. The mina itself is a six-foot-long hollowed trunk set upon a cross brace of two poles (Fig. 3). It is played with sticks on both the body of the drum and its deerskin head and is accompanied by the smaller, upright curbata. The second set comprises

Figure 2. San Juan Bautista. (Photograph by David M. Guss)

Figure 3. The mina. (Photograph by David M. Guss)

three cylindrical, double-skinned drums called the *culo e' puya*. Of probable Bantu origin, these three-foot-long instruments are nestled between the legs of the drummer, who plays them upright with a stick in one hand and with the bare fingers of the other.[8]

The corpus of rhythms, dances, and songs of each of these ensembles is completely different, as is its structural relation to the saint. For it is the music of the drums that satisfies the promesas that are repaid during the three days and nights of the festival. These promesas, which may be based on any favor granted by San Juan, require that a *velorio* be offered, with the sponsoring household paying for all the alcohol and food consumed. During the velorio, which lasts an entire night, the image of San Juan, dressed in red and covered with flowers, is installed in a place of honor. Immediately in front of it, the culo e' puya drums are played, while outside, in the street, another group of celebrants dances and sings to the mina and curbata. These velorios continue from house to house until the conclusion of the festival.

SAN JUAN NACIONAL

While local colonial authorities may have seen an advantage to encouraging this unusual celebration of San Juan, the earliest written records reported it with horror. Not only were the borders between San Juan and the African deities he seemed to represent dangerously blurred, but so were those between male and female. In short, the celebration appeared too erotic. Hence when Bishop Mariano Martí visited the parishes of Barlovento in 1784, he concluded that all such celebrations should be strictly prohibited. Of Curiepe in particular he wrote:

> These people are led by a passion for dancing, not just at parties or celebrations on holidays or when some baptism occurs but also at what they call *velorios*, both for dead children and on the eves of festivals;[9] all of which leads to a sorry disorder, with men and women in a confused mess, especially at night. And they go on this way during these festivals with endless dancing for nearly the whole night, so that they wake up worn out and tired, unable and prohibited from satisfying the

Precept of Mass, burdening their consciences, and, knowing the risk to which they expose themselves, still do not avoid these ridiculous and earthly diversions. Therefore, in order to end these so-called disorders, we must of course prohibit under penalty of excommunication such velorios, in which wild dances and other suspect gatherings occur; and we must send and order that the priest of that congregation in frequent sermons and exhortations make his parishioners understand the pernicious effects resulting from such dances of which one Church Father has said, "They are a circle whose center is the Devil and circumference his Ministers." (Chacón 1979: 33)

Such behavior was not entirely new to the Catholic Church, of course. As Enrique González pointed out, a fundamental role of saints had always been as substitutes for ancient deities.[10] In medieval Europe in particular, they not only provided a more direct access to God but also, through the dances with which they were celebrated, a critical re-access to the body (González 1989). The church, then, would seem to have vacillated between tacit acceptance of such rites and, as Bishop Martí implored, unequivocal repression. As Michael Taussig noted in his work among African-descended groups in neighboring Colombia, such ambivalence between license and restraint led to "almost insuperable contradictions that made social control difficult for colonialists everywhere" (1980: 44). It also led to the paradox of dominant groups appropriating the very magical powers they were purportedly trying to destroy—the image of the Inquisitor with his African healer (1980: 42). Yet most significant of all were the consequences of this attempted repression. With numerous examples from throughout Latin America, but in particular the Andes, Taussig shows how religious repression, time and again, has stimulated cultural creativity, leading to the fashioning of new forms of resistance from old structures of belief. And so it is too that, despite the interdictions of Bishop Martí, the celebration of San Juan has continued in Barlovento to the present day, responding rather than yielding to the changing conditions in which it is performed.

Nearly 160 years elapsed between Bishop Martí's unflattering report of the festival and any other written mention of it. In 1939, however, a young poet from Caracas named Juan Liscano began making regular journeys to the village of Curiepe, in the heart of Barlovento. Curiepe had changed little since the bishop's visit there in the late eighteenth century. To reach it, one still had to go either by mule or by foot or to take a steamer to the port of Higuerote, just a few miles away. Its population too had changed little, rising to just over 3,000 people (Acosta Saignes 1959). As in Martí's time, the villagers were mainly farmers with small orchards of cacao, citrus, and avocado. And festivals too were still times for social ties to be renewed, for families who spent much of the year isolated in the mountains to come to town to visit friends and to pay debts, both religious and otherwise. They were also times for people to drum and sing, activities at which Curiepe was said to be the very best. It was for this reason that Liscano went there, dragging his antique record-making machine with him.

Liscano had grown up in France and Switzerland. His stepfather, who had an enormous influence on him, had been the Venezuelan ambassador to the League of Nations. When Liscano returned home as a young man in 1934, Venezuela was like a foreign country to him. After studying law for three years, he decided to dedicate himself entirely to literature, associating with a movement known as Nuevo Mundismo. This movement, in response to the chaos that was engulfing Europe, sought to discover a new spiritual ideal disengaged from both war and politics. The New World for these artists and intellectuals was to be an "Americanist Utopia," free from all the contaminating ideologies now destroying the Old (Machado 1987: 40–41). This desire to discover an authentic American experience led Liscano to Curiepe and to the investigation of its Afro-Venezuelan music and lore. Although Liscano is now credited with initiating the scientific study of folklore in Venezuela, he insists that this was never his intention. In a 1987 interview, he stated: "I began studying folklore as a real life experience, in order to get close to the primitive, down-to-earth man, to what I thought to be that 'integrated' Venezuelan, because he was integrated with nature and tradition" (Machado 1987: 47).

With this predisposition, it is little surprise, perhaps, that the Sanjuanero described by Liscano is strikingly similar to that portrayed by Bishop Martí a century and a half before. But his sexually liberated celebrants were not objects of scorn to be condemned. Rather, they were ideals for a newly emerging urban population who, dominated by European cultural values, perceived in them an unrepressed and joyous alternative. As Liscano wrote in *La fiesta de San Juan el Bautista*, "Among the blacks of Venezuela, the celebration of San Juan has lost almost all religious inspiration and has been overcome by rhythmicity, orgiastic power, and drunken energy. . . . The vital release achieved through frenetic dances, collective songs, velorios, and processions gave relief from the tensions created by an exploitative social regime" (1973: 47, 51).

Liscano's views, which reinforced not only the rupture between spirit and body but also the stereotype of black eroticism and licentiousness, were to have an important impact on both the future of Curiepe and the celebration of San Juan. Continuing to work in the area of folklore, Liscano was selected to head the Folklore Service when it was formed by the revolutionary junta in the fall of 1946. And then, two years later, when Rómulo Gallegos was inaugurated as the first popularly elected president in Venezuela's history, it was Liscano who was asked to organize the five-day Festival of Tradition, featuring the most representative groups from throughout the country. Of course, at this time the notion of "groups" was foreign to those who performed out of religious devotion in small and isolated rural communities. But Liscano, with the help of a choreographer and dress designer, succeeded in presenting sixteen different acts. There were Indians from the Guajira, Tamunangueros from Lara, the Parrandas of San Pedro, the Giros of San Benito, *comparsas, jinetes,* Diablos, Chimbangueles, and, of course, the drums of San Juan. The event, held in a Caracas bull ring and attended by thousands of people, was an extraordinary success. It was as if Venezuela had suddenly discovered itself and, responding to the need of a new democracy, created a people.[11] None of the groups presented had been known nationally or even outside the particular regions in which they resided. Yet, as a result of the festival, they had embarked on a long transformation into national identity.

Within ten months Gallegos was in exile in Mexico, and the dictatorship of Pérez Jiménez was installed. Liscano would renounce his position at the Folklore Service and then, four years later, also flee. But the image of San Juan, and particularly that associated with Curiepe, had become part of the national consciousness forever. The changes brought about by this new association were nearly imperceptible at first. A group was formed to represent the community nationally. Called the Conjunto Folklórico San Juan de Curiepe, it played at festivals in Caracas and elsewhere. In 1950 the first paved road was completed, making it possible to journey to and from Caracas in a single day. Four years later electricity arrived. Dancers like Yolanda Moreno created arrangements based on San Juan to be performed on television. Articles, records, and even books appeared (Aretz 1953, 1955; Liscano 1947, 1950; Liscano and Seeger 1947; Ramón y Rivera 1951, 1963a, 1963b; Sojo 1943, 1959a, 1959b). The media began to refer to the entire month of June as the "Days of San Juan," treating it as if it were a national holiday. And little by little, tourists began to appear. By 1960 there were so many that the customary velorios, held in private households, could no longer be performed. As a result the community, under the leadership of a local doctor, decided to construct a cultural center in which the saint would be housed. They called it the Casa de Folklore "Juan Pablo Sojo, Hijo," after the man who had assisted Liscano and been the first to write about local folklore.

San Juan would no longer be an intimate celebration, sponsored by grateful individuals repaying promesas to a miraculous saint. It would now, befitting its new national status, be a public event organized by the community at large and open to all. The three culo e' puya drums would still have a privileged position beside the saint, but it would be in front of the stage at the Casa de Folklore. The mina and the curbata, meanwhile, would remain a half block away on a corner of the plaza. The structural relation of the two drum ensembles would remain the same. However, the space in which it occurred would move from the inside out, that is, from private to public or household to square. While this new manner of presenting the festival was certainly a radical change, it was but a prelude to even greater transformations about to come.

SAN JUAN MONUMENTAL

Not all the tourists who came to Curiepe for the celebration of San Juan were drawn by interests that articles or television programs had generated. Many were actually Curieperos who had migrated to Caracas and were now returning to experience contact with their regional heritage. Even blacks from other Barlovento communities began coming to Curiepe, convinced by both media and friends that this was the festival's most genuine expression. The fact that so many participants were emigrants on an annual pilgrimage to their homeland mediated San Juan's adaptation to its new conditions. Unlike descriptions of other festivals that have been converted from local and subregional holidays to national and even global ones, the increased popularity of San Juan did not result in what John Kelly refers to as a "heritage spectacle" (1990: 65), a staged event with a small core of "traditional" performers surrounded by a sea of passive onlookers. Here the majority of those labeled "tourists" did not come to observe and take photos. They came to participate, to dance, to be transported from a life of enforced marginalization to one of active centrality.[12]

Although Barloventeños had been migrating to Caracas for generations, it was not until the mid-1950s that this movement took on large-scale proportions (Pollak-Eltz 1979: 34). Attracted by new jobs in services and construction, immigrants attempting to re-create the conditions of family and support they had left behind began to fill up whole neighborhoods. One such neighborhood was San José, located just blocks above the Pantheon, where the national hero, Simón Bolívar, is buried. It was here that the great majority of those arriving from Curiepe settled. And it was here too that a group of them began to meet in 1969 to discuss ways to "help their community." It was the era of the Alliance for Progress, and Venezuela, like the rest of Latin America, was obsessed with the notion of development. But Venezuela, unlike its neighbors, was on the verge of an enormous boom. The price of oil alone, Venezuela's main export, would rise by more than 700 percent between 1970 and 1974 and then double again over the next eight years (Ewell 1984: 194). The Curieperos who met in the barrio of San José in Caracas thought it unforgivable that their community should be bypassed by this economic miracle. Their philosophy, as Pedro Roberto Ruíz, the self-proclaimed leader of the group, explained, was simple: "A village that does not progress lives abandoned forever. Which is to say, communities must progress.

It's obvious." Yet exactly how to incorporate this remote agricultural community into the growing economy of the rest of the country was not clear.

After several months of discussion, Ruíz's group concluded that Curiepe's main resource was culture, particularly the festival of San Juan. They believed that it would be possible, with proper organization and publicity, to promote this festival to the rest of the country. If they were successful, enough tourists would arrive to generate a permanent infrastructure of hotels, restaurants, and jobs. Eventually they dreamed of an enormous "drum park," so that tourists, as Ruíz put it, "could view the festival in an orderly fashion, with better execution and preparation." Drummers would be brought from all over Barlovento, and at the end of each festival prizes would be handed out. Of course, at the time (and even today), Curiepe had no accommodations whatsoever for tourists. But the Curiepe Prodevelopment Center (Centro Prodesarrollo de Curiepe), as Ruíz's group was now known, felt the most important thing was to first put the village on the map.

The nine-member core of Ruíz's group included individuals uniquely situated to mount a national publicity campaign. Two were journalists, while another worked in advertising, and still another in the census bureau. Ruíz himself was an officer attached to the accounting office of the air force.[13] It was therefore not difficult for him to gain access to the highest levels of government. After winning support from both the national and state congresses, he entered into an agreement with the National Tourist Board (Corporación Nacional de Turismo), which had just adopted a policy to promote festivals and other manifestations of local culture as tourist attractions. They decided that the 1970 San Juan celebration in Curiepe would be the centerpiece of an enormous folklore festival rivaling that organized by Juan Liscano in 1948. It would be promoted both in Venezuela and abroad and would be known as San Juan Monumental, the greatest San Juan ever held.

Working together, they designed a poster that would soon become the symbol of the festival. It showed three drummers playing culo e' puya. Shot from below like three great giants, they were dark and sweaty, the image of the black campesino caught in a moment of authentic celebration. But the poster, which won a national award for photography, was by no means the only form of advertising. Ruíz went on a tour throughout the country, speaking to local groups and government officials. Ads appeared on television and radio. There were articles in magazines and newspapers. Automobiles with loudspeakers circulated throughout Caracas and other cities, announcing the festivities. And handbills floated through the streets everywhere. As Ruíz recalled, "We were really proud of the advertising we did. It got all the way to Japan. The Venezuelan ambassador there contacted us to say that the word was reaching them and that the people there were really interested in finding out more about San Juan Monumental."

The advertising campaign was so successful that it brought more than 100,000 people to the village of Curiepe in the course of an eight-day period (Fig. 4). For San Juan Monumental included much more than the three days of traditional drumming. It was a Semana Cultural, a "Culture Week," with performances by musical groups from every region of the country. As in the Fiesta de la Tradición, there were Diablos from Yare, comparsas from the Oriente, and the Parrandas of San Pedro. There were also groups that had not appeared there, such as the Calypso from El Callao and Luis Mariano Rivera, a famous folksinger from Carupano. And in the center of all the acts were the drummers of San Juan, playing nonstop for three entire days. As described by one of the festival's organizers:

> It was much greater than 1948. What we did was much more extensive. Of course we respected that one, yes. But what we did was to put a type of parentheses around our own folkloric tradition, which was on the 23rd, 24th, and 25th of June, the days of the drums of San Juan. There were no other folklore groups performing then. The days they performed were the 20th, 21st, and 22nd and the 26th and 27th. Because the 27th of June, by coincidence, fell on a Sunday. And so that day we presented Flor García, a popular lyrical singer, who closed San Juan Monumental at nine in the evening, singing his lyrical songs.

The strategy of locating the festival at the center of a new national culture effected a brilliant recontextualization of meanings. From a local saint's day celebrating both religious piety and ethnic heritage the fes-

Figure 4.   San Juan being carried from the church, preceded by the culo e' puya and celebrants. (Photograph by David M. Guss)

tival was converted into the main act of a national variety show. The "parentheses" within which it was now enclosed formed an essential part of the new meaning the festival organizers were trying to construct. Illustrating what Goffman characterized as the problem of "brackets" in relation to spectacles and games, San Juan Monumental had encased one ritual event (the game) within another (the spectacle). The resulting ambiguity, as to "whether the outer or inner realms [were] of chief concern" (Goffman 1974: 263) was one the village of Curiepe was not yet ready to confront. For those who had organized the event, however, the festival had been an unqualified success. Their goal had been simple: to incorporate the community into the national economy. Yet their strategy was to start with the culture, and to relocate it as squarely as possible at the center of the national one. While San Juan Monumental clearly achieved this end, its effect on both the festival itself and the local economy was one neither the organizers nor the villagers had foreseen.

The following year, 1971, the festival was celebrated in much the same way. A new committee, composed entirely of people living in Curiepe, took over its organization. To differentiate their events from those of the year before, they renamed the week of cultural activities San Juan Sensacional. For most Venezuelans, this name evoked one of the country's most popular television shows, an eight-hour extravaganza of variety acts broadcast on Saturdays and called *Sábado Sensacional*. This link to the state media was yet another step in the nationalization process begun by Juan Liscano in the 1940s. The government also continued its contribution to this process by naming Curiepe the "National Folklore Village" and at the same time instituting a system of nominal payments for many of the festival's drummers, thus tying local performers not simply to the patronage of the state government but, in a more dangerous way, to the particular party that was giving it out.[14]

While San Juan Sensacional was not quite the success of the previous year's event, it nevertheless established the festival as an annual attraction for people throughout the country. Hence, when the Culture Week program was suspended altogether in 1972, it had little impact on the number of visitors who still came to Curiepe to celebrate. Many of those who came, however, were attracted less by an interest in folklore than by what they perceived as an African bacchanal dedicated to drums, drugs, and free love. It was the image Liscano himself had fabricated twenty-five years earlier, of a people "overcome by rhythmicity, orgiastic power, and drunken energy" (1973: 47). These stereotypes of black hedonism and sensuality generated a new audience for the festival, which in turn imposed its own carnivalesque definitions. Visitors from Caracas regularly spent the day at the beach and then in late afternoon appeared scantily clad in bikinis or shorts. They replaced the traditional dance, in which couples gracefully moved forward and back, with long chains of whirling groups, all howling and shouting in unison. Motorcycle gangs began to arrive, and knifings and fights were not uncommon. Villagers were scandalized and, by the mid-1970s, were spending most of the festival sheltered in their homes. As Angel Lucci, a community organizer who was then a young man growing up in Curiepe, recalled:

In the final years people didn't even participate. Motorcycle gangs came and took over the town. It was an incredible disaster. . . . No one could sleep. My mother and grandmother hid. They were totally terrified because it had become really ugly. Curiepe had handed its San Juan over to the tourists.[15]

But it was not merely the tourists who had invaded San Juan. Commercial interests had begun to arrive as well, particularly tobacco and beer companies. On the days preceding the holiday, they sent groups to hang posters and pennants, not simply to advertise their products but to associate their names as closely as possible with that of the saint. As the tourists entered, they passed beneath enormous banners welcoming them to the drums of San Juan, courtesy of either a cigarette or a rum. And the drummers were now dressed in T-shirts with the name of a beer on the front and that of San Juan on the back. Those setting up stalls to sell alcohol and food were not from Curiepe either, and none of their profits remained in the community. The vision of Ruíz's group had not materialized. The village, which numbered less than 3,000 people (Brandt 1978: 10), still had not a single hotel or restaurant. And instead of enjoying the economic miracle it had been promised, Curiepe now braced itself once a year to be invaded. Those studying the festival at this time all wrote of its serious decline, predicting that, unless changes were made, it would likely disappear (Brandt 1978: 333–338; Chacón 1979: 110; Liscano 1973: 52).

SAN JUAN CIMARRÓN

The mid-1970s was a time of enormous change, not simply in Curiepe but throughout Venezuela. The tremendous influx of foreign currency caused by the rapid inflation of world oil prices was resulting in a massive demographic and cultural transformation. In her book *Venezuela: A Century of Change,* Judith Ewell refers to this period as "the petrolization of the national problems" (1984: 193–226). It gave birth, she notes, to a long list of new programs and organizations initiated by the governments of both Carlos Andrés Pérez and his successor, Luis Herrera

Campíns. Many of these programs, such as the formation of the Bibli-oteca Ayacucho in 1974 and the Consejo Nacional de la Cultura (Na-tional Council of Culture, or CONAC) the following year, were attempts to distribute this new wealth to the cultural sector.

Other programs, however, were responses to the various forms of social dislocation that had accompanied the economic boom. One such program, sponsored by the Ministry of Justice, was the "Cultural Divi-sion of Crime Prevention." Despite its somewhat inauspicious name, this small pilot program was a type of urban Peace Corps, sending out small cadres of idealistic men and women to targeted marginal neighbor-hoods. Their plan was to create "centers of activity" that in turn would generate community leadership, pride, and autonomy. Although Cu-riepe fell outside the urban mandate for this project, one of its organizers, Jesús Blanco, suggested that it nevertheless be included.[16]

Blanco was aware from previous visits to Curiepe that its youth were extremely disaffected from any organized cultural activities. In fact, the predictions of Max Brandt (1978: 335) and others concerning the future of San Juan were based on the lack of participation or interest of any of the younger generation. Blanco began with an ambitious sports pro-gram, bringing young people together to compete on basketball, volley-ball, and other teams. It was the first time that such sports had been introduced in any organized way, and the youth of Curiepe responded with enthusiasm. Once these groups had been formed, Blanco had little trouble in translating their energy into other cultural realms. Many of those who participated in the new sports program had been upset by the invasion of tourists and the exploitation it had engendered. With Blanco's help, they developed a plan that would not only limit the im-pact of these visitors but also restore the community's control over the festival. The group, with twenty-two core members, would eventually become known as the Centro Cultural y Deportivo de Curiepe (the Cu-riepe Culture and Sport Center).

The initial activities of this group, which began with the celebration of 1975, were both educational and supervisory. They believed that if tourists were only informed of the festival's history and religious sig-nificance, much of the destructive behavior would disappear. They distributed lengthy pamphlets with histories of the community and detailed descriptions of each aspect of the festival. A small museum was created in an old house just off the plaza. Brigades were formed to patrol the village and to enforce a new dress code that would be more respectful of a religious holiday. Shorts and swimwear were now forbidden, as was the use of alcohol in the presence of the saint. The group also attacked the festival's commercialization, and when attempts to discourage the hanging of pennants and banners failed, members pulled them down themselves.

In time, the sale of food and alcohol was also controlled. In order to prevent profits from leaving the community, organizers restricted concessions to local charitable and educational groups. And when drummers were finally convinced to reject all government stipends, a system of food and beverage coupons was established. It was a brilliant rerouting of reciprocity, giving the traditional velorio system new life. Instead of being paid directly by a family sponsoring the velorio, drummers now registered with the festival directorate and, after playing, were given vouchers that could be used at the concessions of other village members, who were in turn receiving payments from tourists. It took several years before these innovations were fully in place. In fact, only after Jesús Blanco left in 1978 did the Curiepe Culture and Sport Center finally assume total control of the festival, replacing the board that had directed it since the time of Pedro Ruíz.

One of the first decisions of the new leadership was to revive the Culture Week of 1970 and 1971. The group's intentions, however, could not have been farther from those of Ruíz and his San Juan Monumental. Instead of trying to recontextualize the festival within a larger, national framework, the Culture Week of 1979 would attempt to restore it to its original one. As such, there were to be no "parentheses," only a single bracket or arrow leading back to what its organizers called "its true meaning." The events presented, therefore, would all precede San Juan, making it clear that the festival should be understood as an end in itself. They would also help to firmly relocate it within a single community and people. The groups invited would no longer be a sampling of Venezuela's most popular folkloric acts. Instead, they would be a carefully orchestrated demonstration of what the festival would now represent. For the Culture Week was no longer meant to be a simple entertainment devised to attract as many tourists as possible. It was now to be a heuristic tool, as the slogan heading the program unequivocally announced:

COMRADE
WE INVITE YOU TO PARTICIPATE
IN A FULL WEEK OF WORK AND RECREATION
JOIN AND STRUGGLE

A wide range of activities was now presented, including movies, plays, lectures, and even a book party.[17] Yet all of them shared a vision of regional and ethnic autonomy. A special symposium on the question of "indigenism" was held, and the film *Yo hablo a Caracas* shown. This film, which Carlos Azpúrua had just completed, was a dramatic appeal by the Yekuana Indians to have their land and culture respected.[18] This show of solidarity with the indigenist movement underlined the feeling of many that Barlovento's culture had also been colonized and was in the same need of protection. The language included in the Culture Week program borrowed heavily from the indigenist literature that was just starting to circulate. The culture now in danger, however, was the Afro-Venezuelan, as statements such as the following made clear:

> The cultural manifestations of the Barlovento area, which is to say those of Afro-Venezuelan origin, have been heavily attacked—at times to the point of disappearing—by so-called civilization. As such, we have seen how the drum festivals of Barlovento have taken on a cheap and commercial meaning, instead of those of solidarity and struggle. At the same time, we have seen how our cultural and moral values have been replaced by cultural values different from those of our Afro-Venezuelan identity. All of which shows the transculturation and domination by other cultures. (Centro Cultural y Deportivo de Curiepe 1979)

The Culture Week would now attempt to reassert these values. Surrounded by a series of aggressively regionalist, Afro-Venezuelan performances, the festival would be symbolically recast. It would shed its image as a national extravaganza and be "re-Africanized." If Curiepe was experiencing a crisis caused by both the loss of citizens through emigration and the influx of strangers through tourism, then the festival would be a tool in reconsolidating its identity once again.[19] To do so, the aspects of San Juan that would be emphasized were those of liberation and resistance. For the Barloventeño, the festival would soon be as much a historical performance as a religious celebration. As such, the focus would now be less on the saint and more on the drums (Fig. 5). Or, as the commonly quoted statement by Juan Pablo Sojo, a local writer, went, "The drum is the cross of the black Christ" (1976 [1943]: 154).

Drums, of course, had served as images of resistance not only in Venezuela but throughout the Caribbean. In neighboring Trinidad they had become the symbol of a carnival that had been transformed from "a high-society affair of elaborate balls" to an ecstatic celebration of emancipated slaves (Hill 1972: 10). When the former European masters attempted to suppress these new expressions of liberation, they did so by outlawing the use of drums, a strategy that was to have disastrous though ultimately unsuccessful results (1972: 6–31). It is interesting that when the steel drums that replaced the originally suppressed ones began to appear in London's Notting Hill Carnival in the early 1970s, their symbolic power was much the same. As Abner Cohen describes, however, there was also an appropriate transformation:

> The steel band has acquired a powerful symbolic significance well beyond the making of loud rhythms. . . . In the first place, there is a feeling of pride and elation at its invention, and many Carnival leaders emphasize that the pan is the only musical instrument invented in the twentieth century. . . . At the same time, with its rust, rough edges, and clumsy appearance, the pan is the symbol of poverty and social disadvantage, a protest that in lands of plenty, endowed with so many sophisticated musical instruments, a people should be forced to pick up abandoned shells to express their artistic feelings. (1980: 71)[20]

The close symbolic connection of drums to expressions of freedom and protest, particularly during carnival, has led more than one government to convert this holiday into a celebration of political independence. In Cuba, for example, carnival has been moved to the beginning of January,

Figure 5.   San Juan drummers playing the mina. (Photograph by David M. Guss)

where it now commemorates the overthrow of the Batista government by Fidel Castro. And in Antigua it is celebrated not during the days before Lent but rather on August 1, the date on which the slaves were emancipated. It is therefore not surprising that its celebration is characterized, as Frank Manning noted, by "regional awareness [and] expressions of racial solidarity" (1977: 269).

Although the Festival of San Juan should not be confused with carnival, it nevertheless has a similar historic relation to the experience of liberation and slavery that many New World carnivals have. In redesigning the program for the new Culture Week, its organizers were attempting to highlight this relation and to present a past not of docile submission but rather of proud, resolute resistance. For them, San Juan embodied this history, and the performance of the festival was a sacred re-creation of it. Its performance was not simply the fulfillment of a promesa or the reenactment of an ancient fertility rite; it was a magical return to a moment of origin, which, as Duvignaud noted, following Eliade (1959) and Caillois (1959), is what "gives life to history" (1976: 21). The transformation of the festival into such a "paradigmatic event" (Eliade 1959: 34) depended on the invocation and recharging of a number of symbolic associations. Most of these derived their power, however, from a concept known as *cimarronaje.*

Difficult to translate into English, particularly because the closest word we have, "maroon," is already a Spanish cognate, cimarronaje is the quality or ethos of a *cimarrón,* an escaped slave. In Venezuela, as elsewhere in the New World, the escaped slave, whether in a *cumbe, quilombo, palenque,* or free village, was a source of inspiration for those still in bondage (García 1990: 53).[21] They represented a refusal to submit either physically or culturally to the brutalizing institution of slavery, for the cimarrón communities hidden away in the mountains and swamps of the Americas often still maintained a rich African cultural heritage (García 1989, 1990; Guerra Cedeño 1984; Price 1983; Price and Price 1980). When invoking the concept of cimarronaje today, the Afro-Venezuelan refers not merely to a past history but to a living tradition still determined to resist the domination of a European ruling class. It recognizes that the black Venezuelan remains a marginalized, economically oppressed citizen who must find solutions within his or her own community.

Conversely, when elements of Afro-Venezuelan culture have already been absorbed into the centralized system of power, it is claimed that the community must *cimarronear,* or "cimarronize" them, which is to say, they must "re-Africanize" them, repositioning both their control and their meaning in the society that generated them. This, of course, is precisely what the new directors of the San Juan Festival were now trying to do. They were attempting to "cimarronize" it by showing the festival's direct links to an ongoing tradition of autonomy and resistance. Several of the strategies used to connect the contemporary reality of Barlovento to that of its cimarrón history have already been mentioned. With its performances, lectures, and conferences, the Culture Week, which has continued with brief lapses up to the present, sought to effect this recontextualization and to provide the people of Barlovento with a new language in which to speak about both their traditions and themselves.[22] It was not long, therefore, before people began to speak of the festival, as Bernardo Sanz did, as the commemoration of the three days of freedom that the slaves had in order to plan either rebellions or individual escapes.

Even the origin of the festival was firmly relocated in the cimarrón experience (see Fig. 6). Participants claimed that the songs and other musical powers of the celebration derived from an escaped slave named José Larito. Larito, also known as José Hilario or Calvarito, had arrived in Venezuela on a French slave ship from the Gold Coast. With him was an African prince who, upon discovering that he was about to be sold into slavery, took a piece of tin and slit his throat. As the prince was dying, Larito reached down and scooped up the prince's blood, quickly covering his entire body with it. After a brief period of enslavement, during which he was particularly abused, Larito fled into the mountains and formed his own *cumbe.* But on the 23rd of June each year he would appear in Curiepe for the celebration of San Juan, leading the drumming and singing, and then, on the evening of the 25th, would escape once more with a new group of cimarrones. The Spanish, of course, did all they could to catch him. But the power of the prince's blood allowed Larito either to become invisible or to take another form.

Figure 6. "Africa Is Also Our Mother Country," mural by Javier Rodríguez on the Casa de Folklore, Curiepe. (Photograph by David M. Guss)

The tale of José Larito, which exists in both written and oral versions, is a perfect example of the "cimarronizing" process (Sojo 1959b; Uslar Pietri 1975). By locating the germinating force of the festival in the deeds of a culture hero such as Larito, there is a transference in the locus of power from that of a Catholic saint's day to one of historical remembrance.[23] This is particularly significant when one realizes that the name José Larito is directly derived from that of Don Joseph Hilario Tinoco, the priest sent to Curiepe in November 1731 to establish the first church there (Castillo Lara 1981b: 144; Chacón 1979: 21). Thus, on another level, the tale is also "cimarronizing" the community's origin, converting the priest credited with its founding into a cimarrón hero. But of all the attempts to identify the festival with an African past of struggle and liberation, none has been so important as the Africanization of San Juan himself.

SAN JUAN CONGO

The pale-skinned San Juan Bautista, with his burnished red cheeks and painted nails, was not always the figure carried through the streets of Curiepe and sung to for three days and nights. In fact, Curieperos, though reluctant to speak of it, acknowledge that this saint is something of a newcomer. Until at least 1870 there was another San Juan, the one claimed to have been the original. Referred to as San Juan Congo, this figure was also carved of wood and coated in plaster. Yet unlike the one that replaced it, San Juan Congo is said to have been black. He also had a phallus, a common feature for many African figures but totally unknown for a Christian one. Like many other icons, San Juan Congo was the personal property of a single family, who, on the saint's day, lent it to the community to be celebrated.[24] Toward the end of the nineteenth century, possession of "the Congo," as he is commonly known, passed to a local doctor named Nicomedes Blanco Gil. At about that time—the precise date is difficult to ascertain—San Juan Congo suddenly stopped appearing. Some say he vanished because an indiscretion was directed toward the doctor's wife as she was walking through the streets. Enraged by such disrespect, Blanco Gil decided to punish the entire community, and he refused to lend them the saint from that moment on. Others, however, claim that the church, upset by the saint's phallus, pressured the doctor to retire it.

Faced with the dilemma of having no saint with which to celebrate their festival, members of the community approached the family of Enrique Moscoso, who had just arrived from neighboring Birongo and was the owner of a much-admired image of San Juan. This image now became the official one of Curiepe, and while San Juan Congo was still celebrated on the fourth of August for several years, it was soon almost entirely forgotten. Passing into the hands of Blanco Gil's illegitimate daughter, María Poncho, the saint remained an almost hidden figure. Then, in the late 1970s, nearly a century after it had been replaced, a group decided to ask Poncho if they could borrow her San Juan and hold a velorio.

Although the velorio coincided with the other innovations surrounding the celebration of San Juan, it was held not during the festival itself but four days later, on the Day of San Pedro. This way, the organizers avoided the intrusion of any tourists and succeeded, as they had hoped, in re-creating the celebration as it had existed before the arrival of Liscano and others. It was to become, as people said, "our festival," "the one of the village," "the real one," and it has been held in relative secrecy since 1979 without any publicity or national attention. For while substantial changes could be made in the organization and performance of the festival as it occurred from the 23rd to the 25th of June, the tourists and national celebrity they represented were now a permanent (and not entirely unwelcome) part of it.[25] The velorio to San Juan Congo, on the other hand, permitted the village to complete the cycle of historical recuperation already under way. The symbols surrounding this event, therefore, were a powerfully orchestrated return to origins.

Instead of celebrating the velorio in the plaza, the participants held it in the ruins of Curiepe's former church, called the *Capilla* (chapel). Sitting atop a hill overlooking the main square, the Capilla was Curiepe's sole church from the earthquake of 1811 until the construction of a new one in the village center in 1959. At one time, members of the community planned to construct a new school in its place, but after tearing down most of the old structure and rebuilding some walls, they simply left it as a shell. Today it sits as a symbol of the surrounding neighborhood of the same name, a neighborhood associated with Curiepe's poorest citizens and best musicians. "The people above" (*el pueblo arriba*), as they are known, have developed a certain resentment for those they call "the people below" (*el pueblo abajo*), the town's more well-to-do and powerful citizens, who live in the larger homes around the square. For many years the people of La Capilla had complained that the celebration of San Juan was too restricted, that it should not be limited to the main square but should also be performed in the upper part of the village. Now, with the new velorio of the 29th of June, "the people above" feel that they finally have their own San Juan. María Poncho herself lives in a small house within two blocks of the Capilla, so this neighborhood takes sole responsibility for organizing the night-long event.

At 2:00 in the afternoon, a mixture of people, old and young, men and women, begin to arrive to decorate the remains of the Capilla. They place palm fronds against the walls, both inside and out, and create a thatched ceiling, from which a selection of local fruits is hung. Above the altar where the saint will be installed is placed the most important crop, cacao, and then, spiraling out in an improvised hierarchy, are all the other locally cultivated plants: a bunch of bananas, a long, curved pod of guamo, shoots of sugarcane, pineapple, passion fruit, guanabana, almonds, cashews, coconut, and a score of other rich tropical fruits that reach back to the entranceway, covering the entire ceiling. A few lights are run from a lamppost, and the altar is modestly decorated with flowers and a painted velvet hanging. At dusk a young boy arrives, nearly unnoticed, with the saint. A group close to the altar begins to play culo e' puya and sing. And outside, 20 yards from the church entrance, others start on the mina and curbata. Both ensembles will continue playing throughout the night, with people coming from the entire village to dance, drum, sing, and drink. And, of course, to see San Juan Congo, to touch him, to ask him for a favor, to simply stand and silently pray.

It is significant that this velorio, held annually since 1979, has escaped the attention given the preceding three days of celebration. For if the consistent arrival of outsiders converted the original Festival of San Juan into a public event to be held in the village plaza, the new velorio has restored it to a private (and, for the participants, "authentic") one. It has also returned the celebration to its original location, the Capilla, where for generations Curieperos worshiped and met. This "return" is especially meaningful when one recalls that the move from the Capilla to the new church coincided with the construction of the Casa de Folklore and, hence, the move of San Juan from individual home to public square. Both of these restorations, to private space and primary location, must be seen as contributing to what is perhaps the fundamental restoration: that of the original community.

But the most important element in this obvious primordialization of the festival remains its return to the original saint, San Juan Congo. As with the events surrounding the new Culture Week, the symbolism underlying this restitution was also powered by its relation to cimarronaje, although not simply because San Juan Congo was said to be black and hence African. The story of his origins also linked him to a past of liberation and struggle, just as that of the festival linked it to the cimarrón hero José Larito. In the version recounted by Juan Pablo Sojo (1986: 168–172), two African princes, who are also brothers, arrive in the port of La Sabana to be sold into slavery. They are brought to a plantation in Curiepe owned by a hacendado named Blanco. Once there, they show a remarkable if not uncanny skill in the growing of cacao. Although treated with particular deference because of this, the younger of the two brothers grows increasingly melancholy and finally takes his own life. The surviving brother continues to bring prosperity to his master and then one day is suddenly given his freedom, along with a small piece of land. Soon after, Blanco dies and the former slave takes his name. The fortune and prestige of the new Señor Blanco continue to increase, with slaves and free blacks coming to him for support and advice. Then, just before the celebration of San Juan, he proposes that they form a society to purchase the freedom of two or three slaves a year. He begins by contributing enough to buy the freedom of at least three of the most expensive. Moreover, he commissions a carver to make a saint for the new order, a San Juan, said to cost 2,000 pesos and to include gold dust.[26]

While this tale may exemplify what John Watanabe refers to as "myths of saintly origins [that] complete the localization of ... once-Catholic figures" (1990: 138), it nevertheless contains many verifiable historical elements. In the record of his visit in 1784, Bishop Martí writes of a slave freed by Don Alejandro Blanco Villegas in order to clear and settle the area around Curiepe (García 1985: 5). And documents brought to light in 1981 by the historian Lucas Guillermo Castillo Lara verify that the village was indeed founded by a group of free blacks. The leader of this group, which arrived in Curiepe a full ten years before Father Joseph Hilario founded his church, was named Juan del Rosario Blanco (Castillo Lara 1981a, 1981b).[27]

Even more significant, perhaps, was the existence, not only in Venezuela but throughout the Caribbean and Brazil, of what were known as "liberation banks." These "emancipation credit unions," as Sheila Walker refers to them, were set up by both slaves and free blacks in order to make funds available for the purchase of "free papers" (1986: 29–30).[28] It is precisely this form of sanctioned subversion that Blanco and his collaborators set up in Curiepe and for which San Juan Congo was to serve as a symbol. By fusing the history of this liberation movement with the origin of the saint, San Juan is not simply Africanized; he becomes the ultimate expression of cimarronaje, a precursor not simply of Jesus but of freedom.

Because of my awareness of the special regard in which San Juan Congo was held and the role that his "blackness" played in creating this esteem, I was somewhat stunned when I finally had the opportunity to see him. For in reality he was not black at all, a bit darker, perhaps, than the porcelain-skinned San Juan of the Moscosos but certainly not black, at least not like Venezuela's other black saints, such as San Benito de Palermo and San Martín de Porres. In fact, in addition to being light skinned and having Caucasian features, the two-foot-high San Juan Congo also had curly blond hair. When I discussed this issue with friends of mine in the community, they appeared quite shocked. How could I not see that he was black? Yes, perhaps a restorer had been a bit overzealous in cleaning him, they confided. Nevertheless, it was still clear that he was black. After several of these discussions, I began to realize that the issues of blackness signified by San Juan Congo were much more profound than simple pigmentation. In fact, I eventually came to understand that it was actually the absence of color that made San Juan such a powerful symbol of it. For the blackness represented here was that of poverty and oppression. It was the economic and social marginalization that had defined the African condition since the arrival of the first slaves in the early 1500s. And indeed, although San Juan Congo might not have appeared black, he was certainly poor. His broken fingers, the lack of any toes, the irregularity of his skin, all were in sharp contrast to the elegance of his wealthy namesake celebrated by "the people below" (Fig. 7).

But like all "dominant symbols," the color of San Juan is loaded with contradiction and ambiguity (Turner 1975). Hence, it also speaks directly to Venezuela's resolute denial of any color at all. In what might be called the myth of mestizaje, historians, philosophers, writers, and even anthropologists have consistently claimed that in Venezuela the issue of race does not exist, that all ethnic groups have blended together in a harmonious and indistinguishable new entity called the mestizo. Juan

Figure 7. San Juan Congo. (Photograph by David M. Guss)

Liscano, one of the first to write about African cultures in Venezuela, stated that "Racial differences were absorbed in the cruel process of our national formation, and today there is no 'black problem' as there is in the United States, with its unforgivable discrimination. What exists is a class problem, just as there is everywhere" (1950: 86).

This commonly held view, that discrimination is the result not of race but rather of class, is the focus of Winthrop Wright's study, *Café con leche: Race, Class, and National Image in Venezuela* (1990). In it, Wright makes a distinction between what he calls the "creed of racial democracy," which maintains that no discrimination based upon color exists, and the "idea of racial equality" itself, a belief somewhat less realized (1990: 111). It is this "seeming paradox" that Wright addresses, showing that if blacks were able to emerge from both racial and economic oppression, they were able to do so not through acceptance but through miscegenation, for "the myth of racial democracy's basic premise [was] that blacks achieved great things in Venezuela only as they whitened themselves and their offspring" (1990: 115).[29] Racial democracy, then, was not the absence of prejudice; it was simply the license to transform one's ethnic identity. The awareness of any prejudice based on color was therefore effectively masked by a belief system that did not recognize racial diversity. Instead, it insisted that anyone discriminated against was selected because he or she was poor. But, as Wright points out, such reasoning was hopelessly circuitous, for "the majority of blacks were poor because they were black" (1990: 5).[30]

So widespread was this color-blind view of Venezuelan society that even social scientists subscribed to it, insisting that even those identified as black did not necessarily consider themselves to be. As one of Venezuela's leading students of Afro-American traditions, Angelina Pollak-Eltz, wrote:

> In Venezuela there is little racial consciousness or discrimination due to skin color. The fact remains, however, that the majority of Afro-venezuelans belong to the lower strata of society. This is due to class differences, lack of educational opportunities for the rural sector, and little spatial mobility until recently. Africa has no meaning for Barloventeños, who consider themselves "criollos" just like Venezuelans elsewhere. (1979: 31)[31]

For the people of Barlovento, such statements, along with the pattern of denial they represent, are but another step in the systematic erasure of the Afro-Venezuelan's cultural and racial history. The fact that San Juan Congo is such a powerful symbol of blackness without actually being black, therefore, reveals much about the issue of race itself in Venezuela. To those celebrating at the Capilla, San Juan Congo is clearly black. Yet it is a blackness that only they appear able (or willing) to perceive. Like the cimarrones who continue to inspire it, it is dissembled and hidden. But the power of San Juan Congo, like that of all religious experience, is the power to make the unseen visible.

Chapter 3 "Indianness" and the Construction of Ethnicity in the Day of the Monkey

It has no European or African roots whatsoever.
This is native. It's the only festival in Venezuela, and
perhaps the world, which is celebrated on just one
day only: the 28th of December. And it has no
European influence nor any African. It's native to
the indigenous Carib culture, and what's more, I'd
say, to the region of Caicara. Descended from the
Chaima, the Guarao, and the Guaiqueri.

EDGAR BAQUERO

They could have called it some other animal, but
they called it "the Monkey."

ARGELIA CARDIEL

THE PERFORMANCE OF ETHNICITY

The myth of mestizaje has affected not only black populations in Latin America, as witnessed in Barlovento, but also people of indigenous ancestry. This has been particularly true in various Andean countries, where the seemingly all-inclusive discourse of mestizaje has been employed for the precise purpose of excluding those who do not conform to national ideals of progress and a market economy. Just as Wright

(1990) and others (Burdick 1992b; Skidmore 1974; Wade 1993; Whitten and Torres 1998) have shown that the language of mestizaje masks unequal social relations between blacks and whites wherein *blanqueamiento,* or "whitening," is the unstated physical and cultural goal, so too in the Andes have Indians been subsumed into a national ideology that continues to exclude them. The most articulate expression of this sinister process, whereby mestizaje excludes not only those who fall outside the "mixed" category but also those who fall within it (specifically, blacks and Indians), may be Norman Whitten's discussion of ethnic and racial politics in Ecuador:

> The practical process of excluding those considered to be nonmixed is carried out by the very persons who espouse an ideology of inclusion based on racial mixture, *mestizaje,* and the resulting contradiction is obvious to ethnically identifiable black *costeño* and black *serrano* Ecuadorians as well as to indigenous Ecuadorian peoples. Additionally, the superficially inclusive claims of *mestizaje* ideology are further undercut by a tacit qualifying clause which ups the price of admission from mere "phenotypical mixture" to cultural *blanqueamiento* ("whitening," in terms of becoming more urban, more Christian, more civilized; less rural, less black, less Indian). This compounds the contradiction by continuously generating internal dissension and dissensus within "mixed categories." . . .
>
> The designation *blanco,* white in terms of national standards, is inextricably linked with high status, wealth, power, national culture, civilization, Christianity, urbanity, and development; its opposites are *indio,* Indian, and *negro,* black. The false resolution of the opposites is found in the doctrine of *mestizaje,* the ideology of racial mixture implying *blanqueamiento.* (1981: 15–16)[1]

In the double-bind situation described by Whitten, those who are included in definitions of *mestizaje* will feel as excluded as those who are not. For the *mescolanza,* or "mix," is never an equal one, and the contributions of blacks and Indians will continue to be undervalued or ignored entirely. For those who retain a strong ethnic identity and either reject or are refused entry into the national ideal, the cost may be even higher. Beyond the likelihood of discrimination and derision are the accusations of unpatriotic behavior and even sedition. Claims will be made that these groups, through their relentless attachment to alternative values, and particularly to alternative modes of production, are impeding the nation's ability to modernize and progress (see Guss 1994). Although these tensions between ethnic and national identities, or what Cohen calls "particularist versus universalist" (1993), may be found everywhere, their resonance in Latin America is particularly strong.

As indigenous groups begin to organize around such issues as land rights, environmental protection, constitutional representation, bilingual education, and health care, initial governmental response, regardless of the country, has been one of denunciation. The simple fact that groups have been demanding consideration based on a collective ethnic interest has been seen as subversive if not treasonous. In 1988, for example, when two Kayapo leaders returned to Brazil from meetings in the United States with World Bank and environmental leaders, they were arrested and charged with violating the "foreigners law." The outrageousness of indicting Brazilian Indians under a law reserved for foreigners who interfere with national politics was further compounded when judges refused to allow the defendants into court unless they wore "white men's clothes" (Cultural Survival 1989: 18).[2] Charges were eventually dropped, and the following year the Kayapo were able to bring representatives of more than forty tribes together in a well-publicized protest against the construction of the Gorotire dam. This successful campaign not only led to the suspension of the project but also helped to promote the eventual demarcation of indigenous territories and the inclusion of various amendments protecting indigenous rights in the new Brazilian constitution.[3]

While the Kayapo's victory in Brazil may have signaled a turning point in rain-forest politics, it also indicates a shift in the strategic use of ethnicity as an organizing tool. In Belém, Brasília, and, most important, Altamira, the site where the dam was to have been built, the Kayapo carefully orchestrated a series of well-publicized demonstrations in which the performance of their ethnicity was the primary focus.[4] It is little surprise, therefore, that Terence Turner, in documenting this process of "cultural self-conscientization and sociopolitical empowerment," referred to the Kayapo as the "consummate ethnic politicians" (1991: 309, 311). Through a self-conscious dramatization of their culture the

Kayapo have been able to mobilize world support and attention for their struggle and in so doing convert ethnicity itself into a powerful symbol of resistance. Hence, even though ethnicity may be oppositional by its very nature, the Kayapo, along with others, are using it to articulate and defend rights that national governments refuse to recognize.[5]

Is it possible, however, for groups identifiable both objectively and subjectively as mestizo to make use of the same ethnic politics that the Kayapo have? If so, what strategies will be employed to differentiate them as ethnically distinguishable? And which element of the three available—Indian, African, or European—will be selected as the most prominent and meaningful? What will determine this choice and, once it is made, give it legitimacy and authority? And finally, what are the historical reasons for such ethnic manifestations? Is it simply, as Werner Sollors claims, that ethnicity is "the acquired modern sense of belonging," replacing all others in an attempt to reestablish the ties of community (1989: xiv)? Or are these ethnic choices "nesting hierarchies," temporary perches from which to assess and redefine new social relations and hence tools of empowerment and resistance (Cohen 1978: 395)? All are questions one must ask when visiting Caicara, Venezuela, a small, uniformly mestizo farming community in the easternmost state of Monagas, where a celebration known as El Día del Mono, or Day of the Monkey, has been used to assert the singular "Indianness" of its participants' pasts. For the Day of the Monkey may not always have been an indigenous celebration and, according to some Caicareños, was very likely not even known by that name. If so, it may be an irony of this festival's current elaboration that, in seeking to establish the purity of its origin, it has underscored its own syncretic invention. And instead of creating solidarity through this ethnic construction, the festival has merely given voice to the many competing interests it had once sought to unite.

SANTO DOMINGO DE GUZMÁN

Like most of Monagas's first towns, Caicara was established by Capuchin missionaries for the express purpose of settling Indians into one location, where they could be both converted and put to work. But historians and local residents are unable to agree as to exactly when this occurred. Some put the date as early as February 1728; others claim that it occurred the following year. Many, however, insist that the town was not established until April 20, 1731, for its acknowledged founder, Father Antonio de Blesa, did not even arrive in Venezuela from Puerto Rico until January of that year. When an official seal was designed for the community, the debate was resolved by displaying all three dates with equal prominence (Chitty 1982: 85–87; Ramírez 1972: 12–28).

The Indians, after whom Father de Blesa was continually chasing, were from various groups: Pariagotos, Coacas, Cores, Kariñas, and, most numerous of all, Chaimas. Carib-speakers like the others, the Chaimas inhabited a territory spreading from the coastal Turimiquire range to the mesas overlooking the Guarapiche River, the site where the new community was to be placed. The town's official name was Santo Domingo de Guzmán de Caicara, and it was Santo Domingo, the patron saint, who was said to have saved the town soon after its founding.[6] As various accounts, both written and oral, tell it, a large group of Indians had gathered at the outskirts of the village and were preparing to overrun it in the middle of the night. But as they approached, they were stopped by the image of a huge figure in gleaming armor seated on a horse with sword drawn. By his side was a snarling dog. So startling was this image that the Indians fled in fear. To confirm what had happened, they returned to Caicara the next morning. Finding the village asleep, they timidly entered, arriving at last at the church. When they entered, they found a statue of Santo Domingo with his dog and immediately recognized that a miracle had happened. The date was August 4th and from that moment on was celebrated as the official Patron Saint's Day of Caicara.[7]

The town grew slowly and more than fifty years after its founding still had only 400 inhabitants (Vila 1978: 97). But its location at the crossroads between larger commercial centers such as Maturín in the south and Cumaná and Barcelona in the north helped establish it as an important stopping point for mule trains and travelers. Even more important was its access to the rich farmlands of the Guarapiche valley, which soon began to attract large numbers of settlers. Cotton, corn, indigo, and tobacco were the earliest crops, but as farms were broken up into smaller holdings vegetables such as tomatoes, cucumbers, and cabbage became even more important.[8] By 1961 there were more than 4,700 people living in Caicara and an equal number in the smaller surrounding communities and hamlets (Ramírez 1972: 7). Almost none of them could be identified as Indians.[9]

Then, as now, the festival cycle revolved around two main holidays, the Festival of Santo Domingo de Guzmán, or Patron Saint's Day, on August 4 and the Day of the Monkey on December 28. While similar in some ways, in most they are structurally opposite. For if the Day of the Monkey, as many of its participants claim, is an expression of all that is indigenous, the Festival of Santo Domingo commemorates the miraculous triumph over the native. During the Patron Saint's Day, all activity emanates from the church. Diversions range from local rodeos to traveling carnivals, but the principal events remain the mass and the lengthy procession following it, in which the image of Santo Domingo is slowly carried throughout the town. In recent years there have also been enactments of Santo Domingo's miracle, wherein children dressed up as Indians are first vanquished and then converted by the sudden appearance of the saint. Throughout the celebration the message remains the same—the triumph of order over chaos and faith over paganism. The Day of the Monkey is an inversion of this triumph and, rather than emanating from the church, begins in the small outlying communities and farms surrounding Caicara. It too is a reenactment of the battle waged against Santo Domingo, except that in this version the outcome is reversed, and the power of the church and the state is defeated. Caicareños are well aware of the oppositional nature of these two celebrations. Or, as one participant summarized it in a rather startling reference to an earlier conflict, "Render unto Caesar what belongs to Caesar, and unto the Monkey what is the Monkey's."

THE DANCE OF THE MONKEY

The performance of the Monkey Dance is relatively simple. Sometime before dawn on the 28th of December, groups referred to as *parrandas* begin to gather in various parts of town as well as in the smaller, outlying hamlets. Most of the groups have danced together for years, with names such as Garibaldo, Zanjón, Gavilán, Eufracio Guevara, and Viento Fresco. Some of these are place-names, indicating the village or section of town from which the group comes; others are derived from famous figures, most often well-known *moneros* (monkey dancers). Many are wearing costumes with monkey masks, while some have simply painted their faces blue with indigo. Ideally, they will be led by a woman in a long flowered dress or a white *liquiliqui*.[10] This is the "mayordoma" or "capitana," who, wielding a large machete, keeps order among the group. But some are not led by women and instead have men parodying "mayordoma," dressed in skirts with oversized breasts and exaggerated wigs. The most famous of these transvestite figures is Chilo Rojas, a seventy-year-old monero who has been dancing for more than fifty years (Fig. 8). Like other groups, his is a mix of men and women. As he leads his dancers, clothed in an elegant dress with purse dangling from his arm, a young woman advances ahead, waving a banner with the group's name and the number 28 painted on it. Equally important to each group is its band, for as the parrandas wind through the streets on their way to the main square, they dance and sing improvised verses:

Allá viene el mono
por el callejón.
Abrele las puertas
a ése parrandón.[11]

Here comes that monkey
down the narrow street.
Open your doors
to those dancing feet.

Arriving at different times and from different directions, the parrandas enter with a flourish, parading in front of the review stand, then mounting the stage to perform. Here is each group's opportunity to display its costumes as well as the skills of its band and the brilliance of its singers' improvisations. The order of the parrandas' entrance is anything but random, and although it does not remain the same each year, it still

Figure 8. Chilo Rojas and the Parranda de Gavilán. (Photograph by David M. Guss)

retains a clear symbolic importance. In 1990 the first group to enter was the Parranda de San Pedro, a group which had not marched for several years and, as Padre Freites, Caicara's priest, told me, "had required a superhuman effort to bring." In reserving this privileged position for the group, festival organizers were able to emphasize the traditional character as well as indigenous roots of the Day of the Monkey. For not only is the Parranda de San Pedro considered the oldest remaining group, it is also the only one composed of Indians. It is also one of the only parrandas still organized around a small rural community in the hills outside Caicara. Following the Parranda de San Pedro was the Parranda de Gavilán, also known as the Negros de Chilo Rojas.[12] As with the San Pedro group, the placement of Chilo, the oldest monero still dancing, was both symbolic and honorific.

But the entrance of the parrandas is not a system of ranking. Many of the larger groups, for instance, prefer to come later in the morning, when bigger crowds have gathered. With much larger bands, such groups as

Garibaldo and Zanjón can also remain onstage much longer. Yet eventually each is replaced by the next and leaves the stage, to be swallowed up by the mass of revelers that has been steadily growing since dawn. It is this much larger group, uniting both the public and the parrandas, which is doing the Monkey Dance. Spiraling and swaying back and forth, long lines of dancers are whipped about, hanging desperately onto the belts or shirttails of those in front. The leaders of these long columns swing belts, which they periodically use on any bystander they happen to see. At times they crouch down, leading the dancers in difficult hopping motions; at other moments they move so quickly that shirts are torn through the mere effort to hold on. Others drink from skins of wine and rum or carry paint cans of blue indigo used to splatter anyone they pass. From the stage come warnings against ripping clothes or other rowdy behavior. Nevertheless, by dusk the plaza is entirely filled with an increasingly chaotic and inebriated mass of dancers. And then the groups begin to drift off one by one, and the festival, as suddenly as it started, without any pomp or ceremony, fizzles to an end.[13]

It may be difficult to imagine at first glance what this apparent free-for-all has to do with the indigenous traditions preceding the arrival of the Spaniards. Without the focus of a recognizable ceremony or the central image of a saint, the celebration seems improvised and undirected. And indeed, my own impression of the dance when I first saw it in 1983 was that of an "antifestival." Yet many Caicareños are quick to insist that the Day of the Monkey represents the same ritual behavior that Carib-related peoples of this area have practiced for hundreds if not thousands of years. As evidence, they point to the style of dancing, claiming that, whereas Europeans hold hands and move in pairs, indigenous peoples, in a more collective manner, form long lines. They also point out that the musical form is a *marisela*, derived from the traditional Carib or Kariña *mare mare*, and that the instruments used are of predominantly native origin.[14] The ciriaco and the conch, the pan-flutes and the maracas, all of them are the same as those played by the original inhabitants of the area (Fig. 9). A further indication of the dance's indigenous origin is the use of face paint, even if somewhat chaotically applied. But the most important link connecting this dance to an Indian predecessor is the figure of the monkey itself. For underlying all of this

Figure 9. A parranda playing the ciriaco. (Photograph by David M. Guss)

activity is the widely held belief that the dance is actually a harvest celebration honoring an ancient simian deity. As one young man explained it:

> It happens that the monkeys protected the harvests that the Indians here in Venezuela had, basically corn, which originated here in Latin America. The monkey was the one that frightened the birds away from the harvest. The birds would drive those monkeys crazy. And so this is what happened. They turned the monkey into a god. In gratitude, the Indian made him a god. And they would dance. El Baile del Mono. The Dance of the Monkey. You know how the monkey swings from branch to branch in single file. And the Monkey Dance . . . the monkey walks holding on to the tail of the monkey in front. And so that's the way the Caicara monkey dances. Understand? Because the Chaima Indians from here used to participate in that harvest. And we're "*culturistas*," followers of the Caicara culture. And we're not going to let anyone from outside come in here and change our tradition.

Another person insisted that although the dance was indeed a harvest festival, it was directed toward the God of Rain:

Look, señor, this is a story that comes from generation to generation. The Monkey goes back to the beginning of Caicara . . . *Caicuara*. Caicuara, the name of the Indian cacique who founded Caicara, before the Spaniards came. Yes, this was an Indian village. And they used to dance the Monkey. But not for entertainment. They danced to the God of Rain. This was their God of Rain, the Mono. And every 28th of December they would dance to him, asking for rain. That's why . . . I don't know if this is your first time here or if you'll believe this, but that's why people say that on the 27th, it's bright and sunny. But on the 28th when it dawns, it's usually overcast and gray. Because this was a rain dance. Well, this is what we know from what we've been able to read.[15]

What explanations such as these resolutely deny is that the Day of the Monkey may also share its origins with an African or European past (Fig. 10). Yet it is not difficult to discern how elements from these cultural traditions have also contributed to the festival. In fact, in many ways, it is the African and European influence that initially impresses the observer. The parrandas, with their marching bands, waving banners, and masked dancers, are much closer to the African-derived carnival tradition from nearby Trinidad than to anything that existed among Venezuela's native peoples. In fact, as Henry Corradini correctly observed (1976), indigenous dance was usually circular and inward, unlike the parranda style with its long lines moving from place to place. Such claims are also supported by Chilo Rojas, who recalled the former importance of black musicians and dancers and the African songs they would bring:

> Yes, they came from outside. There were lots of blacks who arrived here from Guiria [near Trinidad] because I remember that black preparing his *negritos* [dancers]. They would sing a chant. He'd come out with a chant and say to them:

> Jalé tamba
> gongo tó

And the dancers would respond:

> Bamba cailá

Figure 10.   Monkey mask. (Photograph by David M. Guss)

Then

>De mi
>Bamba fe menor

And the dancers:

>Bamba cailá

. . . the *negritos,* I remember them as if I were seeing them right now, understand? Which means there's an origin to that. That black came here with his thing from someplace else.

In addition, it is possible that even the long bamboo ciriaco, that emblem par excellence of "Indianness," may be traced back to an origin in the West African carángano (Hernández and Fuentes 1992: 96; Méndez 1978: 11; Ramírez 1986: 60).[16] Yet equally if not more pronounced than these African influences is the relationship of the festival to one of Europe's oldest church celebrations—the Day of the Holy Innocents.

THE FEAST OF FOOLS

Known also as Childermas, the Day of the Holy Innocents was established to commemorate King Herod's slaughter of every male child in Bethlehem under the age of two. Although the Bible gives no date for this event, the early church fathers established it as December 28, thereby associating it with the four-day Roman Saturnalia concluding the year. In many parts of Europe it was considered the unluckiest day of the year and was commemorated by giving children (in order to remember Herod's deed) a sound thrashing (Hatch 1978: 1157). Called Cross Day in Ireland and other parts of the British Isles, it was an inauspicious day, on which altars were draped in mourning and no major event, such as a wedding or a coronation, was ever held. A more common tradition did not punish children but elevated them into a position of power. It is quite likely that this latter custom began in abbeys and monasteries, where the youngest cleric or nun was placed in charge for the duration of the holiday. This inversion was soon to spread, however, into a more generalized burlesque of all power. In England and France, young boys were chosen to be bishops with all the authority that position entailed (Mackenzie 1987). In Belgium, children locked up their parents, requiring them to pay a ransom before they could be freed. But it was not only children who joined in these games. Peasants, women, and other disenfranchised groups also took advantage of this holiday, not only to assume power but to mock it. What was once the unluckiest day of the year was now the most absurd, and so the 28th of December also became known as the Feast of Fools.

The church, it should be noted, did not appreciate becoming the target of its congregants' humor and as early as the seventh century began an active campaign to prohibit it. But it would be nearly a thousand years before the Feast of Fools finally began to disappear in Europe (Bakhtin 1984: 77).[17] In the New World, however, it had already taken hold, and in countries like Venezuela it was extremely widespread. There December 28th was a type of April Fools' Day in which newspapers ran false headlines, wives put salt in their husbands' coffee, and children were sent on pointless errands. The names of objects were also changed. Rum might be called "water" and the flag, "dishtowel." In the coastal towns of Barlovento entire "governments of women" were set up, parodying male authority with absurd decrees and other actions such as cross-dressing. In the highland communities of Lara, masked figures known as Zaragozas danced through the streets behind miraculous images of the Holy Innocents' massacre. And in Caicara workers from the outlying haciendas paraded into town, singing and dancing in the homes they passed, until finally arriving in the plaza, where the landowners had set up tables covered with liquor and food. At least this, according to some accounts, was the way the Day of the Holy Innocents was celebrated until around 1925.[18]

It was at this point, elderly Caicareños say, that an innovation in the dance occurred. Indians arriving from the community of El Cerezo suddenly grabbed onto each other, forming a long line of hopping figures. One man, who claims to have witnessed the event, says it was in fear of getting separated from one another. In fact, Jacinto Guevara says, it was

Balbino Blanco's daughter Veronica who first clutched onto her father, giving the dance its distinctive step. Then a bystander, perhaps Celestino Palacios, screamed out, "Allá viene el mono." "Here comes the monkey." Although he meant it derisively, others took up the dance, and within several years, it was the only step being done.

Chilo Rojas also insists that the Monkey Dance is a recent innovation, but he remembers its origins somewhat differently:

> How did that begin? There was a family around here named Palacios who lived around El Cerezo. They lived up around the Río de Oro. Okay, and on the Calle de la Casualidad there was a man named Jorgito Taylor who had a business. And he sold ponsigué rum, rum. A Mr. Peña Guzmán lived over there as well. And Felix Díaz. And those people, because that was the main street here, the Calle de la, de la . . . that was the town . . . the Calle de la Casualidad!
>
> Okay, they, well, they began to drink rum over there. That was an enormous family, that Palacios family. Incredible. There were, no shit, at least fifty. And they were living in the farmworkers' camp. There are still a few old guys living over there on Calle Tracadero. They began to drink rum, and they bought a carafe of rum. They're an enormous family. And so they began to drink rum. And the old man said, "Hell, whoever doesn't leap from there to here, doesn't get a drink!"
>
> They were all over there crowded into the middle of the street. I was just a kid then, around 17 years old.[19] And so they began coming. One would leap and grab onto the bottle and take a drink and then stay in front. And then the next. And they started in with that and before you know it they were just about at Felix Díaz's corner with the carafe of rum. They went on grabbing one another and then they really got going with that. They grabbed onto one another's belts. Jesus! They belted one another. They'd jump, grab the carafe, take a drink of rum, and keep on going. No shit, they took over the whole street. They held onto one another's belts and just kept on dancing. And monkey, by God! And drinks, no shit . . . and I took off my own belt because that stuff . . . that's the problem.
>
> And that's the way the monkey began. But they didn't dance the monkey before that. I remember . . . look, it's as if I were watching it today.[20]

What is clear from these multiple versions of the festival's origins is that Caicareños do not agree as to what the celebration represents.

For even upon hearing the first-hand accounts of such respected elders as Jacinto Guevara and Chilo Rojas, many still claim that the festival has absolutely nothing to do with the Day of the Holy Innocents. Even the official state historian, Juan José Ramírez, has chosen to ignore these sources and instead construct an origin based on the uncorroborated account of a single eighty-two-year-old man. In it, Balbino Blanco also appears, but the year is 1895 and it is to honor Santo Domingo that he revives the ancient Monkey Dance beneath a giant ceiba tree in front of the church. What is interesting in this depiction is that Ramírez also reported interviewing such elders as Jorgito Taylor and Domitila Campos Guzmán, both of whom insisted that there was no Monkey Dance. What did exist, they claimed, was a simple *mare mare*, performed annually as part of the Holy Innocents celebration (1972: 62–63).

In order to understand these conflicting claims, it is important to consider who is making each of them. Those who state that the Monkey Dance was simply a craze that took over in the 1920s and eventually silenced any reference to the Day of the Holy Innocents are predominantly older people with strong ties to Caicara's agricultural past. However, those insisting that the Day of the Monkey is a completely indigenous celebration, with no link whatsoever to any European or African tradition, are, for the most part, young men who have left Caicara in order to study or work. For this group, which continues to grow with the changing face of Venezuela's economy, the Day of the Monkey is a homecoming celebration or, as they themselves say, "un día de retorno." It is on this day, conveniently situated between Christmas and New Year's, that every Caicareño, no matter where he or she is, will make every attempt possible to return to the village. Such sentiments are strongly reinforced by the many lyrics now incorporated into the dance welcoming these Caicareños home. The following example, credited to María Maita de Guevara, is but one of many:

> Caicareño si estás lejos
> vente corriendo el 28
> no importa que tú estés viejo
> o tu burrito está mocho

Caicareño, si no vienes
es porque no eres de aquí

tú sabes que el mono tiene
muchas cosas para ti

Caicareño if you're far away
come running on the 28th today
it doesn't matter if you're old
or if your burro's lame

Caicareño, if you don't come
it's because this isn't where you're from

you know full well
the monkey has many things in store for you

For those returning to *la Patria Chica,* or "the Little Country," as it is
sometimes called, the dance is a symbol of identity, distinguishing them
from (rather than joining them to) a larger national tradition that continually threatens to engulf them. The "Indianness" of the Day of the Monkey, therefore, is the quality of being native and rooted. It is the ability
to localize the no longer local. Or, as a young dentist dressed as a priest,
who was also a Caicareño living in the Andes, claimed, "For me the
monkey represents the beginning, the essence. Why? Because it's my
identity as both a Caicareño and a native of this community."

The use of "native" here (*indígena* in Spanish) is intentionally ambiguous. It indicates that he is native because he does the dance and a
Caicareño because he is native. The fact that since the 1920s "indigenous" aspects of the festival have been selected as the most characteristic
and meaningful is no doubt a response to the socioeconomic changes
that have been occurring throughout this area. It is little surprise,
therefore, that the appearance of the Indians dancing in from El Cerezo
should coincide with the sudden appearance of another band of strangers—Standard Oil of New Jersey, who at the same moment was drilling
its first wells in Monagas.

THE SULTAN OF THE GUARAPICHE

The effect of the oil boom on the state of Monagas, one of Venezuela's main oil-producing areas, has been tremendous.[21] It is significant, therefore, that Jesús Guevara Febres begins his monograph on the Day of the Monkey, *Sobre las huellas de El Mono* (1974), with an analysis of the impact the oil industry has had upon Caicara and other rural communities in Monagas. After describing the original irresistibility of working in the nearby oil fields, he tells of the tragic results when mechanization arrived and this new labor force was suddenly unemployed.[22] Unable to return to agricultural employment, the former oil workers soon became part of a growing underclass in such exploding urban centers as Caracas and Puerto Ordaz. What is particularly revealing is the illustration Guevara Febres included in his study to dramatize this process: a drawing of oil fields and refineries with a long row of hopeful campesinos, identifiable by their straw hats, entering them (Fig. 11). One of them has his hand raised as if to signal "onward." Yet on the other side is the same row of men (now wearing hard hats) coming out. No longer campesinos, they are now workers, despondent, unemployed, and with their hands in their pockets. Above this whole scene and filling the sky is the godlike figure of the monkey, arms outstretched in an embrace of the entire landscape (Guevara Febres 1974: 7). The symbolism of this image is both powerful and clear. The oil industry has been a factory for the production of urbanism, unemployment, and destabilized social relations. And in such a world, it is tradition alone (particularly that of the monkey) that can hold these various disintegrating elements together.

The illustration reproduced by Guevara Febres indicates another powerful explanation for why this festival suddenly became a celebration of indigenous values and what exactly those values signify. For in addition to being native, as suggested above, the "indigenous" is also being used to indicate an Edenic pastoral past that no longer exists. It is a reminder of another festival and another era, in which the dancers did indeed come from the surrounding haciendas and hamlets. They were campesinos who worked the land and used the festival as an important occasion to join together on an annual basis. Yet today almost all of the

Figure 11. Transformation of the workforce, 1974. (Courtesy Jesús Guevara Febres)

parrandas come from the town and are largely composed of urban workers who return simply for this day. As the man who claimed that the
monkey was a celebration of his "nativeness" also admitted, "The San
Pedro Parranda is the only native one left that comes from outside. The
others now are all from town, and they're like us. We're mestizos, but
they aren't."

If it is true that the Day of the Monkey is being used to invoke the
memory of another, less-industrialized, reality, then it is one that many
Caicareños insist was a much more prosperous one for their town. Caicara before 1920, before the arrival of automobiles and the oil industry,
was still a rural hub for traders and travelers, a town with restaurants
and hotels, none of which it now has. As Freddy Natera, a longtime
Caicara resident, said:

> Look, Caicara was even more important than Maturín [the state capi-
> tal]. Caicara had an ice plant. It had a soda-bottling plant. Caicara de
> Maturín, that's what it was known as. And why? One simple reason, it
> was the agricultural capital of Monagas.[23]

Chilo Rojas was even more emphatic in recalling the glories of this
former golden age, when Caicara serviced the needs of the many campesinos and traders who depended upon it:

> It was an amazing town, filled with activity. Caicara had so much. . . .
> Maturín was a pigsty compared to Caicara. And on the weekends . . .
> even the president of the state would come to spend his weekends
> here. Because Caicara was so important! Caicara had a tobacco shop,
> which Maturín didn't, two shoemakers, four or five sandal makers [al-
> pargaterías]. It had saddle and harness makers where they even made
> buckles. It had a blacksmith. It had four soap makers. It had cotton
> gins, corn mills, four or five corn mills. And the first soda-bottling
> plant, where was it? Right here in Caicara de Maturín. "La Libér-
> tico. . . ." Caicara had everything and now it has nothing. Look, now
> there's not even a single store to buy a handkerchief in. In a town that
> had more than a hundred shops!

But economic realities are always bound to social ones, and if the
"Indianness" of the monkey celebration is being used to signal an era

of pastoral plenty and well-being, it also resituates the participants who wish, at least for the day, to recover that reality. In this sense, "Indianness" may be seen as a classic instrumental use of ethnicity to restore relations that have been ruptured or destabilized.[24] It resuscitates the memory of a forgotten "tribe" long dispersed throughout Venezuela's various urban centers. It creates distinctions where distinction has been lost and makes Caicareños unique among all others. Or, as Caicareños continually proclaim about their Monkey Dance, "It has nothing to do with the Day of the Holy Innocents or any other holiday, because the only place where it is danced is here."[25]

What is fascinating about the way the Day of the Monkey has been used to express this new ethnicity is that those who identify with it most closely do not consider themselves Indian or, for that matter, black or European. They are mestizos.[26] Hence, not only do they see themselves as unrelated to the members of the San Pedro Parranda, which is composed of Indian-descended campesinos, they also see no contradiction in the fact that their performance of the Monkey Dance is in many ways unrelated to that of the group championed as both the oldest and the most authentic (Fig. 12). For the aspects they claim make the Day of the Monkey an indigenous celebration are generally absent from the San Pedro presentation. Instead of dancing in long lines with each person holding onto the one in front, the San Pedro performers dance in couples, or, as many would say, "European style." Even more significant is the absence of any reference whatsoever to the supposed Monkey God. Masks, when they do appear, are fashioned from simple gourds. More common are large straw hats with colored ribbons hanging from their brim and fruits and flowers on their top. Wearing the skirts of dried banana leaves, these dancers evoke images of fertility and nature. It is the same image Jacinto Guevara recalled when describing Balbino Blanco and his dancers from El Cerezo in the 1920s: "With Balbino all you could see was his hat. That's all. A straw hat all covered with wildflowers piled on top."[27]

But Caicareños are not disturbed by such discrepancies. Although they claim that the "Indianness" of the Day of the Monkey is supported by such traditions as the collective style of dance, the instruments and whips, the face paints, and the reverence for the monkey itself, it is not

Figure 12. San Pedro Parranda with gourd masks and straw hats. (Photograph by David M. Guss)

"authenticity" as normally defined that gives it its real authority. In fact, it may be an irony of this insistence on local, indigenous culture that the most important validation is that derived from both national media and the state. Without the historical depth or textual and artifactual records of a festival like San Juan, the Day of the Monkey has had to legitimate itself through other means.[28] This "folklorization" process has taken a number of forms, all reiterating the same "objective" claim: that "the Mono is eastern Venezuela's greatest folkloric treasure." In fact, it is this identical expression that has been used by one author after another to describe the festival (Abreu 1984; Pérez and Bermúdez 1978; Ramírez 1972, 1988; Zuloaga 1990). It is also the phrase used to announce one's arrival in Caicara (Fig. 13). For at the town's entrance is an enormous billboard with a monkey on it, accompanied by the following message:

Está llegando a Caicara
Tierra del Mono
Máxima Expresión

Figure 13.   Billboard at the entrance to Caicara. (Photograph by David M. Guss)

Folklórica del Oriente
Salud Amigo

You are entering Caicara
Land of the Monkey
Maximum Folkloric
Expression of the East
Welcome Friend

Such sentiments go well beyond the simple rhetoric of civic pride or commercial promotion. They have become part of the vernacular which Caicareños employ to locate the festival and hence themselves. Or as one member of the Parranda de Zanjón put it: "On the 28th of December in Caicara, all roads lead to the monkey, which is the Rome of tradition and the Mecca of Eastern Folklore. . . . The monkey is the Sultan of the Guarapiche." Frequent statements such as these reflect the way in which an officializing discourse has been transformed into the common language of shared perception. The strategies through which this has occurred are a complex blend, mixing elements from almost every medium. One of the most significant of these is that of public art, discovered not simply in the billboard at Caicara's entrance but on the walls throughout the town.

If it is the case that the Day of the Monkey cannot be confirmed through any historical or written evidence, the murals which now line

Caicara's streets may be said to provide this textual record (Fig. 14). Created over the last fifteen years, these murals tell the history of the festival, aggressively asserting both its traditionalness and its "Indian-ness." Paintings commissioned by individuals, parrandas, political parties, cultural organizations, and commercial interests, such as rum companies, provide an inventory of the festival's diverse elements. The most common of these images is that of the monkey, either its body contorted in dance or a portrait of its head. Many paintings, however, simply depict the instruments or a bowl of indigo with the image of a blue hand next to it; others show famous costumes, such as that of Perucho Arcilla and his twins. Yet there are also more complex images, such as the tableaux of parrandas being led through the streets behind the leaping figure of a monkey playing a cow's horn. Almost all of these are accompanied by messages, exhorting participants to "take care of your monkey," to "maintain your tradition," or to "defend your cultural identity."[29] Together these paintings form a body of knowledge, a catalogue on walls detailing exactly why the Day of the Monkey is such a unique and important tradition.

The culmination of this complex public text, which has been added to year after year, was the erection in 1990 of an official "Monument to the Dance of the Monkey" (Fig. 15). Designed by José Roca Zamora, a Caicareño now living in Puerto La Cruz, it was placed at the end of the main square opposite the church. Standing on a pyramid-shaped base, the monument depicts a two-headed monkey atop a 20-foot-high column. On one side the monkey is smiling, while on the other he is frowning. Sculpted into the concrete column are the dance's most emblematic symbols—the instruments, the belts, the cans of indigo paint, handprints, the number 28. Although many Caicareños have expressed disappointment with the statue, insisting it is either too phallic or looks too much like an ape instead of an indigenous monkey or simply was too expensive, the monument remains a source of pride, an affirmation once again of Caicara's specialness as the only place in Venezuela where this festival takes place. It is also an important passage into what Eric Hobsbawm claimed is one of the principal ingredients in the invention of new traditions. For the establishment of "an alternative 'civic religion'"

Figure 14.   Mural dedicated to the Day of the Monkey. (Photograph by
David M. Guss)

demands the creation of new sacred spaces in the form of public monuments (Hobsbawm 1983: 269).[30]

The billboard, murals, and monument were generated from within
the community, or at least in collaboration with its members, but many
forms of legitimation come from without. Such recognition has been
extremely important in confirming claims of authenticity. The fact that
radio stations regularly transmit the holiday throughout the state or that
television and film crews come to record it is proof that the Day of the
Monkey exists as a unique folkloric entity. Similar importance is attached
to both national and regional folklore festivals in which parrandas from
Caicara have occasionally participated. To be invited to perform beside
such well-established groups as the Sanjuaneros of Curiepe or the Tamunangueros of Lara is recognition in itself of the special status of the
monkey tradition. Members of the community are conscious of this and

Figure 15. Monument to the Dance of the Monkey. (Photograph by David M. Guss)

can easily cite the events at which moneros have danced and even won awards. They also cite with mixed pride the names of performers, both national and international, who have adopted the Monkey Dance for commercial use: the Orquestra Típica de Venezuela, Billo Frómeta and his Caracas Boys, the Dominican merengue star Wilfrido Vargas, and Yolanda Moreno, the dancer who Guevara Febres claims is now a "capitana" (1974: 26). Each of these is but one more demonstration of the undisputed place of the Monkey as "a national folkloric dance." Even my own presence as an anthropologist was converted into a symbol of authentication. If it was worth being studied, it must be real. Singers would frequently comment on my presence in their quatrains. And announcers, whom quite often I had never met, would repeatedly acknowledge me from the stage:

> Welcome to the anthropologists from everywhere. Because today we have an anthropologist with us from the United States . . . forgive me if I can't remember from where . . . an anthropologist who has come all this way to be here for the great folkloric expression of the Mono.

This modern sense of authenticity as bestowed by either the media or academic recognition is regularly parodied by a group of performers dressed as a television crew (Fig. 16). Despite the fact that their camera is made of cardboard and their microphone an inverted beer bottle, it is difficult to tell at first glance that the three men dressed in blue coveralls with official identification tags are not from a national television network. As they move through the crowd conducting mock interviews, they never once break character. Although comic, their message is also very serious. It announces that the Day of the Monkey is a momentous folkloric and cultural event and hence must be documented and studied. For those participating in the festival it dramatizes precisely those elements that the Monkey Dance is performed to evoke. Here play is put in the service of the real work of creating an identity that only the weight of authenticity will sustain. It is an identity where symbols are collapsed together and the construction of ethnicity so tightly wound around the town of Caicara that to be "Indian" and Caicareño are the same. For in the end it is neither race nor work nor ethnicity that unites these dancers

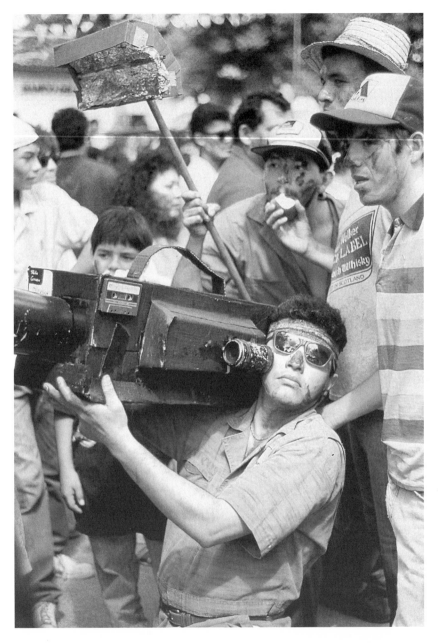

Figure 16. Mono performers dressed as a television crew. (Photograph by David M. Guss)

but rather a sense of place. And while it is this sense that distinguishes the monkey dancers, if just for an instant, from a larger national identity, it is only by linking the festival to this greater reality that such sentiments can be achieved.

The "Indianness" of the Day of the Monkey, however, is not simply an oppositional strategy used to distinguish one group of mestizos from another. It is also a powerful symbol of subversion, which, when joined to the antisocial character of the monkey, succeeds in redefining the Day of the Holy Innocents in a way that is indeed unique to Caicara. Like every Feast of Fools celebration, it maintains inversion as its most important element, mocking all symbols of authority and power with equal abandon. Yet it does so in a way that evokes Caicara's own history. Now, more than 260 years after its founding, the Indians succeed in overwhelming the city. They finally triumph over Santo Domingo and the power of the church he represents. And what is most significant is that they do so in a way that is indeed Carib, that celebrates the triumph of nature over culture and elevates above all that most enduring symbol of anticulture, the monkey.

The anticlerical nature of the Day of the Monkey is clear, of course, to many of the celebrants as well as to the Church itself. However, if the church was able to suppress the holiday in Europe, it has been unable to in Caicara. Instead, it has tried to appropriate it as best it could and has instituted a special open-air mass to "los moneros difuntos" (the dead monkey dancers). But the transparency of this strategy has fooled few. And as one monero stated:

> The monkey's a challenge to the Catholic Church, and if they say a mass to the departed dancers . . . look, the Catholic Church with all its stuff, with its intrigues, may accept the monkey. But what is the monkey? The monkey is a manifestation of before . . . a manifestation so great that the people just overwhelmed the church. And so the church realized this. Okay, and they used that old saying, "If you can't beat them, join them."

It is here that Caicara's history of Spanish-Indian conflict is wed to the traditional ecclesiastical subversion common to all Feast of Fools celebrations. Yet the inversion is not that derived from Europe's rigid monastic orders or courtly aristocracies, inversions characterized by the weak and disenfranchised being given temporary power. Instead, it is the inversion of a world where hierarchies are barely visible and festive reversals are signaled not by parodying political or class distinctions but by turning culture itself on its head and allowing nature to overrun it. Such celebrations can still be found today among Carib groups in Venezuela. In the *Wasai yadi ademi hidi* festival of the Yekuana, for example, travelers who have been away for long periods of time indicate their inverted status by dressing as forest spirits. Clothed in palm skirts and headdresses, they dance into the community, only to be attacked by those who have remained behind. Similar costumes are also worn by the Pemon as they perform the *Parishira* ritual in order to summon the wild boar. Here dancers are transformed into wild and dangerous animals who suddenly pounce on those who sit apart holding bows and arrows (Guss 1977, 1985, 1989). It is in traditions such as these, perhaps, that the true Indianness of the Day of the Monkey is to be found, not in the long line of dancers clinging to one another's shirttails nor in the memory of some long-lost simian deity but in the specter of chaos which only the monkey, with all his antisocial pandemonium, is able to conjure.[31]

Chapter 4 "Full Speed Ahead with Venezuela"

THE TOBACCO INDUSTRY,
NATIONALISM, AND THE BUSINESS
OF POPULAR CULTURE

Bigott's other crop.

To project our roots

We plant culture

and we harvest art.

THE BIGOTT FOUNDATION

This is what "popular" culture really is, and not
some alien corpus, anatomized for the purposes of
exhibit, prepared and "quoted" by a system which
reduplicates upon these objects the same situation it
has prepared for its living subjects.

MICHEL DE CERTEAU,
"ON THE OPPOSITIONAL PRACTICES
OF EVERYDAY LIFE"

If the histories of San Juan and the Dance of the Monkey appear to be triumphant narratives of resistance and local autonomy, it should be remembered that they continue to exist in real time and that it will not be long until new forces arise to suggest alternative interpretations and meanings. While these interpretations may continue to coexist and compete with one another, each will attempt to naturalize itself and, in so doing, portray the other as both inauthentic and spurious. Such conflict can lead to serious community divisions. Just as Blanco Gil removed San Juan Congo from the annual celebration in Curiepe, so too have factions removed themselves, choosing either to celebrate alone or perhaps not at all. Even more common is the type of accommodation achieved by Chilo Rojas and his Parranda de Gavilán. Although he criticizes the current manner in which the Dance of the Monkey is celebrated, disputing even its name, he still leads his dancers through Caicara's streets and into the main square. But he refuses, in subtle protest, to mount the review stand as all the other parrandas do. Such multiple readings are the norm, and no matter how dominant any interpretation of a festival may become, some members of a community will always challenge it.

Festivals, however, are no longer limited to the interpretations of a single community. The enormous economic, demographic, and technological changes that have occurred throughout Latin America over the last quarter of a century have guaranteed that such events as San Juan and the Dance of the Monkey also engage in a national and even global discourse. It was with this in mind that García Canclini claimed that all traditional or popular forms in Latin America today are "doubly enrolled" in two systems of cultural production, giving them simultaneous significance at both community and extralocal levels (1988: 486; 1993: 45). As already observed, San Juan and the Dance of the Monkey have each articulated and responded to numerous historical and economic changes. Among them are the consolidation of a democratic form of government, the increasing dominance of an oil-based economy, and the rapid urbanization that has been taking place since the late 1960s. In each instance, the festival became a vehicle through which participants could dramatize such concerns as race, ethnicity, marginalization, and oppression. And yet, as popular forms become increasingly "doubly enrolled," they will also be subject to appropriation by new and unforeseen audiences.

Until now, most discussions of the enlistment of popular culture by new and nonautochthonous forces have been dominated by concerns surrounding the state. And without doubt, the desire to develop a coherent identity has been a driving force in the way many popular forms have been reconfigured. This nation-building model, however, may have more relevance to Europe, from which so many of these studies have emerged (Herzfeld 1982; Hobsbawm and Ranger 1983; Wilson 1976), than it does to Latin America. Although it is true, as the present work attests, that states throughout Latin America have appropriated these forms as "instruments of ideological cohesion" (García Canclini 1993: 45), there are other forces which must be given equal if not greater attention. The domination of multinational interests in cultural apparatuses as well as in basic economic production has created conditions that did not adhere during the period of state formation in either Europe or North America. As a result, William Rowe and Vivian Schelling argue, it has been the electronic media rather than the state that have been the greatest homogenizing agent in Latin America (1991: 100, 196).

Although it is certainly clear that global market forces are transcending national boundaries everywhere in the world, it is important to recognize that these forces do not act uniformly in every country. In recognition of this, Ulf Hannerz distinguished between what he calls multinational and global corporations. Although each might strive for the homogenization of its consumers, the former recognizes and exploits local differences, whereas the latter steadfastly ignores them (1992: 234–235). Closely related to this process is what Arjun Appadurai identified as "production fetishism," the manner in which multinational corporations "localize" themselves. Or, as he defines it:

> An illusion created by contemporary transnational production loci, which masks translocal capital, transnational earning-flows, global management and often faraway workers (engaged in various kinds of high-tech putting out operations) in the idiom and spectacle of local (sometimes even worker) control, national productivity and territorial sovereignty. . . . The locality (both in the sense of the local factory or site of production and in the extended sense of the nation-state) becomes a fetish which disguises the globally dispersed forces that actually drive the production process. (1990: 16)

Such "production fetishism," which Appadurai does not elaborate upon, could encompass a number of corporate strategies, from a "Buy

American" campaign to Nestlé's establishment of infant-oriented rest stops throughout Europe.[1] What concepts like those of Hannerz and Appadurai make clear, however, is that multinational corporations can no longer be seen as simple cultural imperialists exporting anonymous Western values at the expense of all that is local and indigenous. Although one should not minimize the negative impact these corporations may have, it is also critical to recognize that in the course of extracting resources and manufacturing and selling goods, multinational corporations have also become extremely important cultural producers. The simple fact that the reserves of the ten largest corporations in the world today are greater than those of the hundred smallest nations suggests that the once undisputed role of the state is now being challenged by another authority. Yet the interests each has in constructing a unified national identity are not necessarily opposed. Whereas the state may wish to achieve allegiance in order to transcend regional and ethnic discord (along with all the power and benefits such transcendence brings), a corporation may wish to become identified with the state in order to win the allegiance of consumers. As the concept of "production fetishism" suggests, if corporations can attach their products closely enough to images of the nation, then to purchase them will be translated into a patriotic duty. In Venezuela this is precisely what one corporation, the Cigarrera Bigott, a subsidiary of British American Tobacco, has done.

The multifaceted campaign initiated by Bigott in 1981 to achieve these goals has converted Venezuela's most important producer of cigarettes into an equally important producer of culture. While the company may insist that it is simply engaged in the disinterested promotion of popular culture in its most authentic and unadulterated form, the reality is somewhat different. The creation of new contexts and audiences, the selection and promotion of particular events to the exclusion of others, and the diffusion and massification through new technologies are only a few of the ways in which Bigott has helped to redefine the manner in which these forms will be appreciated and understood. This does not mean, however, that Bigott is simply another invasive force contaminating the otherwise pristine and folkloric. What it does mean is that a powerful multinational corporation has now become an active participant in the ongoing debate over how cultural expressions should be performed and interpreted. They join all those in communities like Curiepe and Caicara, where musicians, dancers, promeseros, community activists, and government workers, to name but a few, have used festivals as a means to articulate a wide range of personal and collective interests. To understand this participation, therefore, one must analyze Bigott's campaign within the same sociopolitical framework that one would use in examining a festival. For just as San Juan and the Dance of the Monkey have responded to an enormous range of historical and economic changes, so too has the campaign that has transformed the Cigarrera Bigott into one of Venezuela's most important cultural producers.

THE ORIGINS OF A FOUNDATION

As its name suggests, British American Tobacco did not grow from a small local concern but originated as a transnational cartel with a specific mandate to enter foreign markets. Founded in 1902, the company emerged from a short but bitter struggle between the world's reigning tobacco monopolies, Imperial of Great Britain and American Tobacco of the United States. In order to preserve control over their territories, they agreed not to sell in one another's markets and to band together to form a new entity to handle all sales of their products outside Britain and the United States. The company, to be called British American Tobacco, would be located in England, while its first chair and largest stockholder would be James Duke of American. But in 1911 antitrust legislation forced Duke to break up his empire, and American Tobacco's interests in the new corporation were sold. British American, however, continued to expand, and before long it was the largest producer of tobacco in the world.

Today, with assets of well over $25 billion and more than 170,000 employees, British American Tobacco remains one of the world's largest manufacturers of cigarettes as well as England's third largest industrial enterprise (Directory of Corporate Affiliations 1999: 78; Tucker 1982: 71). Like many tobacco corporations, British American began to diversify its interests in the 1960s. Since then, it has invested heavily in cosmetics, retailing (including Saks Fifth Avenue, Gimbels, and Marshall Field), packaging, paper, insurance, and financial services. In 1976 the company recognized its new makeup by reorganizing into six divisions and changing its name to BAT Industries. Yet despite these changes, tobacco remains the corporation's most important concern. With manufacturing in seventy-eight countries and sales in more than 130, BAT continues to expand, opening new markets in Eastern Europe and China.[2] In at least thirty-six countries (including Brazil, Mexico, India, Nigeria, Germany, Malaysia, and Indonesia), it is the brand leader. And in the United States, where its largest subsidiary, Brown and Williamson, markets Kool and Viceroy, it ranks third (Chai, Campbell, and Spain 1993: 142–143; Corina 1975: 304–305; Tucker 1982: 71–84).

Although British American Tobacco has been equally successful in Venezuela, few if any of its citizens could identify it. Following a tactic used in other countries, it acquired an already existing corporation with a national reputation and simply adopted its name. This strategy proved particularly successful in Venezuela, where Cigarrera Bigott, the company British American purchased in 1922, was not only the leading producer of cigarettes but also recognized for its record of progressive philanthropy. Founded by Luis Bigott in 1898, the company had a long history of investing in the welfare of its employees and their families. After selling the company, Luis Bigott went on to a long career as a distinguished philanthropist. In addition to constructing schools and homes for workers, he also aided in the resettling of Dominican refugees and the development of a national education program (Fundación Polar 1989: 375–376). Needless to say, the company continued to benefit from whatever good deeds its former owner undertook. Yet British American never entirely abandoned the activities of its founder and in 1963 set up the Bigott Foundation (*Fundación Bigott*) to aid workers in the procurement and financing of homes. Not until 1981, however, did the new owners begin to pay serious attention to the work of this foundation.

By this time Bigott and its perennial best-seller, Belmont, had firm control of more than 80 percent of Venezuela's tobacco market. Its only real competitor was the Tabacalera Nacional, a much smaller company which, despite partial ownership by Philip Morris, was still Venezuelan run (Gerente Venezuela 1990). In 1981, however, a different challenge arose when the government of Luis Herrera Campíns outlawed the advertising of all tobacco and alcohol on both radio and television (Licausi 1981). Bigott reacted immediately, deciding to use its foundation as a means to promote its name without actually advertising cigarettes. As Agustín Coll, one of the foundation's first directors, recalled, "From the moment of the presidential decree we knew we had to find a way to continue in broadcasting, and so we decided—because the idea was to stay on television, but without mentioning the name of the cigarette— that the way to do it was through the Bigott Foundation, and so we said, 'Let's change the whole focus of the foundation.' "

Bigott's parent company, of course, had been faced with an identical crisis ten years earlier in the United States, where similar legislation had been passed.[3] There, major tobacco companies had banned together to form the Tobacco Research Council as well as the Tobacco Institute, the first to oversee efforts in all health-related research and the latter to co-ordinate lobbying activities (Miles 1982: 58–90). Bigott was still not sure what area its redesigned foundation should promote. Yet, as Coll confirms, three criteria guided its search. First, whatever theme was chosen should not conflict with the issue of tobacco. Youth or sports-related activities, for example, would be inappropriate, given the health concerns that had already alarmed the public. Then there was the fact that Bigott was a multinational corporation. The environment in Venezuela, as in many other Latin American countries, had grown increasingly hostile to foreign-owned companies throughout the 1970s. Some of these companies had actually been nationalized, and it was with this in mind that Bigott resolved to choose a sphere as closely associated with the values of Venezuelan identity as possible. In short, it wished to nationalize itself before anyone else did. And finally, the area selected should appeal to the masses. It should not be restricted to concert halls or museums nor to special audiences. As Coll himself said, "It should not be elitist."

The search for this new focus had actually begun in the late 1970s, which explains how Bigott was able to react so quickly once antismoking legislation was passed. As with all of the company's public relations efforts, it was directed by Corpa (Corporación Publicitaria Nacional, C.A.), the largest advertising firm in Venezuela. Like Bigott, Corpa is a multinational corporation, owned by the Anglo-American giant Ogilvy and Mather. Its director, James Steel, had foreseen the difficulties that tobacco advertising would soon face and had suggested that a contingency plan be explored.[4] A survey was therefore conducted asking people what area they would most like to see private industry support. Based on the results of this survey, Steel convinced Bigott to restructure its foundation. The previous loan program for employees would now be part of a newly created foundation called Los Ruices, while the Bigott Foundation, which bore the all-important name of the company, would dedicate itself to the promotion of popular culture. So successful would this campaign be that Bigott would not only nationalize itself but, through it, become a synonym for all that was most authentically Venezuelan.

The survey that Corpa conducted for Bigott, however, provides only a partial explanation for the choice of popular culture as the foundation's new focus. To understand why this was perceived as such a fertile area of exploitation, one must also recognize the tremendous convergence of political and economic forces that came together in Venezuela at the end of the 1970s. Some of these forces, such as those of demographic change and technological innovation, have already been alluded to. Yet it is important to reemphasize how much rapid urbanization throughout Latin America and not simply Venezuela has helped to redefine the nature of traditional and popular forms. No longer the preserve of oral-based rural communities, these traditions, once relocated in the city, become active participants in new modes of production. Or, as García Canclini points out:

> Urbanization and industrialization not only generate new cultural forms but contribute to the reorganization of all symbolic processes. The fact that 60 to 70 percent of the population is now concentrated in big cities and is connected to national and transnational networks means that the contents, practices, and rites of the past—including those of migrant *campesinos*—are reordered according to a different logic. (1992: 33)[5]

Part of what determines this "different logic" is the availability of new media for both production and dissemination. Yet access to such media as television and radio is often difficult, particularly for such historically marginalized groups as those identified with folklore and popular culture. By the time Corpa conducted its survey, the pressure to respond to these groups, now a large part of all audiences, had been mounting for well over a decade. In the vanguard of those calling for this "democratization of culture" were the many leftists formerly active in Venezuela's guerrilla movement. In fact, the pacification of these groups in 1969, after ten years of armed struggle, was directly related to the growth of interest in popular culture throughout the country. Most of these guerrillas were university students from middle-class, urban backgrounds. Their years in the countryside and mountains had been their first exposure to the diversity and richness of campesino life. It is little surprise, therefore, that, once demobilized, these former militants were among the primary agitators for the interests of popular culture. Many of their ideas were articulated at the historic three-day Cultural Congress against Dependency and Neo-Colonialism. Held in December 1970 in the western oil town of Cabimas, the congress outlined what became known as *El Nuevo Viraje* (the New Direction). Participants argued that it was time to move from armed to cultural struggle and called for "the recolonization of Venezuela" (Chacón 1973: 60).

At the heart of the Cabimas strategy was the conviction that popular culture (which was the perfect union of the rural campesino with the urban proletariat) represented the essence of Venezuelan identity and, as such, was also a powerful agent of resistance. It alone could combat the forces of cultural imperialism that had colonized the very souls of the Venezuelan people. In fact, many Venezuelan leftists believed that only through an initial cultural revolution would citizens be sufficiently liberated to imagine a true economic one. As Esteban Emilio Mosonyi, a leading theorist, wrote, "Without underestimating in any way the other mechanisms for struggle, we categorically state the need for a *cultural revolution* as the first step in the creation of a truly integrated revolutionary movement designed for the radical and definitive transformation of our reality" (1982: 180).

All of these discussions, which continued throughout the 1970s in various forms, recognized that the crisis in Venezuela was as much cultural as economic. This became even more apparent during the tremendous oil boom beginning in 1974, when prices quadrupled in a single year. Over the next five years public spending alone increased at an annual average of 17 percent (M. Rodríguez 1991: 246). Arriving with this sudden wealth was a massive importation of Western, and particularly American, consumer goods. For many, it was the age of the *Miamero*, the Venezuelan who slavishly mimicked an American lifestyle, or the couples who flew to New York City to shop for the weekend. It was, as Carmelo Vilda put it, the era of "the cultural dictatorship . . . when even our hearts beat to the rhythms of Houston," a reference, of course, to the numerous Caraqueños with American cardiologists (1984: 15–16). Yet many were also alarmed, warning that this new materialism was obliterating all evidence of Venezuelan culture. The historian Briceño Iragorry echoed these concerns when he wrote:

> We've come even further now on our unconscious journey to destroy the character of this nation. The wave of Anglo-American commercialism has taken over our criollo values and replaced them with exotic symbols. . . . Today even Christmas in Venezuela is no longer the old holiday of our criollo grandfathers. It's a holiday of invading Yanqui grandfathers. No one wishes "Felices Pascuas" any more. Today they send cards with English jingles wishing "Merry Christmas." (quoted in Vilda 1984: 15)

Eventually a second wave of congresses was held, repeating for a new generation many of the same ideas expressed at Cabimas. The first of these, billed as "A Meeting for the National Defense of the Culture," took place in Barquisimeto in 1977. Once again performances of music and dance were interspersed with discussions about popular culture and the need to develop an alliance among campesinos, workers, and students that would be based on true Venezuelan values. Or, as the organizing document stated it: "To arrive at a dynamic and transformative definition of Venezuelan culture in all its diversity and potentiality, and to find the bases for an alternative cultural project that is aligned with our own anti-imperialist and patriotic process of struggle" (Comisión Nacional 1977: 1). Out of these meetings came a new national organization, El Movimiento sobre los Poderes Creadores del Pueblo, "Aquiles Nazoa." Its name was taken from the line of a poem by the beloved writer and humorist Aquiles Nazoa, who had died in a car crash the year before. "I believe in the creative powers of the people," it read, expressing with eloquent simplicity what for many was the essence of popular culture, both as an alternative culture of resistance and as a unifying force in the struggle against imperialism.[6]

Movements and organizations were now springing up everywhere, each one professing solidarity with the culture of the masses. Many of these were music or theater troupes dedicated to the study and promotion of what they considered the true national art forms. Un Solo Pueblo, Madera, Luango, Convenezuela, Vera, all of them crossed the country many times, searching for the best examples of this work. It is likely that the efforts of these groups in not only reviving and adapting but also performing and educating did more to fuel the interest in popular culture than did those of any others. Another important stimulus to this explosion of interest was the model provided by the many artists and musicians forced into exile from the south. For several years, groups in countries such as Chile, Argentina, and Peru had been transforming popular musical forms into expressions of solidarity and protest. When a wave of military dictatorships forced many of them to flee, Venezuela became an asylum of choice. Like the numerous artists and intellectuals who fled Europe for the United States during World War II, these exiles were also to have an enormous influence on the culture of their adopted country.[7]

By now, the government too was starting to play an important role in what was quickly becoming a national crusade for cultural renewal. The nationalization of the steel industry in 1975 and the oil industry the subsequent year helped unleash a groundswell of patriotic fervor. It also stimulated adoption of Venezuela's first comprehensive cultural plan, a key aspect of which was the formation of CONAC, the council empowered to coordinate cultural and artistic activities for the entire country. Groups actively working in the area of popular culture were now given support for the first time. Much of this assistance was earmarked for "projection groups" (*grupos de proyección*), such as Un Solo Pueblo and Luango, who were engaged mainly in performance. But efforts were also made to establish workshops where students would be taught a variety of these popular forms. Most of these activities, however, remained extremely localized or were suspended altogether with subsequent changes in the government.[8] In 1980 an attempt was made to institutionalize this instruction for all Venezuelans with the passage of the Ley Orgánica de Educación, a national education plan which required, among other things, that "folklore and popular traditions" be taught as part of the curriculum in every school (Ley Orgánica de Educación 1986: 12). Resources for implementing this plan never materialized, however, and by 1980 years of overborrowing and reckless spending had finally caught up. The debt crisis had begun.

It was into all of this that the Cigarrera Bigott entered in 1981, when a presidential decree banned all advertising of tobacco and alcohol on television and radio. In many ways it was a perfect equation: a decade of escalating interest in popular culture, a huge vacuum left by a government unable to respond, and a large multinational corporation in search of a theme with which to reinvent its own identity. There was also by now an availability of experienced people from both government and academia who were eager to find new outlets for their skills. Of course, working for a multinational corporation, particularly one that produced tobacco, presented certain moral and political concerns. After all, if popular culture was by its very nature an oppositional strategy with which to resist imperialist domination, then how could a British-owned corporation such as Bigott be responsible for its production?

The tensions surrounding these questions about the definition of popular culture, as either counterhegemonic discourse or an apolitical expression of a simpler folkloric age, were to remain central to the development of the foundation for a number of years. The debate over this issue also replicates in many ways the type of contestation that performers commonly articulate through festivals. In this sense the history of the foundation is much like that of a festival, a performative reality in which competing interests are continuously challenged and negotiated.

As Tulio Hernández, a sociologist who studied the history of the foundation, said about this period when all interests seemed to collide, "Each one was looking for a solution, an enrichment, a pretext, a key, a road. Which is to say, there was a gold mine there [in popular culture] . . . and each one approached it in his own way."

To understand how Bigott was able to resolve these conflicts and in so doing transform itself into an actual site of cultural production, it is best to focus on the histories of the two principal aspects of the campaign: the workshops and the television programs. As already noted, Corpa, the company responsible for Bigott's public relations and advertising, had been planning for this contingency for some time. When the presidential decree was passed in 1981, therefore, Corpa was prepared to redirect the foundation into its new role as an advocate of popular culture. The campaign that followed, however, grew as much from trial and error as it did from any single master plan. As a result, the five major areas in which the foundation is currently active each developed in response to different needs and circumstances. The publications program, for example, continued the work of the in-house magazine, *Revista Bigott*. By 1985 the magazine was dedicated entirely to popular culture and, with its well-researched articles and beautiful illustrations, was a highly coveted journal. Added to this program was a series of calendars and deluxe annual books, each one concentrating on a different folkloric theme.[9] Although these works were distributed free of charge, their audience has rarely extended beyond the company's favored clients or the handful of intellectuals and artists who search them out.

A different though equally restricted audience is that for the agricultural program. Although the only area of the foundation not dedicated to popular culture, it maintains the company's historic ties to farm-related issues. Administered at a separate location in Valencia, this program was initiated in 1986 to provide technical assistance to farmers in the tobacco-growing states of Cojedes, Portuguesa, and Guárico. It has subsequently become involved in tree planting as well as a special radio series entitled *My Friend the Agricultural Producer*. But this program remains extremely small, accounting for only 4 percent of the foundation's annual budget.

Slightly larger, though with a much broader outreach, is the foundation's grant program. Open to any individual or organization wishing to apply, the program is exceptionally competitive, funding just over 1 percent of all requests. In 1992 more than 5,000 applications were submitted, but only 60 won support.[10] While most of these grants were for culture-related activities, those chosen included cinema clubs, museums, folk groups, schools, aquariums, children's books, and libraries.

As important as these three programs have been, it is the remaining two, the workshops and the television campaign, that have been the most instrumental in accomplishing the goals for which the foundation was established. Not only has two-thirds of the budget been devoted to them, but it is primarily through these that Bigott has succeeded in both constructing and projecting its new image.[11] Of course, it was the desire to remain on television that had originally inspired Corpa to suggest popular culture as a focus for the foundation, but the programs produced did much more than simply keep the company in the public eye. In documenting and presenting these traditions, they also helped to redefine them. And in the end Bigott also redefined itself, becoming for many a symbol of national values and identity. The lengthy process by which this occurred can be traced through the three generations of television series the foundation produced. Yet just as important were the Talleres de Cultura Popular, the "Popular Culture Workshops," where so many of these ideas were first tried and developed. It was here that the initial struggle over the very nature of popular culture was first waged. And it is only through analyzing the history of both of these programs—the workshops and the television campaign—that one can begin to understand how the world's largest manufacturer of cigarettes also became Venezuela's leading agent of cultural production.

THE WORKSHOPS: "WHERE THE PAST AND THE FUTURE COME TOGETHER"

Although the primary purpose of the foundation was to maintain Bigott's position in both radio and television, it was not with the media that the new program was launched. In fact, it would be a number of years before any of the now famous documentaries or radio series were aired. In the meantime, Bigott sponsored an ambitious program of workshops in which traditional forms of Venezuelan music and dance were taught. Within months of the creation of the new foundation three *cuatro* workshops, two for adults and one for children, were being offered, beginning what would become one of the most successful educational experiments in all of Latin America.[12] As already noted, the demand for such courses had been felt for some time, and with the ready availability of personnel to direct them, it was not difficult to launch a program. Even so, the response was overwhelming. In just seven years, the number of students would grow from less than 200 to 1,300 and the workshops offered, from 3 to more than 80. But such growth would also bring many problems. For while it may have transformed Bigott into the country's primary sponsor of traditional arts, the nature of this sponsorship would remain extremely contested. In addition to the issue of curriculum would be the even more difficult one of deciding how the new school was to be structured. Would the fact that its content was popular culture demand that the relations among faculty, administration, and students be redrawn? And how important was context and "lifestyle" in teaching what until now had only existed in an alternative realm of society? Such questions would soon become critical in the debate over how the first school ever of popular culture should be organized and run. They would also signal an even deeper division between two radically different views as to what popular culture was.

As with much of the foundation's early operations, Corpa, which had suggested the workshops, was now entrusted with setting them up. But they were publicists, not art educators, so they contracted Rafael Salazar, a leading arts administrator who had worked to promote popular culture during the first presidency of Carlos Andrés Pérez. Since leaving government, Salazar had organized a national association of musicians and artists called the Federación Nacional de la Cultura Popular. It was this group that Salazar now wished to use in an ambitious nationwide program wherein workshops would be established throughout the country to teach different regional forms. In Maracaibo, for example, they would teach *chimbangueles* and *gaitas;* in Barquisimeto, Tamunangue and

golpes; and in the llanos, *joropo* and *bandola.* Beyond recognizing the pluralistic nature of popular culture, this plan would also maximize Bigott's
exposure, for the company's investment would not be limited to one
school situated only in the capital. Salazar, however, was never able to
coordinate this complex program, and, within three months of being
named director, was let go.

The Clavija and the Cultural Reforestation of the City

Corpa now turned to three musicians who had established their own
musical institute just over a year before. Known as "La Clavija" (The
Peg), a name referring to the fact that each of its members played a
stringed instrument, the institute had been created to confront the problem of teaching traditional musical forms.[13] It was the Clavija's contention that Venezuelan popular culture would only be respected once it
was taught in the same way that other artistic styles were. At the same
time, they recognized that these traditions were integrally connected
with the religious and social matrices that had produced them. In fact,
it was these alternative modes of social organization, as much as the
music itself, that had attracted them. Until now, conservatories and other
art schools had been unwilling to make the type of changes necessary to
accommodate these popular forms. But the Clavija was determined to
discover a pedagogy and structure appropriate to the demands of what
until then had been considered either unworthy or incapable of being
taught. It is little surprise, therefore, that the press quickly dubbed the
Clavija "the school that teaches the music that other schools don't."[14]

For the members of the Clavija, teaching was to be much more than
simply a professional commitment. It was to be a total expression of
one's reality, in which transformed social relations would be as important as any other element in the learning experience. Hence, if popular
culture was to be apprehended at all, it would have to be embodied,
becoming as much as possible a lived experience. The Clavija continually
emphasized this integrated approach, claiming:

> We don't teach popular culture. We are popular culture. Or let's just
> say, what we're proposing has to do with our lives. It forms a part of

our life's work. . . . It's not an experiment. It's life. It's a way of being. For us it's just everyday life and when you're living you can't say that you're an experiment. . . . And so when we moved the Clavija over to the talleres we moved a lifestyle.

Such statements clearly placed the Clavija in the vanguard of the "cultural revolution" Mosonyi and others had been insisting would have to take place if Venezuela was to transform itself into a more democratic and egalitarian society. Here were the ideas of Cabimas and Barquisimeto put into practice, the "alternative cultural project aligned with an anti-imperialist and patriotic process of struggle" (Comisión Nacional 1977: 1). Yet it was completely reliant upon the support of one of the world's largest multinational corporations. Given such a scenario, it is not surprising that this unlikely alliance eventually came apart and that the interests of each collided in a series of bitter accusations. However, the final rift did not take place until the fall of 1989, giving the Clavija a full seven years of almost unlimited support within which to experiment.

In part, it was the administrative structure that allowed the talleres to continue operating under the leadership of the Clavija for as long as it did. With Corpa in charge, Bigott had almost no contact with the day-to-day operation of the workshops. Beyond the annual Christmas concerts, company executives rarely if ever visited them. Even Corpa had little contact, for all communication was the responsibility of a single administrator. This position was held by Teresa Zapata, the wife of a well-known Venezuelan artist and a childhood friend of Cristóbal Soto, one of the cofounders of the Clavija.[15]

It was Zapata who had initially promoted the idea of the workshops at Corpa. And although the advertising firm is said to have doubted whether the project could actually succeed, it authorized Zapata to go ahead. She immediately contacted Soto, asking who he felt could best direct it. But when his suggestion, Rafael Salazar, failed, Zapata returned to offer the job to the Clavija itself.

While Soto characterized the events that brought the Clavija to the Talleres de Cultura Popular as something of an accident, their success once there was meteoric (Fig. 17). Expanding on the original three cuatro

Figure 17. The Talleres de Cultura Popular, Caracas. (Courtesy Fundación Bigott)

workshops, they quickly added courses in harp, bandola, guitar, mandolin, maracas, percussion, violin, voice, dance, mask making, and even theory. They brought the best musicians and performers from throughout the country to offer seminars and intensive workshops. Conferences on folklore and popular culture were presented by the nation's most outstanding scholars and writers. Within a year the first of many groups was formed, giving students and teachers the opportunity to present the work they were learning. Like other projection groups, such as Un Solo

Pueblo and Madera, the ones from the Bigott workshops became important forces in a process of cultural renewal. Touring throughout Venezuela, they were to bring both the workshops and the foundation increasing renown. Before long it would be nearly impossible to find a single musical group without some members trained at Bigott. It would also be difficult to visit a festival or dance where a busload of students from the foundation was not in attendance to observe it.

Enrollment soared. With courses costing only a nominal amount and lasting the entire year, it soon became necessary to hold auditions. But the success of the workshops cannot be judged simply by the number of offerings or the quantity of students. It was the social experiment that converted them into a magnet for students and musicians from throughout the country. Here for the first time was a school devoted to Venezuelan culture, free and open to all, where students, faculty, and administration were each treated as equals. The lack of hierarchy and sense of social belonging, the feeling of mission and excitement, of great national purpose, all of these created an environment that participants simply did not want to leave. As Tulio Hernández said:

> The level of voluntarism and cooperation, the sense of belonging and unity that were there at the talleres is something I have rarely if ever seen in a Venezuelan social organization. People were there because they wanted to be, because there were people there who just refused to leave, people who had finished their courses and then wanted to start another instrument. The solidarity was absolute. It was an explosive, electrifying movement.

Such loyalty and sense of community was precisely what the Clavija intended their teaching strategies to instill. By being flexible, spontaneous, and direct, they would approximate as much as possible the dynamic conditions of everyday life.[16] Large meetings, bureaucracies, and paperwork were to be avoided at all costs. In fact, according to them, they were "agraphic, like the Selknam or other peoples who didn't like to write." This distaste for publishing anything, from long-term project goals to class plans, would eventually contribute to their undoing. But for the moment it was an essential ingredient in creating an open, intuitive space, one that mirrored as much as possible the orality of the popular cultures they were trying to teach. It also reinforced what they commonly referred to as their commitment to "horizontality," an organizational structure that would guarantee maximum access and equal treatment for all. The success of this commitment was attested to in a statement made by Arturo García, a harpist from Tuy and one of the first teachers recruited:

> We were one big family. . . . Everyone was connected. There was a perfect democratic structure where no one was more than anyone else, even if you were my boss . . . the camaraderie that's born from true democracy or the democracy that's born from that camaraderie, because it's an ambivalent thing, that.

As conceived by the Clavija and their supporters, this horizontality would eventually extend well beyond the confines of the workshops. It would promote an *efecto multiplicador*, a "multiplication effect," whereby graduates of the workshops would teach what they had learned in less formal settings. Bands, street corners, schools, city plazas, all of them would be converted into new workshops where Bigott-trained musicians would continue to pass on traditional forms of Venezuelan popular culture. Only then would the Clavija's real vision of a "cultural reforestation of the city" start to be realized and the most disenfranchised elements of society be reempowered as musicians and artists once again. But this "reforestation" would not simply mean colonizing the urban with the rural, nor the imported with the native. It would represent the triumph of a "new synthesis," a union of local, popular forms with the many new ones that had now taken root in the Venezuelan cultural landscape (Escauriza 1989: 7). It would mean that those elements discredited as folklore would end their long exile at the margins of society and become the dynamic centerpiece of a new national form.[17]

Commodity versus Community, or Popular Culture Goes to School

By 1987 the success of the Talleres de Cultura Popular had become so great that Bigott no longer wished to leave the administration of the

program in the hands of Corpa. The foundation itself would now assume
responsibility, and although Teresa Zapata would remain as administrator, she now reported directly to it. For the first time the Clavija was
starting to be monitored, and the freedom they had formerly experienced
challenged. It was clear to Bigott that the workshops had become too
great a resource and could no longer operate independently of the rest
of the foundation. Tensions mounted. At Bigott concern grew that it had
lost control and that the direction of the Clavija might no longer represent the company's interests. In order to decide what course to take, the
foundation commissioned Tulio Hernández, a young sociologist and former student of Alfredo Chacón, to undertake a detailed study of the
operation, goals, and effectiveness of the workshops. It was this investigation, along with a shorter, follow-up one (Hernández 1986, 1989),
that helped determine the workshops' fate. For in late 1989, while meeting with Bigott to negotiate their contract, the Clavija suddenly read in
the newspapers that INDASE (Instituto de Asesoramiento Educativa),
an educational consultant, had been hired to take their place.

It was soon after this that I first met the Clavija and began my investigation of the Bigott Foundation. I had been attracted in part by the
similarities to my own experiences at the California Institute of the Arts
when it was founded in Los Angeles in the early 1970s. Although not a
school of popular culture, Cal Arts was driven by similar utopian ideals
of the 1960s (Adler 1979). The combination of radical avant-garde artists,
many of them transplanted from New York, and a conservative board
of trustees dominated by the Disney family, who were the school's primary sponsors, had concluded in an equally disastrous fashion. Yet in
the North American case, many faculty and administration members did
not survive the first year, as the trustees, eager to reassert control, fired
them.[18]

I recounted these events to the Clavija during our first meeting, when,
in a reversal of roles, they cautiously interviewed me. The conflict with
Bigott had left them understandably anxious, and they wanted to know
why this American was so curious about the fate of an obscure experimental music school in Caracas. In addition, each party had agreed as
part of the final settlement to refrain from making any public statements

about what had transpired (a condition making ethnographic fieldwork particularly difficult). With time, however, both sides made it abundantly clear that the primary issue was that of control. From the moment administration passed from Corpa to Bigott in 1987, relations had quickly deteriorated. The Clavija, like many at the workshops, had been forced to reconcile the fact that their radical project was being completely underwritten not only by a multinational corporation but by one that manufactured cigarettes. To do so, they had maintained as much independence as possible, treating the support as if it were a grant and insisting that their efforts not be co-opted in any way to promote the interests of the company. On the other hand, Bigott also experienced difficulty in reconciling its support for what was commonly identified with leftist interests and hence hostile to corporations such as itself. It was a delicate balance for both and as Enio Escauriza, one of the Clavija's founders, made clear, worked only as long as each felt it was using rather than being used by the other:

> There's a reality. Bigott's a company with a very high social cost. It's a harmful product. And one has to think about that. We were developing a project around popular culture and having a real impact. But we were doing it through a company that sells dangerous products. That's something that has to be considered. Now, we had the opportunity to do this through Bigott and as far as possible, we've tried to separate ourselves, one thing from the other. However, they were able through the workshops—let's say the workshops as an important part of their campaign, of their corporate image project—to rescue the image of Bigott. Because the product had swallowed the company. Bigott didn't exist. What existed was Belmont. . . .
>
> Now the anxieties that were generated in them over financing a project devoted to popular culture, which was actually turning into a center full of activity and life, where there *was* popular culture, perhaps that was uncomfortable, just as for us the question of cigarettes is uncomfortable. Yet we could create some distance between one thing and the other. We don't know how uncomfortable the issue of popular culture was for them, because maybe they had no idea what popular culture was. And clearly they still don't know, but whatever it is, they don't like it very much.

Others, less hindered perhaps by the gag order of a separation agreement, were more candid in elaborating on the conflict between the two parties. Arturo García, for example, who was present during all seven years of the Clavija's direction, saw the issue as that of popular culture's ongoing struggle against the forces of neocolonialism. For him, a final confrontation was inevitable, especially when Bigott realized the monster it had created was about to devour it. Like Dr. Frankenstein, the scientist had simply lost control of his experiment or, as García described it:

> What happened is that when Bigott opened the door there was a gigantic monster there who was devouring the company, which is to say, it was swallowing it. That is, the Bigott Foundation with its popular culture workshops was swallowing the cigarette corporation. And from a publicity point of view, from an image point of view, it wasn't working. . . . It was slipping out of their hands. Look, let's be clear about this. It was slipping out of their hands from an ideological point of view. Even though Bigott is the British Tobacco Blah Blah Blah Multinational Neocolonialist, they were supporting a project whose members were famous for being communists and so on. And what they were preaching through the popular culture workshops was the recovery of our identity, which is to say, anticolonialist values.

Although officials at Bigott were somewhat more circumspect in discussing what had transpired, they too acknowledged that the issue of independence had helped accelerate the final rupture. The Clavija's refusal to provide detailed budgets and written plans, along with their general ideological unaccountability, had continued to infuriate the company, leaving them to feel like little more than clients in receipt of a service. The Clavija, of course, maintained that this was the proper relationship, and it might have been had Bigott simply been interested in training musicians in popular forms. But British American Tobacco was primarily interested in producing an image. To be separated rather than linked to the project they were sponsoring would therefore be counterproductive. Agustín Coll, the director of the foundation during this period, explained Bigott's frustration with the Clavija in the following way:

They kept saying it was a service we'd contracted, and the comparison they'd use was that it was like taking your car to a mechanic, that one paid when the car was fixed but that you didn't ask how much the mechanic made or how much this cost or how much that was. You just paid and got it. That was the comparison.

But we said, look, that's not possible. You can't make that comparison in our case because this involves a problem of the Bigott Foundation's image. Each one of the professors of this institution is one of the bearers of our image, because they're representing the foundation in front of the students and in front of the entire community as well. So it's not so easy as just saying, "You give me that money and I'll give you this." It doesn't work that way.

In its public statements, Bigott claimed simply that the problems were "administrative." And indeed, the most common criticism voiced against the Clavija had been their highly personalized and informal management style. From the documents produced by Hernández (1986, 1989), it is clear that the foundation no longer wanted the future of the workshops to depend on the charisma of several individuals. The extraordinary energy and communitas of the first seven years would now have to be channeled into institutional norms and rules. As Hernández concluded, "The workshops simply can't go on being administered and directed in a random fashion" (1989: 20). If the reproduction of the workshop experience was to be guaranteed, either in Caracas or elsewhere, then it would have to be taken out of the hands of individuals and placed in the norms of an institution. It is little surprise, therefore, that every one of Hernández's recommendations required that the activity be carefully committed to writing. Whether class plans, evaluations, catalogues, or mission statements, each aspect of the school would now have to be systematized and codified (Hernández 1986: 55; 1989: 11–13). In some cases, the difficulties of applying such standards to popular culture were enormous, especially when they required campesino artists with no formal training to begin submitting detailed course plans.[19] To Arturo García, this idea was particularly offensive:

I don't have any written method. My method's not written down! Anyway I'm very jealous with that. When I die no one will know shit about how I gave classes, or what I based my classes on. Method? Are you crazy! Where? Ask the people at NASA to give it to you. That's the way they do things. It's like asking for formulas. It's the same thing. . . . Besides, people have been learning music without writing it down for ten thousand years, so why do I have to now?

Underlying these issues of systematization was much more than a simple conflict of leadership styles or even the yearning for structure, which Victor Turner has claimed all such "spontaneous communitas" will inevitably provoke (1969: 131–140). It was part of a much larger debate, in which orality and literacy became markers for two very different points of view as to what the nature of popular culture and folklore was. For the Clavija was not simply mimicking popular culture with its aversion to writing; it was trying to ensure a context in which the most important thing produced would be social relations themselves. In this process-oriented environment, popular culture and folklore would be determined by neither authenticity nor content. They would be byproducts of a dynamic social reality, what de Certeau called "a style of social exchange" (1980: 4) in which every individual is actively engaged as a creative and participatory being. Unlike other programs organized to promote popular culture, the workshops would not be concerned with simply bringing art to the masses. Their preoccupation was to turn the masses into artists.

While Bigott was also concerned with providing excellent training for workshop participants, its notion about what was being produced was radically different. To the foundation, folklore was primarily an artifact, a set of discreet traditions bound by either rural isolation or religious superstition. It was an entity defined not so much by social relations as by content and origins. This view of folklore as commodity became particularly apparent with the administration that succeeded the Clavija. Although attitudes toward folklore like those of the Bigott Foundation are often characterized by a great deal of fetishizing around issues of purity and authenticity, the new directors actually spoke of the need to "de-folklorize." Through this concept the folklore event would be cleaned up. It would be colorfully recostumed and dramatically rechoreographed. In short, it would be repackaged so that it could compete onstage with other art forms no matter how classical or refined. Only then would folklore finally be "de-marginalized" and, taking its rightful place in the pantheon of the arts, be able to be appreciated by all strata of society, from the highest to the lowest. While this notion may seem more progressive than the normal strategy of consigning these expressions to the status of a museum, underlying it is the same assumption that folklore is a detachable object, to be harmlessly moved from one social context to another.[20] In fact, rather than being defined by its environment, the implications of "de-folklorization" are that it is handicapped by it. However, Bigott would now be its liberator, making available to the middle and upper classes what until now had been too unkempt to be appreciated. Such views, of course, were critical to Bigott's campaign if the foundation was to successfully market the products of its philanthropy.

To Nelly Ramos, who also conducted a study of the workshops independent of that of Hernández, the difference between these two views of folklore is what distinguished the Clavija from any other cultural program (Ramos 1987). For her, the workshops had been a direct response to the very notion of an alienated bourgeois art in which audiences are relegated to the role of passive consumers, too apathetic to engage in any critical thought. They had been a radical cultural alternative to this paradigm, reempowering people with the tools to create their own culture.[21] Unlike other conservatories, therefore, the workshops did not focus on the soloist or the virtuoso. Here the emphasis was on participation and the need to generate a new cultural ideal, particularly among those who were rarely able to attend such schools. The Clavija had referred to this process as "the cultural reforestation of the city." For Ramos it represented no less than a revolution, in which the working class would once again regain control of the means of cultural production (1987: 2–6). And in the end, it was the struggle over this control that was the true source of conflict between Bigott and the Clavija and the critical element that led each to define popular culture in the manner in which it did.

The workshops reopened once again several months after the Clavija left. Almost all of the old teachers remained, and demand among students continued to grow. INDASE undertook the restructuration that Hernández had recommended. A clear division among faculty, staff, administration, and students was now set in place. Evaluations, along with limits as to how long individuals could remain in the workshops, were also imposed, but in most ways little changed, at least outwardly. Students, from mainly working-class neighborhoods, still flocked to the workshops, enthralled with the privilege of learning an instrument that their grandparents had often played in the countryside just a generation before.[22] Teachers too continued to come, gaining certification for the folklore component required by the public schools. And while musicians, dancers, mask makers, and others were brought in from the countryside to lead special workshops, other cities like Valencia and Maracay continued to implore the foundation for talleres of their own. More projection groups were formed, with larger tours and international performances. And within all of this, it was difficult to recognize the loss of energy and excitement of those first years, when the Clavija had created a community inspired by a vision of popular culture as a transforming and liberating agent. But if this strange partnership between big business and popular culture continued, it would now be popular culture as British American Tobacco defined it. For the company had decided it was time to integrate the workshops into a much more unified and public promotional campaign. Attitudes toward multinational corporations and foreign investors were beginning to change dramatically. It was time for Bigott to come out of the closet and, as Hernández advised, "start maximizing its investment" (1989: 26). The Talleres de Cultura Popular could no longer exist independently of the rest of the foundation. Instead, they would be promoted as one of its greatest triumphs, particularly in its television series, where the workshops were about to become a star.

THE IMAGE OF CULTURE

Although it was more than four years before the first television series began to appear,[23] Bigott quickly reestablished itself as a presence on the air. In place of mentioning the name of its most popular brand, each program prominently displayed the company's logo of three tobacco leaves, along with the name of the Fundación Bigott. In all, 140 programs were produced over the next five years. Organized into three formats or series, each one built upon the others until the foundation became much more than a simple cultural apparatus. For, in the end, it was to become the subject of its own study, a producer of popular traditions like the communities it had originally sought to document. Essential to this transformation was the creation of a unified campaign incorporating not only the workshops but all of the foundation's projects, from publishing to tree planting. In this sense, Bigott was applying the same strategy of vertical integration used by its parent company, British American Tobacco. Producers, suppliers, and distributors, in this case of culture, would now have to be subsumed into a single organization if profitability was to be maximized. Key to understanding how this process occurred is an analysis of the different television series and the manner in which each promoted a new vision of the foundation and its work. Only then can one begin to understand how Bigott, in wedding its name to popular culture, was able to convert itself into a synonym for the nation's most traditional values.

Encuentro Con . . .

The great majority of the programs were part of Bigott's first series, called simply *Encuentro con . . .* (Encounter with . . .). The initial encounters, which would eventually total 120, did not distinguish between popular and mass culture and were dedicated mainly to presenting the work of such pop urban musicians as Billo Frómeta, Guálberto Ibarreto, and Cecilia Todd. While several of these performers did draw heavily on folk traditions, it was only in the series' third year that the programs assumed their exclusive focus on traditional forms of popular culture. It was these final *Encuentro con*s, aired between 1987 and 1988, that eventually became most associated with the series. Shown each Saturday at noon, they presented a steady weekly catalogue of every major folkloric genre in dance and music throughout Venezuela.[24]

Each program, produced by Corpa, had the same half-hour format, with twenty-seven minutes devoted to exploring the subject and three minutes reserved for publicizing the work of the foundation. It was for these three minutes of "commercial time" that Bigott paid the television stations to have its programs aired. And yet, if Bigott was promoting itself, it was careful, during this first series, to remove any mention of its name from the main body of the program. Only at the beginning and end did the company's logo of three tobacco leaves fill the screen (Fig. 18), and a narrator announce in a deep baritone voice:

The Bigott Foundation, as a contribution to the diffusion of our nation's music, history, and traditions, presents *"Encounter with . . . Our Musical Expressions."*

The creation of this distance between content and sponsor was an important element in the overall strategy used to establish Bigott's legitimacy as well as that of the programs. For these were not meant to be sound bites but serious documentaries chronicling as faithfully as possible the nation's most important, if neglected, cultural treasures. Everything was calculated to reinforce their objectivity—the narrator's deep reverential tone, the experts' thoughtful, if often ponderous, analyses, the interviews with performers, even the monumental backdrops of castles and churches. Wherever possible, performances were filmed on location and songs and dances presented in their entirety. In the program devoted to the Tamunangue celebration, for example, a short history of the colonial community of Tocuyo precedes the actual dance. A local scholar then comes on to explain the performance's structure and meaning. Specialists as well as local participants continue to appear throughout the program, offering both commentary and insight between segments. It is a careful, didactic style, whose sole purpose seemingly is to educate the Venezuelan public about the origins, beauty, and depth of its own traditions. How could one help but believe the narrator, therefore, when, at the conclusion of each program, he announces: "Fundación Bigott . . . en pro de la cultura popular," "the Bigott Foundation . . . in support of popular culture."

The Micros

In 1989 Bigott introduced a new series. With *Encuentro con . . .* completing its fourth season and the foundation's other programs gaining increasing recognition, Bigott decided it was time to embark upon a new campaign. In many ways, it was the conflict with La Clavija that precip-

Figure 18. Bigott-sponsored concert, showing the company logo, Caracas. (Courtesy Fundación Bigott)

itated this decision. Hernández and others who had analyzed the first several years of the foundation's work concluded that Bigott was not deriving as large a return on its cultural investment as it should be. Foundation projects were simply acting too independently of one another. What Hernández in particular recommended was that a "global campaign" be initiated, in which each aspect of the foundation be used to promote every other (1989: 39). Only by creating such synergies, in the language of contemporary corporations, would Bigott begin to take advantage of the considerable symbolic capital it had now accumulated. For it was clear that the workshops, documentaries, and publications had all attained large followings among the Venezuelan public and, in so doing, had dispelled many of the early suspicions with which they had been greeted. The new television series, it was hoped, would now begin to exploit the special relationship that had been firmly established between Bigott and popular culture.[25]

One of the first considerations of the new series was that it be aired during prime time. However, the current format was too slow and ponderous for most Venezuelans, especially if it was to compete with the popular *telenovelas* shown during that hour.[26] There was also the question of cost. Until now the networks had classified the programs as educational and charged Bigott only a nominal fee for airing them. If they were to be shown on Sunday nights, as Bigott wished, the stations would insist that they pay for a full thirty minutes of advertising. The solution to these problems was the *micro,* a slickly edited two-minute slice of folklore in which Bigott and popular culture were so brilliantly interwoven that the viewer could not distinguish between them. Unlike the previous generation of documentaries, which were shot in video in a slow, deliberate style, the micros were to be state of the art. The first were actually filmed in 35 millimeter and made by some of the country's leading directors. But the costs soon exceeded those of the half-hour programs, so 16 millimeter was used for the remainder of the series.

Even more significant than this technological innovation and the programs' increased visibility was the organization of the information itself. For each of the micros conformed to a precise structure, heralding a new stage in the relation between Bigott and popular culture. The objectivity of the first series was now replaced by a radically altered image, in which Bigott was inextricably linked to the production of popular culture itself. The site of this production, of course, was the Talleres de Cultura Popular, which, free from the obstructive leadership of the Clavija, could now be incorporated into the larger designs of the foundation. Although Bigott still travels out to the *campo* in these programs, it is no longer simply to document the performance of traditional forms. Now, in an eerie parallel to the manufacture of cigarettes, the forms are "harvested" like any other raw material and brought back to the workshops to be processed.[27]

This theme is repeated in each of the micros, where simple titles first announce the names of the artists, along with their specialization. The artists are then shown in their native habitat, surrounded by images of campesino life—barnyard animals, horses, cows, rows of corn, dramatic landscapes. As they play their instruments, often surrounded by neighbors, the narrator comments on the history of the tradition, as well as its location. Then, as if by magic, the performers are suddenly transported to the workshops, where, in place of neighbors, eager students surround them. The narrator now affirms that it is at the Talleres de Cultura Popular that these traditions are passed on from one generation to the next. Although these statements are tailored to the individual artist, they are the key moment in each program, consecrating the workshops as the legitimate site of cultural transmission. In the program dedicated to the Tuyera harpist Fulgencio Aquino, for example, the narration states:

> In the Popular Culture Workshops of the Bigott Foundation, under the wise guidance of Maestro Aquino, the rich Tuyera tradition of music and dance flows into the blood of new generations.

The organic metaphors encourage the audience to associate the workshops with a living community and the traditions discussed with age and naturalness. And yet, if the participants are portrayed as members of a single family, it is the invocation of the nation that ultimately binds them together. The ever-present tension between regional traditions and national identity is both resolved and mediated by the workshops, as the structure of each of these minidocumentaries makes clear. In the program on Anselmo López, one of Venezuela's most famous folk artists, the musician is first shown playing his bandola in front of a campesino house with cowboys chasing cattle nearby. After a description of his instrument, along with his contributions to it, López is transported to the workshops, where enthusiastic students greet him. Then, as the class begins, the narrator says:

> In the Popular Culture Workshops of the Bigott Foundation, where the present and the future come together, Anselmo López transmits the secrets of the bandola llanera to the followers of a musical tradition with deep Venezuelan roots.

The image now shifts back to the llanos, with López once again surrounded by cattle and horses. As he lies in his hammock, playing the bandola, the final words of the narrator are heard:

In Anselmo López's hands the bandola llanera has transcended the western plains and become an instrument of universal dimensions.

As the screen goes black, the company's logo of three tobacco leaves appears for the first and only time. Then, with the words "Fundación Bigott and *Encuentro con . . .*" flashing quickly beneath it, the program ends. It has all taken just two minutes. But the uniform movement from country to city and back again presents the viewer with the unequivocal if multilayered message that culture is now mediated by the large centers of urban power. Although Bigott's new programs introduce the workshops as the symbol of that power, it might as easily be that of any number of multinational corporations, or the state, or the mass media in general. What is certain is that they are all partners, willingly or not, in a new cultural equation where local and global, regional and national, popular and elite, oral and electronic (La Clavija and Bigott, the list is endless) are constantly interacting in the reinvention of self and nation.[28] Of course, the fact that these programs were emblems of a new cultural paradigm was of little importance to Bigott. To Bigott the micros simply chronicled the evolution of the foundation, signaling its new role as both a transmitter and producer of popular culture. They announced that it was now at the Talleres de Cultura Popular that the nation's most important folk artists came to pass on their traditional knowledge and wisdom.

The Cuñas

After producing ten micros, which were aired regularly at 8:20 on Friday and Sunday evenings, Bigott decided to introduce yet another series.[29] Exactly ten years had passed since the foundation dedicated itself to popular culture, and the situation in the country had changed dramatically. No longer were politicians and others calling for the nationalization of foreign enterprises. A wave of neoliberalism had swept the entire continent, and multinational firms such as British American Tobacco were suddenly more welcome than ever. The original motivation of the company to conceal its British identity had lost its urgency. On the other hand, the success of the campaign had encouraged others to start their own programs in popular culture. Bigott was beginning to experience competition. If it was to maintain its preeminence, it would have to become more aggressive in both promoting its accomplishments and staking out the field as its own. Antonio López Ortega, the foundation's new director, explained these developments and their influence on Bigott's decision to change course in the following way:

> When the foundation chose popular culture as its niche in 1981, it was a very clear choice. In this country in that year, at that time, no one was interested at all in the issue of popular culture. Right now, though, we're starting to see something else. We're starting to see a growth of interest from other private-sector companies in the area of popular culture and also a growing interest in city and regional governments in supporting popular culture events. . . . All this would have been impossible ten years ago, but right now we're in an area where we're starting to feel a little competition. And the foundation has to watch out. Because fortunately up till now we've been all alone in this field, and that has really let us stand out. Which has been the fundamental change from 1991 till now, when the foundation decided to completely abandon its old course and start coming out in public and begin speaking really clearly about our programs, our achievements, and the various objectives we've accomplished.
>
> Look, this is a multinational corporation, with British and American capital, and I think that at the beginning, in 1981, it was very smart for a multinational corporation to create a socially responsible program associated with the country's most traditional values. But right now the situation has changed. Today the concept the country has of a multinational company is very different. Today the government is telling the world, "Come on, foreign investors. This is the place." And so the situation is a little different.[30]
>
> The most important decision I think that the foundation has made is to speak out very clearly about its programs. Before we hid them. But now we've decided we have to speak. We have to put them on display and keep on doing it. Because in the end it's been a program that's lasted over time, a costly one, yes, but one that's brought a lot of recognition to the company. And so that's the policy we're going to continue to follow from now on.

Of course, Bigott had already shifted the emphasis of the television programs onto the workshops, focusing only on artists who worked directly with them. It was a strategy Hernández had referred to as "closing the circle," a way in which each foundation program was used to champion the accomplishments of the others. But the micros still portrayed the workshops as intermediaries in a cultural process. The talleres may have had the power to transform local artists such as Anselmo López into national (if not "universal") figures, yet they remained a place where great musicians and dancers visited, and then left. In the new series about to be introduced, all of this would change. Now the foundation would become the tradition itself and the object of its own study. The countryside and the mediating role of the workshops would merge into one, and, after ten years of cultural intervention, they would be viewed, as would all of the foundation's programs, as a single, self-contained space in which production, consumption, and distribution all took place.

The new programs were called *cuñas* (spots) and were even more condensed than the previous two-minute series. Only forty-five seconds in length, each one focused on a different area of the foundation's work—the calendars, the publications, the workshops, the agricultural projects. In all, Bigott made nine of these programs, airing them during the same Friday and Sunday evening slots as they had the micros. Like the previous programs, these too adhered to a consistent format whose closely repeated structure communicated a single message. At the heart of this new structure was the image of a book, its two covers symbolizing the self-containment with which Bigott was now beginning to represent itself. Of course the book also indicated knowledge and wisdom, and the passage of its traditions from one generation to the next. As such, each cuña was organized as a small story, a tale told about the way the foundation was transmitting the country's most cherished values.

The opening image of each program shows the same enormous green book lying on a table. Its title, clearly visible above the corporate logo of golden tobacco leaves, is *La otra Siembra de Bigott*, "Bigott's Other Crop." As the book begins to open, suggesting the unfolding of a story, the narrator's deep voice wraps the title into a quatrain of neat organic metaphors, wherein past meets future and producer, consumer:

Bigott's other crop.
To project our roots
We plant culture
and we harvest art.

Or, in the program on publications:

Bigott's other crop.
To preserve the country's living memory
We plant testimonies
and we harvest history.

The subject of the program is identified, and as the next page appears, a carefully framed black-and-white photograph comes into view. The camera zooms in, and the photograph not only comes to life but also turns to color. The figure, with less than half a minute to speak, makes a statement about the history and importance of his or her activity at Bigott. After displaying several aspects of this work, the image suddenly freezes, returning to the original black and white. As the book closes once again, the narrator repeats the title and then the slogan, "Una semilla más de la Fundación Bigott" (One more seed from the Bigott Foundation). A small toy passenger train now rolls into view. As its steam engine turns to fill the screen the corporate logo can be seen once again displayed on its front. The booming voice of the announcer concludes by reading the message that appears below it, "A todo tren con Venezuela!" ... "Full speed ahead with Venezuela!" (Fig. 19).

The *Encuentro con . . .* title has now been replaced with the powerful new image of a train. The fact that it is a steam engine representing the technology of another age enables the program to identify with both progress and tradition at the same time. In place of a backward image of folklore there is a dynamic view, in which popular culture seems to catalyze the nation into action. Within the cyclical confines of the book (and hence Bigott) there is a constant movement between past and future, young and old, black and white and color. The text too resolves this same polarity, making it clear that Bigott is in the vanguard of supporting popular culture for the benefit of the nation. Inspired, perhaps,

Figure 19.   The Bigott train. (Courtesy Fundación Bigott)

by the Clavija's original slogan calling for the "cultural reforestation of the city," the cuñas now employ a steady barrage of telluric references, in which the word "culture" is once again reunited with its agricultural origins (Wagner 1981: 21). According to the new programs, it is a natural resource which, if properly cultivated and cared for, will continue to bear fruit. Yet the metaphor of planting the past in order to harvest the future is employed to evoke other associations as well. As López Ortega explained, Bigott was now using these programs to stake out its territory and, as such, was announcing in no uncertain terms that this was its crop. The message not only unites the past with the future, therefore; it also joins Bigott to popular culture and, what is most significant, in a way that suggests the company's historic ties to the land. The effect of all this polysemy is a calculated confusion in which viewers are suddenly uncertain as to exactly what it is this corporation produces: tobacco and cigarettes, or culture and community?[31]

In the program devoted to the Talleres de Cultura Popular, the narrator's voice announces:

> Bigott's other crop.
> To preserve the country's living memory
> We plant tradition
> and we harvest the future.

After the title page is shown, a black-and-white photograph of a young girl around eleven or twelve years old appears. As the camera zooms in, the image comes alive with dance and song. She is then shown in a sequence of activities—participating in a workshop with other students, writing at her desk, leaving home on her way to the talleres. These snapshots quickly locate her as coming from an Afro-Venezuelan working-class background. As the images roll by, she speaks of the things dearest to her—family, friends, school, and music. She explains that she first came to the workshops at the age of six and that it is here alone that all of these things come together. She is then shown happily surrounded by friends, singing at a rehearsal of the Grupo Zaranda, the foundation's concert group for youth. The image now freezes, returning once again to black and white. As the book starts to close, the announcer says, "The Talleres de Cultura Popular . . . Another seed from the Bigott Foundation," and then as the toy train rolls toward the center of the screen, "Full speed ahead with Venezuela."

In a macabre transformation of the Clavija's vision, the workshops have become a community based on the democratizing values of popular culture. It is where the program's young and underprivileged protagonist receives, produces, and transmits knowledge. It is the center of her social relations, her education, and her creativity, the extended family with whom she has now spent more than half of her life. As a locus of social and cultural production it replicates the national community, becoming the legitimate heir to traditions that were formerly associated with small, rural villages. It is only logical, therefore, that a television series that once scoured the countryside for examples of such expressions should now turn its cameras on the work of the foundation itself. And yet in doing so, the circle has truly closed. While the company may have begun its association with popular culture in order to promote its name and conceal its foreign identity, it has now become its very embodiment. As the language of the cuñas, with its reliance on the epitomizing symbol of the land, makes clear, the nation and the tobacco company are now one.

Chapter 5 From Village Square
to Opera House

TAMUNANGUE AND THE THEATER
OF DOMINATION

San Antonio went out

from the city where he was,

taking just a little drum.

Up to the mountain he came

playing oh so sweetly

singing to them the *yeyevamos*.

And the ones in the mountains

said, "What is this?"

And Antonio answered, "Estangüé,

the same thing you'll dance to."

VENEZUELAN DÉCIMA

Tamunangue, flower of our mestizo nation.

JUAN LISCANO, "FOLKLORE
DEL ESTADO LARA"

THE POLITICS OF PERFORMANCE

The Bigott Corporation may have initiated its ambitious program of cultural sponsorship in order to identify itself with Venezuela's most traditional expressive forms, yet the consequences of this campaign were to be much more far-reaching. As the foundation intervened in more

129

and more areas of popular culture, its responsibility for the production and circulation of these forms continued to grow. Magazines, books, calendars, concert groups, grants, workshops, and, of course, the daily televising of documentaries and micros guaranteed that Bigott would now play an increasingly important role in how these traditions would be interpreted. Until recently most scholars discounted the aesthetic importance of such cultural interventions, insisting that they marked the passage into an antiseptic, dehistoricized reality. Once disembedded from the communities that inspired them, popular traditions have become suspect. Dismissed as little more than bourgeois spectacle and tourist art, these performances have been considered too inauthentic to have any real communicative power or to participate in the ongoing elaboration of new forms.[1] But recent scholarship has begun to challenge such views and, while acknowledging that these mediations do change traditions, argues that they also be considered a part of them. As discussed earlier, recent theories of "hybridity" (García Canclini 1990, 1995; Clifford 1987), "creolization" (Hannerz 1989b, 1992), "cultural reconversion" (García Canclini 1992: 33), and "public culture" (Appadurai and Breckenridge 1988, 1992) have resisted previous stereotypes of popular forms as fragile constructs unable to exist outside a limited cultural biosphere. Instead, a rich process of resemanticization is offered in which new meanings are constantly being negotiated.

In the case of the Bigott Foundation, much of this negotiation centered around issues of performance and presentation. Beyond the question of repertoire and the selection of forms to be taught or presented were the many directorial decisions—choreography and staging, amplification and sound, even the role of a master of ceremonies.[2] In each instance, choices were made that would eventually affect the entire tradition from which they were derived. For these performances were not simply for the benefit of urban audiences curious to learn more about the beliefs and customs of their rural forebears. Whether onstage, in a workshop, or mediated through print and the electronic media, the performances invariably returned to the communities in which they were originally performed. Just as an *Encuentro con . . .* or a micro could be seen on the television sets of those participating in a festival in any part of Venezuela, so too could the same participants be found in the foundation's workshops and concert groups in Caracas. This does not mean that the directorial interventions imposed by Bigott and others have been either welcome or positive. It does mean, however, that the type of folkloric aestheticization discussed by Barbara Kirshenblatt-Gimblett (1998: 75) and others ought to be recognized as an important part of the ongoing practice of these traditions.

As noted above, such acknowledgment has rarely been forthcoming. Yet, as the analysis of popular culture and folklore continues to shift away from one of origins and authenticity to that of social relations and practice, forms previously ignored are beginning to be studied. Along with such changes has come the recognition that festive behavior is not simply multivocal but also multilocal.[3] As expressive forms are repeatedly appropriated by the state, political parties, the church, the entertainment industry, multinational corporations, and other such forces, the notion of privileging a single site becomes less tenable. This is not to say that a San Juan celebration performed in a secular context in Caracas is the same as one that takes place in Curiepe on the 24th of June. Yet if the same musicians and dancers perform in both, then the strategies demanded by each will invariably influence the other. Also influenced will be those who watch the event in one context (be it on television or stage) and then later perform it in another. In this sense, meaning is not only historically but also spatially contingent. For while it may be obvious that a specific context will determine the aesthetic choices employed by the performers, it has not been obvious how these choices affect the overall meaning of the tradition itself. In large part, this is because most analyses of such performances have insisted on the separation of one from the other, maintaining that they be understood either as instances of pure, local production or as dislocated, contaminated ones.

For the Colombian scholar Jesús Martín-Barbero, the importance of seeing all such performances as part of the same tradition is twofold. Not only does it undermine a hierarchical, progress-driven notion of culture in which forms are defined as either preindustrial and rural, or urban and modern, it also recognizes the particular condition of emergent cultures in the postmodern reality that is Latin America. Martín-Barbero claims it is this cultural phenomenon, rather than any ethnic or racial one, that is the determining feature of mestizaje. As he explains:

> Once we take as the starting point of observation and analysis not the linear process of upward social progress but *mestizaje,* that is, *mestizaje* in the sense of continuities in discontinuity and reconciliations between rhythms of life that are mutually exclusive, then we begin to understand the complex cultural forms and meanings that are coming into existence in Latin America: the mixture of the indigenous Indian in the rural peasant culture, the rural in the urban, the folk culture in the popular cultures and the popular in mass culture. In this we are not trying to avoid contradictions but move them out of established schemas so that we can take a fresh look at them in the process of their composition and decomposition. We are looking for the revealing gaps in the context and the context of the gaps. (1993a: 188)

An important element in this new orientation, as Martín-Barbero conceives it, is a focus on the key role of communications systems as spaces in which these new forms are negotiated. No longer seen as mere agents of a hegemonic discourse, the media, whether radio, television, or film, provide a complex arena in which a range of cultural interests are not simply appropriated but also "mediated" (1993a, 1993b). It is in this sense that hierarchical notions of high and low, popular and elite, urban and rural (the list goes on) are simultaneously challenged and recycled. Similar discoveries were also made by Julie Taylor in her investigation of Brazilian Carnival, where competing cultural interests often reproduce one another in the very attempt to establish distinctiveness. Yet, as Taylor indicated, the circularity of these expressive forms only intensified the debate over tradition, making "the politics of aesthetic meaning a central part of carnival itself" (1982: 301).

Studies such as these by Martín-Barbero and Taylor clearly reinforce the need to track the movement of expressive forms through both space and media. While it has been shown how festive behavior has continually responded to historical changes, enabling it to address such issues as race, ethnicity, and nationalism, it must also be shown how concurrent versions of the same tradition are employed to present competing messages. By doing so, one can begin to appreciate the aesthetics of performance as more than simply a response to new technological demands or a result of the degeneration of the tradition itself. Instead, formal aspects of performance are to be seen as part of a highly charged ideological process, participating in the same discursive behavior as every other aspect of the tradition.[4] Although the embrace of such varied expressions under the banner of a single tradition may prove difficult, it will be necessary if festive forms are to be portrayed as they are—complex, emergent, and even contradictory. It is also essential in order to recognize that today festive discourse occurs across communities, classes, technologies, and even national borders and that the elaboration of one contributes to the creation of the other. Or, put another way, with every deterritorialization comes a respatialization.

In Venezuela there are a number of festive forms whose study now requires that they be acknowledged as participating in several symbolic systems—San Juan, the Devils of Yare, the music of the llanos. Yet none has been as successfully and frequently adapted to as many different performative contexts as has that of Tamunangue, a suite of dances performed in honor of San Antonio de Padua on the 13th of June.[5] Although originally restricted to the southern part of the western state of Lara, Tamunangue has now been presented at folklore festivals, state fairs, popular culture workshops, international concert tours, museums, presidential inaugurations, television, radio, and even the Caracas opera. The dramatic transformations that have accompanied this ongoing migration, however, have not eliminated the form's ability to communicate new and rich ideas. In fact, by multiplying both its audiences and venues, Tamunangue has increased the scope of this dialogue. Hence, it has become an important focus for debates on issues not only of race, class, and national identity but also, and even more significantly to those who perform it, of gender. In this sense, one could easily say, as did Taylor about carnival in Brazil, "Debate about the corruption or destruction of a symbol of national identity does not signal that its significance is diminishing. Rather, the debate itself raises the scale of the social space within which the symbol is meaningful" (1982: 311). Yet to understand this meaning requires that one also increase "the scale of the social space" to be investigated and that the entire range of performative contexts be included.

Cultural promoters and folklorists have long recognized the difficulties in extracting religious celebrations from the communities in which they originally evolved. Not only are these events characteristically long and repetitive, demanding great numbers of actors, but they are often ritually obscure, lacking the dramatic focus required by a theatrical context. While Tamunangue was not immune to such difficulties, it nevertheless proved an ideal subject for appropriation. Apart from its intrinsic beauty, it already combined those elements most prized by the stage: music, drama, song, and dance. It was also organized around a small, easily transportable troupe, providing numerous opportunities for individual virtuosity. Unlike with many other rituals, it was easy to create a dramatic focus and to rearrange the dancers on a proscenium stage, where they would now face an audience instead of a saint. Just as important, it could be performed in forty-five minutes to an hour and was divided into discrete segments that could be interrupted for intermissions or announcements or, if need be, abridged. This modular quality proved invaluable as performances were either expanded or contracted, depending on the demands of the situation. For Tamunangue was no longer performed for the sole pleasure of San Antonio. It was now an event with multiple audiences and, not surprisingly, multiple meanings as well.

However, in the communities of southern Lara—in Sanare, Curarigua, El Tocuyo, Carora, and San Miguel—the festival remains a time when individuals and families repay the saint for a gift or blessing he has bestowed.[6] Although certain variations occur within each of these communities, the core elements around which every Tamunangue is organized are still easily recognized. The household that is to pay the promesa first invites a Tamunangue group to play at their home, preferably on June 13, the saint's day. The group itself, which is often organized around a single family, comprises between seven and nine musicians, who play three or four cuatros, a six-stringed *cinco,* a maraca, and at least one or two drums. One type of drum is small and double skinned, and is hung from the shoulder. A second, a long, hollow one known as a *cumaco* or *tamunango,* is laid on the ground and is played by two musicians, one beating the trunk and the other the head. The dance also requires at least three couples, often supplied by the household paying the promesa (Fig. 20).

As musicians and other visitors begin to arrive, the sponsors busily prepare the altar, at its center the image of San Antonio with the child Jesus in his arms and flowers and fruits carefully arranged around them. It is to this household image, whether statue or painting, that the Tamunangue is directed. This special relation between performer and saint is immediately established with the solemn chanting of the Salve Regina, a traditional part of church liturgy learned with the catechism of every child.[7] As the prayer concludes, the musicians begin the lengthy preamble that will accompany the *Batalla* (Battle). Separate from the suite of seven dances that follow, this highly stylized sword fight is acted out by a male couple wielding two-and-a-half-foot-long sticks called *varas* or *garrotes.* Their handles braided with rope, hair, and colored tassels, the sticks are first crossed and then, as the men sweep and lunge at each other, gracefully pushed away (Fig. 21). As this martial ballet continues, with other dancers periodically relieving those who have been fighting, the musicians sing four-line duets, each one punctuated by the haunting refrain:

Adorar, adorar, adorar
y adorar a San Antonio[8]

To adore, adore, adore
and adore San Antonio

The Battle ends with a dramatic flourish as the dancers kneel together in front of the altar and cross themselves with their heads lowered. This signals the start of the seven *sones,* or "dances," that make up the main body of the tradition. The first is appropriately named the *Ayiyivamos,*

Figure 20.   Musicians performing a Tamunangue. (Photograph by David M. Guss)

no doubt from "Ahí la llevamos" (Okay, let's go).[9] In this extremely high energy dance filled with twirls and quick steps the man retains the wooden vara and, with hands periodically raised, tries to encircle the woman. As in square dancing, the couple follows the instructions of the lead singer, while the other musicians respond to each call with the phrase, "Oé bangué." Like most of the sones, the length of the Ayiyivamos is not fixed and can simply be extended by adding more verses to accommodate the new dancers who replace those at the center.

La Bella (The Beauty), which in some communities precedes the Ayiyivamos, is the next in this suite of dances. Considered by many to be "Tamunangue's *son* par excellence" (González Viloria 1991: 96), La Bella has many similarities to the Ayiyivamos yet is more graceful and fluid. The woman, dancing with one hand on her hip while the other delicately lifts her skirt, takes small, rapid steps as the man, with the stick cradled in his arm, continually approaches, withdraws, circles, and spins. As in the other sones, the dancers rarely touch, yet the dance is filled with

Figure 21.   The Batalla. (Photograph by David M. Guss)

coquettish and suggestive movements. The music, on the other hand, is arranged in couplets and quatrains which are performed as duets. Combining both fixed and improvised verses, the singers continually return to the main theme, La Bella:

> Ay bella bella,
> a la bella bella
> ay bella va;
> ay bella bella,
> ay bella va.

> Ah beauty beauty,
> to the beautiful beauty
> ah there goes the beauty;
> ah beauty beauty,
> ah there goes the beauty.

La Juruminga, which follows, contains its own special music and choreography, as does each of the Tamunangue's other sections. The musicians do not sing in alternating duets but, similar to the Ayiyivamos, respond in choral form to the lead singer's instructions. These direct the dancers through a set of carefully orchestrated movements, each one mimicking the tasks appropriate to the performer's gender (Fig. 22). As such, the dance is divided into two parts: In the first the man is instructed to clear the land, plant, harvest, and build a home; in the second the woman is commanded to cook, wash, sew, iron, and clean.

The next son, *La Perrendenga,* is also sung in responsive form. However, the instructions issued by the lead singer are more like those of the Ayiyivamos, telling the dancers how to move their feet and in which direction to turn. The music for this section is also much slower, permitting an intimacy and suggestiveness that has led many people to label it the most flirtatious and erotic of all the Tamunangue's parts. Juan Liscano, in particular, called it "a passionate dialogue" in which the varas, wielded in some communities by both the man and the woman, "become like Cupid's arrows in a game of love" (1951: 21).

The fifth section returns to the narrative style of La Juruminga, acting out a different set of relations between men and women. Like the earlier son, the *Poco a Poco* (Little by Little), is divided into two parts, each one an elaborate pantomime filled with both humor and tension. The first is called *Los Calambres* (The Cramps) and tells the story of a man who falls in love with a woman and then becomes so sick he almost dies. The woman must now nurse him back to health and, following the detailed instructions of the lead singer, gives him herbs, injections, drinks, and even an enema. Finally the man is seized by an uncontrollable fit of shaking ("the cramps"), which only the woman's tenderest strokes and care can cure. At this point the music suddenly changes, signaling the recovery of the patient and the return of the couple to their former selves. This stirring finale, which also concludes the second part of the Poco a Poco, is called the *Guabina,* after a common Venezuelan fish. As the chorus sings:

La guabina me mordío
en la palma de la mano.

Figure 22. Directing a dancer in the Juruminga. (Photograph by David M. Guss)

Si no me quieres creer
mira la sangre chorreando.

The guabina bit me
in the palm of my hand.
If you don't believe me
look how the blood ran.

The Poco a Poco's second part, called *El Caballito* (The Pony), now begins. While the man gets down on all fours in imitation of a horse, the woman takes out a kerchief to be used as both a bridle and a rope (Fig. 23). The lead singer now instructs her in the taming of the horse, warning that he is both wild and dangerous. As she tries to approach, the horse kicks and tries to bite. The musicians respond to each command with a loud "Así," and the audience screams its approval with laughter and mock advice. Then, as the horse settles down, the woman loops her kerchief around his neck and prepares to mount:

Now you've tamed him
Steady horse
Ah good horse
Ah what a devil
Ah what a thoroughbred
Pat his shoulder
Be careful now
he's got a bad foot
Be careful
Pet his shoulder
Pet his mane
Didn't I tell you
he's really tame
Try the saddle
and the blanket
You know how to get on
Go ahead and try
   (*González Viloria 1991: 118*)

If the Poco a Poco is the Tamunangue's most amusing section, then the *Galerón*, which follows it, is its most athletic. Related to a widespread

Figure 23. Attaching a kerchief in the Caballito. (Photograph by David M. Guss)

tradition that Luis Felipe Ramón y Rivera claimed is part of Venezuela's oldest dance form (1953: 24), the Galerón introduces elements not seen in the first five sones.[10] As the musicians return to singing alternating duets, the couples join hands and, instead of dancing independently, actually embrace and twirl one another. But it is the men who use this section to exhibit their great physical strength and agility. As Liscano wrote, "It is a time for the men to show off" (1951: 21). With their feet moving at a quicker and quicker tempo, they crouch down like dancers in a Russian ballet. Then, just as suddenly, they rise and, lifting their legs high, clap their hands beneath their thighs with each step. It is an exhausting, frenetic display that is not only a great crowd pleaser but also an excellent preparation for the great finale about to come.

Whereas the first six movements of the Tamunangue limit the dancers participating at any given time to a single couple, the final son, known as the *Seis Corrido*, is performed by six dancers, three men and three women (Fig. 24).[11] In what is clearly the dance's most complex part, they execute a series of figures with names like "the Wheel," "Basket," "Corners," "Chain," and "Arch." The singing is in a responsive form similar to that of other parts of the Tamunangue, but the lyrics are not tied to the steps themselves. Nevertheless, the complicated figures appear to be related to other traditions, such as square dancing and contradancing, in which callers guide the performers' movements. Here, in a whirl of intricate bridges, circles, and columns, the dancers gracefully move through one baffling formation after another until finally, with hands over each other's shoulders, they kneel in a row before the image of the saint and cross themselves. After this dramatic flourish, the only remaining part of the Tamunangue to be performed is that of the final Salve, a restrained and solemn coda that once again focuses attention on the main purpose of the dance, San Antonio de Padua.

During the entire performance of the Tamunangue, one usually finds a large crowd pressing in around a semicircle organized so that it faces the altar of the saint. For once again, it is San Antonio who is the main audience for the event, not the onlookers who have squeezed into the patio of those who are paying the promesa. This large crowd often follows the musicians and dancers from one home to the next, particularly

Figure 24. The Seis Corrido. (Photograph by David M. Guss)

on June 12 and 13, when the demand for individual Tamunangues is at its highest. But Tamunangues can be repaid at any time, and they can also be performed in front of churches, on street corners, or in open fields. In some instances promesas require that two Tamunangues be played consecutively or that a particular son be repeated. Given this highly compact and mobile structure, which can so easily be reconfigured, it is no surprise that Tamunangue has been so readily adapted to situations beyond the original context in which it developed.

Yet even more important than the structural pliability of Tamunangue has been the form's aesthetic reception. From the moment it first came to national attention in the early 1940s, it has been repeatedly hailed as "Venezuela's richest and most beautiful dance" (Tamayo 1945: 77). In fact, not only do many writers claim that it is the country's premier folkloric form, they also suggest that it may be one of the continent's. As the Chilean music scholar Eduardo Lira Espejo proclaimed upon first seeing it performed in 1941, "Tamunangue is one of the most original dances in the entire Americas" (Lira Espejo 1941; also see Briceño 1990a; Salazar n.d.; Silva Uzcátegui 1981 [1941], 1990 [1954]).

While there is little dispute that Tamunangue's unusually complex and varied structure merits the type of attention and praise it has received, it is also clear that this adulation has been charged by a much larger discourse about the nature of Venezuelan identity. For Tamunangue has not been promoted as the nation's most beautiful dance as a result of its choreography, music, and lyrics alone. Just as important has been its ability to synthesize and project a set of values that, for many, captured the essence of a new national ideal. In short, its beauty, as well as its Venezuelanness, is in the fact that it is so resolutely mestizo and that it joins together the three primary ingredients of national identity: the indigenous, the African, and the European. It is this mestizoness that has impressed nearly every critic and writer who has observed the tradition, beginning with Liscano in 1940. Even before his work with the Sanjuaneros of Curiepe, Liscano had traveled to Lara to both record and film the dance.[12] It is little surprise, therefore, that when in 1948 the new president, Rómulo Gallegos, asked Liscano to organize a folklore festival to celebrate his inauguration, he immediately included Tamunangue. Particularly revealing are the comments Liscano made in the program accompanying this event:

> Tamunangue constitutes one of the most important expressions of our folklore inasmuch as all the elements that came together in its formation have lost their original physiognomy and assumed a completely new one: the Venezuelan criollo. Tamunangue is a true crucible of cultural forms, affirming through its very existence and the process of its formation, the dynamism of American folklore and its endless power of creation. (1950: 212)[13]

Such sentiments were echoed by one observer after another, with Tamunangue serving as a metaphor for the creation of the Venezuelan nation itself. Its very performance was likened to an alchemical act whereby three races were magically transformed into one. "A synthesis of Americanness," wrote Olivares Figueroa, "in which our great spiritual currents converge" (1960: 121). Folklorists and other scholars meticulously dissected the dance, demonstrating the provenance of each of its elements. Some names, like Juruminga and Perrendenga, were said to clearly be African, as was the use of call and response and the presence of such refrains as "Oé bangüé," "Tombirá," and "Tomé ay to." Even the name "Tamunangue" was said to be of African origin, derived, according to Liscano, "from certain parts of Yaracuy where blacks and mulattos do an African dance to the sound of a drum called '*tamunango*' " (1947: 24).[14] Of course, the drum music, along with the rapid dance style of certain sones, was also identified as unmistakably African.

In contrast to these elements were the many traces of European court dances, of fandangos, square dancing, and contradancing. There were La Bella and the Galerón, with their interlocking pairs and more reserved styles; and the Seis Corrido, with its various complex figures, directly related to a number of Spanish forms. Equally identifiable with European traditions was the stick fighting found in the Batalla. Buffones, Matachines, Moriscas, Danzas de Espadas, Paloteo, Seises, and even Morris dancing were but a few of the many forms found throughout Europe that employed the use of sticks or swords in a similar way.[15] But the most European element was the devotion to the saint and the employment of such liturgical forms as the Salve.

The indigenous element of Tamunangue, beyond its originating in Venezuela, was not so evident. Some writers, like José Anselmo Castillo Escalona (1987) and Raúl Colmenárez Guédez (1966), claimed that it could be detected in a certain reticent, if not somber, attitude.[16] Still, many noted that the maraca was an indigenous instrument, which, when combined with the African drum and the European chordophone, created a perfect musical synthesis. However, in the end, it was the union of all these elements that helped transform this extremely local Larense dance into a paradigm of the national racial ideal. The poet and dance promoter Manuel Rodríguez Cárdenas summarized it best: "Today one could say that Tamunangue is as black as it is white, as Indian as mestizo, as colonial as republican, because there are elements from every age and every race in its deep roots. Because Tamunangue is a foundational dance . . . which is to say, an ancient expression of our collective soul" (1966 [1956]: 13).

There is a striking similarity here to the Brazilian discourse around samba, whose elevation to the status of national dance also required that it be linked to the origins of mestizaje. According to Barbara Browning, not only is the ideal female sambista a mulatta, but, in popular mythology, the term "samba" is claimed to come from "*zamba,* mean[ing] a mestiço child, offspring of an African father and an indigenous mother" (1995: 16). According to one early account of the origin of samba,

> The dance is a function of dances: the samba is a mixture of the *jongo* of the African percussive ensembles, of the Sugarcane dance of the Portuguese and of the *poracé* of the Indians. The three races are melded in the samba as a crucible. The *samba* is the *apoplexy* of the court, it is the pyrrhic victory of the bedroom. In it, the heavy sovereign conquers the light *mameluca* [a woman of mixed African and indigenous race]. In it are absorbed the hatreds of color. The *samba* is "if you will permit me the expression" a kind of pot, into which enter, separately, dark coffee and pale milk, and out of which is poured, homogeneous and harmonic, the hybrid *café-com-leite:* coffee with milk. (Quoted in Browning 1995: 17)

As in all invocations of "racial democracy," however, one wonders just how "homogeneous and harmonic" this new hybrid mix really was. In Venezuela, there were some who still challenged the view that Tamunangue was the result of a perfect synthesis of three unique traditions. On one side were those like Rafael Domingo Silva Uzcátegui, who refused to believe that something as sophisticated and beautiful as Tamunangue could be anything other than European. A native Larense from a wealthy, landowning family, Silva Uzcátegui was one of the first intellectuals to write about Tamunangue. In various articles, as well as in his two-volume *Enciclopedia Larense* (1981 [1941]), he attempted to disprove that Tamunangue had any African origins whatsoever. In support of his argument that the dance had been introduced by missionaries, he pointed out various stylistic parallels to a number of Spanish forms, particularly from Galicia and the Canary Islands. The nonvocables he located in different Andalusian songs of Arab origin. He even suggested that the term "Tamunangue" was not African but Indian, derived from an indigenous site near Curarigua called Los Arangues (1981 [1941]: 175). But it was the grace and beauty, the sheer nobility of the form that convinced him more than anything that it must be of European derivation. Or, as he confidently wrote: "The elegance of these dances clearly states that they must have come from a culture far superior to our own Indians or African slaves" (1990 [1954]: 2).

Although Silva Uzcátegui's position may be considered extreme, even those who have rhapsodized over the multiracial virtues of the dance have often done so by reinforcing various negative racial stereotypes. The African contribution, therefore, was always said to be sensual and frenetic, whereas the indigenous was submissive and downcast. The European element, on the other hand, was invariably dignified, reserved, and cerebral. And it was not only folklorists and social critics who held such views. Performers too were soon describing the dance as transcending racial and local boundaries, yet, ironically, by doing so they unconsciously reaffirmed them. A good example is the following statement by Colmenárez Guédez, one of the first Tamunangueros to perform nationally: "In Tamunangue one finds the melancholy of the Indian, the joy and sensuality of the black, and the royal and spiritualized attitude of the white" (1966: 8).

One group that has begun to challenge the popular mythology surrounding Tamunangue's rapid diffusion throughout Venezuela over the last fifty years is the Afro-Venezuelan community. They question not only its appropriation as a national dance but also how mestizo it is and whether its enshrinement as a symbol of racial harmony is but another example of the erasure of African-American culture and identity. Such views, which have been expressed by various scholars and community activists, cite a range of evidence linking the dance's origins to the slaves who worked the sugar plantations of southern Lara. As part of this evidence, they note that the term "Tamunangue" was only introduced with the work of Juan Liscano and Isabel Aretz in the 1940s and that before then the dance was commonly known as *Son de Negros* or *Baile de Negros,* "The Dance of the Blacks."

THE CHOREOGRAPHY OF RACE
AND THE DANCE OF THE BLACKS

The difficulty in determining the legitimacy of the name "Tamunangue" is compounded by the lack of any historical records. According to Aretz, who began her exhaustive study of the form in 1947, "the childhood memories of elders who saw it performed as adolescents is as far back as we can go" (1970 [1956]: 20). Even then, Aretz believed that Tamunangue as presented in the 1940s was already a choreographic reconstruction of a number of dances collected by unknown sources. What some of those dances may have looked like is described briefly in Julio Ramos's 1936 novel *Los Conuqueros*. However, real documentation of the dance only started four years later, with Liscano's expeditions to Curarigua and El Tocuyo. Within a short time a flurry of articles began appearing from such writers as Lira Espejo (1941), Silva Uzcátegui (1941, 1954, 1956), Francisco Tamayo (1945), Olivares Figueroa (1949), and of course, Liscano himself (1947, 1950, 1951). Then, in 1956, Aretz's book-length study was published as a special issue of *Folklore Americano*.[17] In each of these works, the dance was unequivocally identified as "Tamunangue," ensuring that it would now be the name used throughout the country.

Yet, in the small towns where the dance was actually performed, the term "Tamunangue" was relatively unknown. For most, "*Negro*," or "black," was enough to identify the dance. Participants simply said "Vamos por los Negros" (Let's go up to the Blacks) or "Vamos a bailar un Negro" (Let's dance a Black). As María González recalled in 1979:

> Before they just said there were "*Negros, Negros* of San Antonio." It's only now that they say "Tamunangue." But for us here, well, before everything was "Let's go dance some Blacks." One got out their wide skirts, their pleated blouses, their embroidered sandals. (Quoted in González Viloria 1991: 55)

José Pérez, from Curarigua, claims that the people in his community could not even pronounce the term when it was first introduced in 1964. They referred to it as "Tamonangue" and greeted it with undisguised resentment:

The name, Tamunangue, was very counterproductive at first. The people in my community didn't even say, they didn't even call it "Tamunangue" but rather "Tamonangue."

A group from Barquisimeto came. I told you how they celebrated the San Antonio Festival in my community. Every year the same people from the community would celebrate it, but for some reason they were sick or something and those people couldn't do it. So a group from some other place came, and I remember, that was when Angel María Pérez came with his group. They were really well organized. Yeh, with liqui-liqui, and the women, the women with long, colorful skirts. It was the first time the community wasn't really able to enjoy a Tamunangue because the group was the only one allowed to dance. No one else was permitted.

Everyone was really disgusted with that, the fact that the Tamunangue was so bad. There was no participation, no one could dance. Everyone there really looked forward to their festivals, just like you wait for your birthday, to have a good time. And the way to do it was to dance, and a lot of people weren't able to . . . at that moment at the end of a son when you're passed the vara and given a chance. That's when Tamunangue stopped being so popular. It started to lose its popularity. And, yes, I think that was in 1964. I was seven years old, yes, '64, '65. I'm trying to remember now, I was in the third or fourth grade.

How was it, then, that "Tamunangue" was so quickly adopted as the term of choice for this complex dance form? Where did it come from, and why was it imposed if the dance was already known by another name? For those attempting to revive what they believe is the form's authentic name, the answer is quite simple. If the dance was to be elevated to the status of national symbol, it would have to be stripped of its historical associations with a single segment of the population, particularly when that segment was so closely tied to a history of marginalization and oppression. Or, simply put, the name "Son de Negros" was too black. "Tamunangue," on the other hand, was not only more exotic and mysterious but, just as significant, had none of the negative associations with black suffering and poverty. As such, it could convey notions of an idealized mestizaje that were impossible for a term like "Son de Negros."

Doing the work of mestizaje has meant that the name "Tamunangue" is used to mask the actual origins of the form as well as the many divisive elements underlying it. One of the people most dedicated to reclaiming this tradition as part of the Afro-Venezuelan experience has been Pedro Linárez, a curator and activist from El Tocuyo. Like many, he has critiqued the discourse of mestizaje, noting that its sole purpose is to serve a national agenda while discouraging any other. As Linárez claims, this is precisely what occurred with Tamunangue:

> They were looking for a way to hide the Negroid character of the Son de Negros or Tamunangue, making it seem like the product of that perfect blending of races in which the main ingredient, of course, was the Spanish Colonial. It's for that reason that J. R. Colmenárez Peraza came up with the definitive slogan for Tamunangue as "The mix of our race, made with a shout and a drum." (1987: 6)[18]

The "they" being invoked here are the folklorists and promoters who, according to Linárez and others, conspired to transform the dance into a deracialized, national spectacle. It was not enough, therefore, to simply rechoreograph the dance for a proscenium stage. Its very history would have to be rewritten, particularly if it was to appeal to a national audience. This "mnemonic imperialism," as Eric Van Young has called it (1994: 367), was the work of specialists like Liscano, Aretz, and Olivares Figueroa, sent out to identify Venezuela's most representative forms. Or so Linárez claims, insisting that the dance could only be successfully promoted once it was detached from its legacy of slavery and exploitation:

> What happened was that Son de Negros changed its name and now, with its spread as Tamunangue, became a profitable business. We still don't know the exact date when its real name was changed to that of Tamunangue. Nevertheless, we have to recognize that with its massive promotion came a new level of economic activity that also demanded the introduction of changes not only to its name but to its choreography and words. (1987: 21)

Others had certainly acknowledged the African contribution to Tamunangue, but it was always characterized as a single element in a larger cultural mix. Linárez, however, insisted that the dance was primarily

African, with only a few European components added. According to him, the dance had originated among the slaves of the colonial sugar plantations surrounding El Tocuyo. Founded in 1545, El Tocuyo was only the fifth Venezuelan settlement established by the Spanish and the first located in the interior. As the Spanish brought increasing numbers of slaves to work their plantations, the black population soon rose to nearly 20 percent (Linárez 1987: 15; Troconis de Veracoechea 1984). And just as in Barlovento, here too blacks were permitted to form their own religious societies, or *cofradías*. Yet instead of adopting San Juan as their patron saint, the black cofradías of El Tocuyo chose San Antonio de Padua.

Linárez believes that the Son de Negros, or Dance of the Blacks, began in the celebrations of these cofradías. As in other areas, African gods were thinly disguised as Catholic saints, permitting old traditions to continue undetected. Linárez supports these claims with various pieces of linguistic evidence, connecting words such as *juruminga, anguá,* and *aí tomé* to Mandingo. Even the word "Tamunangue" is given African provenance, as poetically deciphered by María Magdalena Colmenárez Losada, the first Folklore Queen: "Dissected by its roots, Tamunangue means '*Ta*' 'people,' '*Mu*' 'our,' and '*Nango*' 'bitterness,' leading us to translate it as 'bitterness of our people.' The word comes from the Mende language of Sierra Leone, Africa, which makes us conclude that at the time of its origin, the dance was already an expression of longing by groups of African slaves" (quoted in Linárez 1987: 16).

Linárez also points to specific lyrics supporting this idea that the original performers were slaves wishing to return to their native land. In the Batalla, for example, one finds the following stanza:

Ay, Father San Antonio,
Virgin of Chiquinquirá,
you took me from my land
now bring me back.
   (*Linárez 1987: 19*)[19]

But the most important piece of semantic evidence is the fact that all of the participants are referred to as "Negros." In each of the sones, dancers are summoned with calls of *"Viene otra negra"* (Here comes another black) or *"Sale otro negro"* (Another black's coming out). Moreover, all of the singers' instructions are addressed to "la negra" or "el negro," as in the following verses from the Ayiyivamos:

> Ayiyivamos
> Ay, let's go
> These are the steps
> of my San Antonio
> The little black's come out
> come out to dance
> Ah, good black
> Now he's got her
> These are the steps
> Listen to me, Negro . . .
> We're good friends
> leave her to me
> leave her to me
> come on, let's go
> come on, Negro
> get 'em up, my little black
> get 'em up, my black
> Now listen to me, Negro
> Let's dance and dance
> to my San Antonio
> (*González Viloria 1991: 93–94*)

Even the musicians are called a "band of blacks" and the director or captain of the dance, the *"negrero,"* "the slave trader." And finally, San Antonio himself is commonly referred to as "El Negro Antonio" and "El Negro de Padua." Of course, many Venezuelans claim that *"negro"* is simply a term of endearment commonly applied without any real racial content. But others support Linárez's argument that the real implications of the dance would be too threatening if its true history were acknowledged. As a result, the recovery of the original name, Son de Negros, has been seen as an act of resistance to an ideology that systematically ignores the place of black culture in Venezuela. One attempt to rectify this was the Popular Culture Congress held in Yaracuy in 1990.

Among the various motions adopted was a demand to "respect the name Son de Negros in the San Antonio cult of the midwest region." There was also a call "to question the term 'folklore' for its discrimination and demeaning treatment of traditional production" (Proposiciones aprobadas 1990).

One of the organizers of this conference was the Barloventeño activist Jesús García, who, not long afterward, chastised me for using the term "Tamunangue." Like many Afro-Venezuelan intellectuals, García has been heavily influenced by the pioneering work of Miguel Acosta Saignes. Trained in Mexico, Acosta Saignes insisted that "Tamunangue had its origins as a black dance." He also recalled a previous minister of education asking, "Why study folklore when it's just about blacks?" (1983: 16–17). Such statements reaffirm Linárez's belief that it was necessary to transform Son de Negros into Tamunangue in order to make it suitable for popular consumption.

Linárez is well aware of the parallels between his argument and that of the San Juan Congo devotees of Curiepe. Both have used their respective festivals to expose the racism in a society where the constant celebration of mestizaje is equated with a false racial democracy. And yet, although the racial politics denounced by Linárez, García, and others may be indisputable, the vehicles for exposing them remain somewhat less determined. Even Aretz, the folklorist Linárez blames most for imposing the term "Tamunangue," insists that the dance oscillates between its European and African roots. It is the performance context, according to Aretz, that determines which aspect of the tradition will dominate. In urban settings, for example, the more courtly, reserved Spanish style seems to surface, whereas in rural environments one finds the more "provocative and sensual" African-inspired elements. "It is the latter Tamunangue," wrote Aretz, "that deserves the name Son de Negros, where the descendants of the slaves dedicated their dances to San Antonio, just as they still do with San Juan" (1970 [1956]: 156).

This ongoing debate over the origin and meaning of Tamunangue may reflect an even deeper struggle, one driven by the agonistic nature of the dance itself. For if Tamunangue is really the perfect expression of "racial democracy," its association with the Spanish tradition of Moors and Christians makes it clear that it was also forged in war and conquest. Only in this version, it was not the forces of a newly united Catholic Spain that had vanquished the Moors but, rather, the lone figure of San Antonio de Padua. Here, as the verses remind us, it was San Antonio who, with nothing but a drum, went to Africa to conquer the Moors. The dances repeat this conquest and, like the act commemorated in the Moors and Christians celebrations, also subjugate all that is wild and untamed.

THE THEATER OF DOMINATION

San Antonio and the Moors

Of all the dance traditions introduced into the New World by the Spaniards, none spread as far and as fast as that of the Moors and Christians. Appearing first in northern Spain around 1150, the dance commemorates the reconquest of the country from the North African Muslims who first invaded in 711. Only when this reconquest was completed in 1492, however, did the dance gain in national popularity. In each area it took on different characteristics and was celebrated at a different time. Often included as part of a village's patron saint festivities, the dance reenacted, in allegorical form, the victory of the forces of righteousness over those of the pagan horde. Some versions included sword fighting and equestrian contests; others featured elaborate pageants and songs known as *embajadas.* In Andalusia the dance took two days to perform. On the first, the Muslims, or Moors, as they were known, attacked the Christian celebrants, absconding with their patron saint.[20] On the second, the Christians counterattacked and, after retrieving the sacred image, either converted or killed the infidels in mock battle.

For Spain, this dance marks the creation of a unified, modern state and, as such, represents one of its most important foundational myths. By joining the political reunification of the country to a higher religious purpose, the new nation was also elevated to a special sacred status. It may be little surprise, therefore, that Franco and the Falangists also attempted to use this dance, casting their forces as the Christian saviors out to reconquer Spain from the new Republican Moors who had overtaken it (Baumann 1988). But the morality tale reenacted by the Moors and Christians was easily transposed onto countless other situations as well.

The recent victory over Muslim forces, encoded in dramatic dances and pageants, was one of the first evangelical tools used by the Spaniards upon their arrival in the New World. As early as 1538, versions of this dance were being performed in Mexico City (Champe 1983: 3). As it spread throughout the continent, the Moors were quickly replaced by other groups in need of conversion, particularly Indians. However, the dance, which pitted good against evil in such stark terms, was able to accommodate any number of adversaries and soon featured Romans, Jews, blacks, monkeys, and even French grenadiers (Bricker 1981; Carrasco 1976). While part of this shift reflects the simple resemanticization into a new environment, it also indicates another dislocation. Performers and audiences were soon to change places, and instead of Spaniards dancing for native peoples, Indians were performing for Spaniards. As this reversal occurred, the message started to change too, and, rather than glorify the work of the conquest, the dance now began to undermine it (Rodríguez 1996: 144 passim).[21]

These new versions were less religious parables than brutal stories of ethnic strife. Like Sylvia Rodríguez, Victoria Reifler Bricker believes that indigenous communities transformed these celebrations into meta-commentaries on both race relations and domination. Analyzing Mexican Carnival plays derived from Moors and Christians traditions, Bricker concludes that the dances have become "rituals of ethnic conflict" (1981: 129):

> All the events dramatized during this festival have in common the theme of ethnic conflict. The towns differ in the conflicts portrayed during Carnival and in their choice of symbols to represent them. But the underlying structure in each case is one of ethnic conflict—warfare, death, rape, soldiers, weapons, fireworks, and the division of people into two groups: the conquerors and the conquered. (1981: 133)[22]

Although Tamunangue's relation to the Moors and Christians tradition may be difficult to ascertain at first, once made, it becomes easy to understand why the themes of ethnic conflict and conversion are so central to it. Among those who have written about the dance, only Norma González Viloria, a folklorist who has studied and danced Tamunangue for twenty years, has emphasized its critical importance. And while Aretz acknowledges the connection, most other scholars ignore it entirely. This is somewhat odd, for participants are quick to assert that the form has its origins in the defeat of the Moors. But instead of taking place in Spain, the events occur in Africa, and in place of a large Christian army, we find San Antonio alone.

In reality, San Antonio did go to Africa in the early thirteenth century to work as a missionary. However, he immediately fell ill and was forced to return to his native Portugal. Along the way, he was shipwrecked by a storm and ended up in Sicily. From there he headed north, eventually joining the Franciscans, which is where he gained his great fame as a preacher, particularly in Padua. It was said that even the fish and animals stood still to hear him preach and that on several occasions he actually stopped the rain. Known as the "Hammer of the Heretics" and "wonder worker," he was canonized in 1232, the year after his death.[23]

In tales recounting the origins of Tamunangue, San Antonio remains in Africa and single-handedly confronts the Moors (Fig. 25). No one has been able to subdue them, yet San Antonio succeeds with the power of song and dance alone. These musical weapons form the basis of Tamunangue. The details of this story are included in the following account by José Humberto Castillo. A famous storyteller from the village of Sanare, Castillo is affectionately known as *El Caiman* (The Alligator). He recounted this tale to me in June 1990, just as the festival was getting under way:

> They say that when the Conquest happened, there was no one who could conquer the Moors . . . a people, they say, who were really, really bad, very wild and savage. So no one, absolutely no one would go, because they'd kill them. . . . Yes, sir, a really wild people. They were savages. And anyone who fell into their hands, they'd chew them up . . . if they were whites, now, because blacks like them they didn't eat. But if you were white . . . well, with yuca no less!
>
> Now, San Antonio was really brave. You have to imagine the courage San Antonio had. He said, "I'm going alone. I'm not going with a

Figure 25. San Antonio being carried through Sanare. (Photograph by David M. Guss)

group. Because if you go with a group, they'll flee. They won't like that."

"Are you so macho you're going to go alone? Because, you know, they eat people."

"They won't eat me," said San Antonio. And he went.

The first day he went, he went there with a vara, like the ones the dancers use [in the Batalla]. So he went and he looked. And of course they were watching too, because those chiefs had lots of lookouts. They were all chiefs of the blacks. . . . They had their army too, and they followed him along. And each time they looked at him in secret like that . . . his clothes so different . . . with his cassock . . . Jesus! And they were all going around completely naked. And what they saw, my friend, was a completely different kind of person. And they all hid with their arrows. At times, they really wanted to shoot him. But no, nothing. That's the courage that God gave him, my son.

Sometimes they'd look at him, because he was black too. He was black. This man was like us, brown, . . . He knew that because of his color they wouldn't do anything. Each time San Antonio approached, nothing. That's what San Antonio said. "What am I going to do, what am I going to do to attract them?"

So he came back, because they wouldn't come, they were so wild. . . . Then he came back, and they asked him, "How did it go, San Antonio? How did it go, Antonio?" Because his name was Antonio.

"It went fine," he said.

"Did you see the gourds there . . . the people, the savages? Didn't you see the Moors?"

"Yes, I saw them."

"And they didn't come?"

"No, they signaled to me, but nothing else, that was all. I'm going back. Tomorrow I'm going to play a little something. I'm going to play some music with a drum because it doesn't work with a vara. They won't come. Let's see how it goes with music. I'll bring a little drum tomorrow and play some things, some pretty pieces . . . for the women." And he took them some presents, a big box like this. . . . Because, look, when you go out you have to be kind too with everyone, with presents and everything.

As he was getting there he started to play the drum. That's why they play the drum, pum, pum . . . ijiii, ijiii. They did it, pum, pum, ijiii, ijiii. That's the way the people did it. Then they started to arrive. They were dancing as they came. They liked the music, and that's what was attracting them.

And with that music he kept on bringing them. He led that whole group back. He led that whole group right into the city, my friend. He tamed them all by playing like that. He played for them, and his gifts. ... And the music went on taming them. With that little drum he brought them all, right up to the prince. That's when he conquered them. That's why they speak of conquering the Moors. That's the story.[24]

In other versions of this event the leaders of the Moors are identified by name, each one corresponding to a different son. La Bella, for example, is said to be the princess of the main chief and "the most beautiful woman the Moors possessed." Poco a Poco, on the other hand, is the most handsome of the chiefs, who arrogantly proceeds little by little. As Castillo explained it, "Each one of the names is a Moor. They are the Moors San Antonio brought back with him. They are the seven sones, each name. ... It all has to do with the Moors. Each one, each one has its own thing. But no one understands that, what it means that music, that all of it, all of it had its name."

Some, such as Américo Escalona, claim that Juruminga and Galerón were friends of San Antonio who actually helped him play the first Tamunangue. However, all agree that it was San Antonio who invented the dance in order to subdue the Moors. As such, the Batalla may represent his initial, inconclusive battle, after which he returned with a new strategy—the irresistible music and dance of Tamunangue.[25] This would also explain the use of the term "Negros," referring not to the slaves but to the Moors who were the first to perform the dance.

Like the Moors and Christians dances of Spain, Tamunangue marks a foundational event, signaling the beginning of a new nation. However, to do so, San Antonio had to do more than simply vanquish a horde of invading infidels. He had to create a completely new people, who, different from the European, African, or Indian, were a unique combination of all three—the Venezuelan criollo or mestizo. This explains why the stories of San Antonio's epic deeds conflate the conquest of the Moors with that of America, converting them into a single event. Such explanations also fuse indigenous peoples with Africans, just as in other Moors and Christians traditions adapted to the New World.[26] Yet here

San Antonio literally uses Tamunangue to blend these groups, along with the European, into a new race, a process which in Spanish is called *enrazar* (to mix, hybridize, or enrace). It is the same term used by Castillo to describe San Antonio's visit to America, particularly the Guajira, where one of Venezuela's fiercest native groups still lives:

> He passed through Spain. He went through various villages. I think he came to the Guajira. Yes, I believe he did. He had to go through there because at the time we still weren't mixed up [*enrazado*] . . . at the time of the Conquest, yes, right, we're talking about the Conquest of America. We weren't enraced [hybridized] yet. We were, we were pure. There were pure, pure Indians, pure stuff. It's certain that San Antonio came as they say.

Like others, Castillo points out that San Antonio was able to accomplish what he did because of his color. At first he claims that the saint was black but then quickly adds, "This man was like us, brown [*moreno*]." This semantic difference is important as Castillo, a typical mestizo, wants to underline the fact that San Antonio was actually creating a new race in his own image. Today people still affectionately refer to this upper-class, thirteenth-century Caucasian as "el Negro San Antonio." But what is significant is not his color. It is his role as a catalyst in joining all races and peoples together. It is for this reason that Liscano and others have celebrated Tamunangue as a triumphant event, signifying the emergence of a new culture.[27] And yet for others, like Pedro Linárez, interpretations such as these simply continue the colonial legacy of racial oppression and denial.

The Choreography of Gender, or the Hegemony of the Smile

In many ways, the debates surrounding the origins and meaning of Tamunangue simulate the agonistic nature of the dance itself. What may have begun as a commemoration of the Spanish struggle to reunify their nation and rid the country of Muslim invaders has become a powerful metaphor for other types of conquest as well. As Bricker and Rodríguez demonstrate, not only did the new conquerors readily transform the

Indians into Moors, but indigenous groups also adopted these dramatis personae, with the role of "savage" being played by any number of actors. As such, Tamunangue is not simply a tale of ethnic conflict but a morality play in a constant state of reinvention—a theater of domination wherein all that is savage and wild is made tame and civilized.

Although the debate over Tamunangue's racial politics continues to rage, it is not the only controversy consuming its participants. For many, an even greater problem has been the performative adjustment imposed upon the dance as it shifted onto a national stage. Many of these issues are mirrors of the same conflict between Son de Negros and Tamunangue. For, as the dance moved into the national spotlight, it too became subject to the same civilizing project. Every aspect of the dance, and not simply its history, would have to conform to a new aesthetic. Performance decisions would now be determined by the needs of the stage rather than by those of community and devotion. To do so would require what Kirshenblatt-Gimblett called "an aestheticizing of the marginal" (1998: 76), whereby all that is wild, improvised, and unpredictable is carefully controlled and choreographed.

For Tamunangue, this process began as early as 1940, when musicians and dancers were invited to Barquisimeto to perform at an agricultural fair. By February of the following year, Tamunangue was already being showcased in Caracas. While many praised the form for its unique and multifaceted quality, others, particularly Larenses, charged that such secular performances were a disgrace. Lira Espejo, who had both studied and admired the dance in Lara, criticized its new adaptation, concluding that "there are some things that should never leave their village" (Ortiz 1983: 33). Even more dismissive was Faustino Moreno, who, after attending a performance at the Municipal Theater, lamented that "one of the country's most picturesque dances had been patiently and scientifically mutilated" (quoted in Silva Uzcátegui 1990 [1954]: 2).

But the changes demanded by this new context had been set in motion, and by the time Tamunangue was selected for inclusion in the 1948 Festival of Tradition many were already in place. Instead of a ritual performance, the dance now became a theatrical spectacle. The distancing that occurred between performer and audience was similar to experiences documented in other cultures and traditions.[28] Dancers and musicians were given a special status, elevated onstage and dressed in uniform costumes. For the men this meant wearing the high-collared, white liquiliqui. The women, on the other hand, dressed in fringed blouses called *garrasi* and wide, colorful skirts that lifted as they spun.[29] Those onstage were invested with special skills, and participation by anyone else was all but eliminated. As José Pérez, who has been both a promoter and devotee, observed, "In the community the excitement and the color is in the participation of the people, but on the stage it's different. There it depends on the costumes and movement."

Now musicians had to be carefully miked and their instruments properly tuned. Improvisation gave way to finely scripted performances, which had to conform to whatever time was allotted. Television programs were particularly demanding, for only brief selections were usually shown. But Iván Querales, a Tamunanguero from El Tocuyo, proudly remembers at least one television appearance in which he condensed an entire dance into twenty-seven minutes. "And we did the Seis Corrido in less than eight, which was a real record!"[30] The flow of the dance was also broken by announcers, who introduced and interpreted each son. Then, after every section, there was loud applause, creating even further interruption. Some performers, such as Nerio Sangronis, considered this response extremely inappropriate: "More than a folkloric act, Tamunangue is an act of faith. Tamunangue is not applauded. You applaud with your heart because faith is great."

However, the public had now replaced the saint as the focus of attention. For the dance was no longer being done for San Antonio, and the audience was not in attendance to pay a promesa. It was there to be entertained. And while an image of San Antonio might still adorn the stage like a prop, the dancers' energy was directed elsewhere. As Sanare's chronicler, Anselmo Castillo, noted, "When it's for exhibition, they eliminate the saint. They eliminate the candle, eliminate the incense and everything. They take all that away and then it has another meaning."

Yet many in the audience at Tamunangue performances are still confused by this distinction. For although such events are driven by the need to create distance between actors and observers, a great number of those who attend are from homes where the tradition is still practiced. Spectators, therefore, are just as likely to cross themselves and chant the Salve as they are to applaud and shout "Viva Lara!" This is especially true in Caracas, where performances are often used to invoke state pride and where the boundary between stage and audience is easily blurred.

This distinction between what Nerio Sangronis calls "the saint tradition" and "the public tradition" is reinforced in a number of other ways, however. In the former, participants are organized into a tight semicircle facing the saint. In staged performances, dancers and musicians are discouraged from turning their backs to the viewers. The semicircle is pried open, and frontality becomes the dominant aesthetic. Everyone onstage must continuously face the audience, with absolutely nothing concealed.[31] Viewers are no longer engaged by inner devotion or a deep emotional attachment to the tradition. What now compels them is the immediacy of the visual experience, the energy and excitement of colorfully costumed dancers furiously whirling about with precise movements and high kicks. Personal religious communication is replaced by a muscular yet sensuous athleticism, unrelenting in its optimism and joyousness. For this experience has no dark side. It is healthy, wholesome, and beautiful. Performers must communicate much more than skill; they must announce with every step and a never-ending smile, "This is fun."

Such performative strategies underline once again the dangers signaled by Kirshenblatt-Gimblett when complex local traditions are reduced to purely aesthetic events (1998: 72). As she correctly observed, issues of conflict, poverty, and stress are inevitably erased. The dancers—all healthy, young, and well dressed—emerge from a magical never-never land, a paradisiacal place where the forgotten world of folklore still exists. This is the same observation made by José Pérez, who said of such events:

> The main purpose of Tamunangue, for me, is in bringing the community together. But that's not the concern in these performances. The concern here is that everyone present say, "Look how beautiful that is." The entire focus is on creating a choreographic work, staged, musical, melodic, strictly technical, the most perfect possible . . . something to be

looked at. It may lack the community element, but that doesn't matter as long as everyone sings well and they're not out of tune.[32]

The external circumstances of the performers' lives, however, are not the only thing sacrificed in these presentations. The hidden, introspective world that is so integral to the ritual experience is also elided in favor of a relentlessly extroverted, up-beat staging. Such changes have demanded that the performers assume what are often dramatically new roles. Nowhere is this more apparent than when dancers and musicians return to their villages to participate in local celebrations. For it is the same performers who are now asked to visit homes in order to pay promesas. Many claim that there is no difficulty in distinguishing between these contexts. As Lucrecia López, an experienced dancer from Sanare, commented: "Folklore is something completely different from promesa. Promesa is one thing and folklore another." Yet mounting complaints suggest that the two have become increasingly conflated.

Along with Tamunangue's commercialization has come the inevitable belief that the dance could provide a means to both wealth and stardom. It is little surprise, therefore, that new groups have proliferated, and with more than fifty in Barquisimeto alone, there is even talk of a union of Tamunangue workers. While this has not occurred, the discussion is symptomatic of a professionalization that many people claim has undermined the tradition. Its worst manifestation is that many Tamunangue groups now charge for ritual performances. They also maintain their special status and distance by wearing their stage costumes. Many spectators, regardless of the setting, are intimidated by recorded artists whom they perceive as famous. As a result, they refuse to participate and complain about the community's diminished involvement in what has always been a religious event.[33] But the greatest number of complaints by far are reserved for the women.

As Tamunangue has moved from the intimacy of a village ritual to that of a proscenium stage and concert hall, the relationship between men and women has been significantly altered. Previously, the women had served as objects to be surrounded and dominated by the men, their movements a metaphor for the proper socialization that all members of their sex must undergo (Berarducci Fernández 1987; González Viloria 1991). Forbidden to lift their feet more than an inch or two, they demurely stared at the floor, displaying almost no emotion whatsoever. But the expectations of a folkloric performance demanded that they now present themselves differently. Movements had to be broad and quick, even exaggerated. The large, colorful skirts that now became part of the women's "folkloric attire" were whirled just high enough so that a bit of flesh was constantly revealed. And all the time, they looked straight at the camera and audience with constant smiles on their faces.[34] Modesty and introversion were replaced with coquettishness and seduction (Fig. 26). And where female sexuality was once a symbol of the "wild" and "savage" that must be tamed, it now threatened to dominate.

At least this is the complaint of many of the male participants in this dance. They state, and I have heard this often, that the greatest challenge to the future of Tamunangue is the way in which the women are reinterpreting the tradition. The fact that they regularly ignore other elements that are transforming this practice, such as tourism, media, and the state, is extremely revealing. For, like most discourses of tradition, its real subject matter is power and the desire to naturalize relationships of inequality. It is little surprise, therefore, that when threatened, as they are by the newly emerging role of rural women in Venezuela, the men will invoke tradition as an ally in their continued domination of them.

Criticisms of women have been lodged from the moment Tamunangue was first presented as a theatrical event. Silva Uzcátegui, in particular, complained that the sensualism and joy expressed by female performers was a sacrilege to the dance's religious meaning. In several articles, he insisted that the proper female dance style was one of complete submissiveness, albeit in the guise of religious devotion. "Anyone who has seen a real Tamunangue knows that this is exactly the way it should be done: the man dances as if he were trying to surround his partner, while she, with arms lowered and eyes steadily fixed on the ground, dances slowly, with the attitude of someone who is praying" (1990 [1954]: 2).[35]

But "praying to whom?" one may ask. For male dancers participating in the same rite are not required to conduct themselves in such a

Figure 26.   María Magdalena Colmenárez Losada dancing with Los Negros de San Antonio, 1978. (Courtesy María Magdalena Colmenárez Losada)

subdued and docile manner. What Silva Uzcátegui identifies as religious fervor, therefore, may be nothing other than acquiescence to the male's dominant role. This is certainly what González Viloria believes, arguing that Tamunangue sacralizes a set of social relations in which men consistently dominate (1991: 140). In this sense, women are to be equated with Moors, blacks, and Indians, another antagonist in a dance whose object is to overcome all that is "other," "natural," and "wild." It is but one more twist in an allegory of conquest, now interpreted as a domestic battle between men and women. As González Viloria explains:

> The lesson of learning Tamunangue prepares the man to exercise his domination over his space, to develop the manly gifts that characterize it. It also prepares the woman to cultivate and adapt to her subordinate role in the male-female relation.
>
> The voice of the man directs the action in it. It is his gestures—the open arms—that mark and delimit the woman's dance space similar to the female's cultural space in real life. In Tamunangue it is the man

who possesses control over the cultural goods related to the playing of
the instruments, the song, and the play of La Batalla, and with his voice
he regulates and establishes the hierarchy of roles and duties: for the
woman cooking, ironing, spinning, sewing, etc. For the man it means
providing the material means for subsistence: he's the owner of the
means of production—the agriculture. (1991: 128, 144)[36]

This vision was certainly accurate until the 1940s, when Tamunangue
was first brought to the stages of Barquisimeto and Caracas. And it is
also true that many of the changes that Tamunangue underwent were
the result of a new performative context. Theatrical interests now demanded that female dancers excite the audience with a more animated,
even lusty, performance. Skirts were raised, feet were lifted, and tempos
were increased. A new flirtatiousness, designed to capture the interests
of a secular audience, was suddenly encouraged. Symbolizing this new
position of women dancers was the institution of an annual Tamunangue
Folklore Queen, initiated at the Lara State Folklore Festival of 1966. The
first selected, appropriately enough, was María Magdalena Colmenárez
Losada, from El Tocuyo's renowned family of Tamunangue promoters.[37]
As musicians and dancers began returning to their communities, aspects of staged performance invariably appeared in the local Tamunangue tradition. Such "braiding" of forms, as Richard Schechner calls
the constant interplay of ritual and theater, is little surprise (1988: 120).[38]
And yet, what has entered into the performance of female dancers is
much more than the innovative stage direction acquired from festivals
and television. For introduced into this new braid is the experience of
women no longer limited by the rural domestic roles that formerly defined them. The women who now participate in Tamunangue are as
likely to work in the city during the week as they are to live on a farm
or in a village. They are also likely to be college graduates, schoolteach-
ers, nurses, accountants, or have any number of occupations. In short,
the set of social relations Tamunangue now reflects is one that men less
easily dominate. And the innovations women have begun to introduce
have clearly announced it.

   Even as men continue to protest the more exuberant and sensual manner in which women currently perform, several other modifications have

become still more controversial. One of these is the adoption of the vara, formerly restricted to male dancers. Now, in nearly every community except Sanare, women dance with the staff cradled in their arms as well (Fig. 27). Speaking for many male participants who have questioned this practice, one man said: "San Antonio didn't give the Virgin the vara, he kept it. So why do women have to take it?" (Berarducci Fernández 1987: 77). Spectators, however, have responded more favorably, as witnessed by a performance I attended at the Teatro Juárez in Barquisimeto. There, during a Perrendenga, a woman trounced her partner so soundly that he was forced to flee the stage. As the audience erupted in wild applause, the master of ceremonies announced that it was a demonstration of how women should treat their husbands should they misbehave.

Another innovation which has been equally popular with audiences yet controversial with many men is the manner in which the Caballito is now commonly performed. In the past, women simply wrapped their kerchiefs around their partners' necks and made a quick, perfunctory gesture, as if to mount them. Today, however, they not only sit securely upon the men but also ride them offstage, waving as they do. This change, whose symbolism is not difficult to interpret, has clearly challenged the machismo of many of the male participants. While the former version may have played with "taming" the wild stallion, the new one unmistakably succeeds. And if the conquest being acted out in this dance is not reversed, the relationship between the adversaries has certainly been altered.

Yet men still appeal to tradition in the hope of maintaining a status quo in which they are the unchallenged rulers. As Orlando Colmenárez, president of one of Sanare's Tamunangue groups, nostalgically put it: "The women seem to be jumping and stomping about now. They dance just like the men, not in that special way they once did." Complaints such as these, however, will have little effect in derailing the enormous changes now under way for women throughout Venezuela. It is little surprise, then, that a dance based on the Moors and Christians is being reconfigured once again. Further evidence of this is the increased participation of women in the Batalla.

Figure 27. A mixed Batalla with men and women at the Talleres de Cultura Popular, Caracas. (Photograph by David M. Guss)

Although less common in smaller communities, Tamunangue performances in Barquisimeto and Caracas have now featured women not only in the ritual sword fighting but in every other aspect of the dance as well. A number of these performances have met with strong opposition. In 1990, when a group of women carried the statue of San Antonio on their shoulders through the streets of Barquisimeto, an angry crowd of male students attempted to block them. The procession was led by Milagro de Blavia, director of the city's museum, and was claimed to have been the first time that women had publicly carried the saint (Briceño 1990b).

But this has been a time of many firsts for Venezuelan women, and it is little surprise that the Tamunangue tradition should reflect it. In fact, the formation of the first all-woman Tamunangue troupes would seem to parallel the struggle of many marginalized radical groups wherein initial separation is followed by eventual reintegration. At least this was the case with Guamacire, the first female Tamunangue group ever organized. Its founder was Luisa Virginia Rivero, a former Folklore Queen, who, like her predecessor, María Magdalena Colmenárez Losada, also came from a well-known Tamunangue family. Encouraged by her father, Benicio Rivero, she began the group in 1987, restricting membership to women. Once established, however, the group began to accept men as well.

Guamacire has not been alone: Other Tamunangue groups continue to break the gender barrier, giving women access to all parts of the tradition. One of the most important of these has been Barquisimeto's Alma de Lara, a group which has incorporated itself as a foundation and now uses Tamunangue as a means of community activism (Ortiz 1998: 28–29) (Fig. 28). Although criticized for being among the first to include women in the Batalla, Alma de Lara continues to encourage them to join as singers and musicians. Domingo Pérez, the group's director, has steadfastly defended this policy, claiming that "Folklore can't be static. It has to change and adapt, and that means making space for women."

Transformations such as these have also taken place in a number of other traditions where women were either excluded or participated in ways that reaffirmed their inferior status. Only recently, with the advent of staged performances and government-sponsored workshops, have women been permitted to dance as devils in Venezuela's Corpus Christi celebrations. And in Cuba and Trinidad, the prominence of women in carnival has escalated to the point of redefining the way these dances are performed (Bettelheim 1993: 151; Miller 1994: 113). Similar changes have taken place in the Cuban rumba, which, prior to the Revolution, highlighted the working-class male's domination over a passive partner. The elevation of this dance into a national form has redefined this relationship, forcing it to conform to the ideals of a modern, egalitarian society (Daniel 1995). The causes for such changes may vary. In Brazilian *capoeira*, for example, it has only been through internationalization and the entrance into American dance studios that this form has been opened to women and female masters have been accepted (Almeida 1986: 3; Browning 1995: 116).

Although numerous other examples could be cited, they all confirm that festive traditions, despite claims to the contrary, are in a constant

Figure 28.   Alma de Lara performing in Caracas. (Photograph by David M. Guss)

state of flux. Such plasticity often reflects the changing social order in which these events are realized. But they are not simply mirrors, for if they reflect, they also create, and the festive state is one in which new realities are also constituted. Whose reality, however, remains a question, for the flexibility of these forms is derived, in no small measure, from their agonistic and contested nature.

Perhaps this is why the Moors and Christians dance was so readily adopted throughout the New World. In a festival constructed around conquest and subjugation, participants found it easy to articulate their own embattled interests. This has certainly been the case in Tamunangue, where the struggle between opposing groups has frequently challenged the way the festival is interpreted. For colonialists and missionaries, it was an allegory justifying their own brutal conquest. For those engaged in the national project of the 1940s and after, it was a realization of the new racial ideal of mestizaje. For blacks, it has become an important symbol of resistance and historical knowing. And for women over the last decade, it has provided a space in which a new-found liberation could be expressed. But this instability and conflict is not unique to Tamunangue. The Festival of San Juan and the Day of the Monkey are also sites where competing groups continue to struggle over issues of interpretation and performance. To those involved, the stakes are high. For, as participants well know, festivals, for all their joy and color, are also battlegrounds where identities are fought over and communities made.

Notes

1.   "Festive forms" can encompass a wide range of public events, including parades, carnivals, concerts, fairs, funerals, patron saint and feast days, caroling, sporting contests, civic commemorations, and even political demonstrations and trials. Many have tried to make a distinction between rituals and festive forms, claiming that the former are religious, obligatory, closed, and serious and that the latter are secular, optional, open, and playful. A number of these scholars, including Gluckman, who used the term "ceremony" for the latter, also tried to contrast these forms by their association with either traditional communitarian or "modern industrial" societies (Moore and Myerhoff 1977: 21; see also Duvignaud 1976; Turner 1982; and Manning 1983).

Public display is always a fundamental attribute to festive behavior, but many of the other distinctions become extremely blurred when considering Latin America. As the examples in this book demonstrate, not only are the meanings and functions of these events unstable but shifting audiences will experience them in a wide range of ways. The focus here, therefore, is less on trying to establish fixed categories than on identifying the changing "social conditions of production" in which these events are performed (Williams 1980: 46).

2.   Among García Canclini's explanations for this phenomenon are the need to generate additional income for increasingly marginalized groups; the market's appetite for new and more exotic products; the increase in tourism; and the state's search for a national identity along with "the establishment of ideological homogeneity" (1993: 43).

For an interesting parallel to García Canclini's argument, see Boissevain's discussion concerning the recent growth of public celebrations throughout Europe since the 1970s. Boissevain argues that the weakening of church and state, ethnic resurgence, reverse migration, tourism, democratization, and even the broadcast of public events have all attributed to this continuing growth (1992: 1–19). And finally, Appadurai and Breckenridge also claim that "Such festivals are on the increase throughout the world and everywhere represent ongoing debates concerning emergent group identities and group artifacts" (1992: 40).

3.   Martín-Barbero has made similar observations concerning the way in which festivals have adapted to the changing socioeconomic reality of Latin America: "The festival is a space for an especially important production of symbols in which the rituals are the way of appropriating an economy which is injurious to the community but which the community has not been able to either suppress or replace with some other possibility" (1993a: 192). This is also the essence of Bakhtin's argument concerning the special role of popular culture and festive forms in particular (1984).

4.   Although the Notting Hill Carnival originated in 1965, Cohen did not begin his investigation until 1976. As he stated in his first published work on the subject, "Most of these studies [of ritual and ceremonials], including my own, suffer from insufficient longitudinal data to permit validation of the analysis in terms of interrelated historical movements. It is principally to overcome this methodological difficulty that I have concentrated on the study of a current London annual carnival, which has developed, both culturally and politically, in full light of recorded publicity" (1980: 66). In his book-length study, *Masquerade Politics,* he divides the carnival into five phases: a diverse, polyethnic phase (1966–1970); a Trinidad-style steel band and calypso phase (1971–1975); a British-born West Indian phase introducing reggae, Rastafarianism, and other Jamaican influences (1976–1979); a period of increased government co-optation and institutionalization (1979–1986); and a diffuse intrusion from a number of sources attempting to regiment and institutionalize the carnival even further (1987–1991). He hypothesizes that the next phase may be increased tourism and commodification (1993: 153).

5.   While Goffman provides some of the best insights into how cultural performances are set apart from other forms of behavior, he also suggests that they may include almost any human interaction. Or as he claims, it is "all the activity of an individual which occurs during a period marked by his continuous presence before a particular set of observers and which has some effect on others" (1959: 22).

See Abrahams (1982, 1987) for a discussion of the specific way in which festivals are initiated and framed as opposed to rituals, which respond to transitional breaks that already exist: "Festivals must initiate their own energies while they organize the celebrants for mutual fun and profit. Thus, festivals begin with a bang, literally, with loud noises produced by drums, guns, firecrackers, and other attention-grabbers. The vocabulary of festivals is the language of extreme experiences through contrasts—contrasts between everyday life and these high times, and within the events themselves, between the different parts of the occasion" (1982: 167). As discussed elsewhere in this chapter, the distinction between festival and ritual that many have tried to make is much more blurred in Latin America, where the multiple uses of festive forms preclude identifying them as stable members of any fixed category.

6.   For analyses of Peru's Corpus Christi and Qoyllur Rit'i celebrations and their complicated relations to one another, see Allen (1988), Cahill (1996), Dean (1993, 1999), Poole (1990), Randall (1982), Sallnow (1987), and Huayhuaca Villasante (1988). For a good comparison of the way Corpus Christi was used in the proselytization of Mexico, see Curcio-Nagy (1994).

7.   Hobsbawm also recognized the important relation between festivals and new secular states, claiming that "public celebrations" were one of the three "invented traditions" necessary for their consolidation (1983: 271). The other two elements that Hobsbawm considered essential in this process were public education and public monuments. One should also see the work of Mosse (1971), who discusses the critical role of festivals and monuments in what he identifies as a new politics of the masses rather than one mediated through parliamentary institutions.

8.   For excellent discussions of the political appropriation of festive forms and their subsequent reduction of meanings, see Cohen on the "irreducible in culture" (1980: 81–84) and DaMatta on the "contamination of codes" (1991: 52–53). Both argue that a festival, or in this case carnival, is by its very definition a polysemous event subject to multiple interpretations and can therefore never be reduced to a single political sign.

9.   Parkin makes a similar observation, that "while anthropologists have wished to remove the essentialism and exaggerated mutual boundedness implied by such terms as tribe and culture, the members and bearers of these same groups and concepts have themselves emphasized such qualities as being at the

basis of their own beliefs and practices" (1996: xxviii). For two examples of this somewhat inverted but clearly postmodern debate, see the Maori response to Hanson's claims that their mythic origins were inspired by anthropology (Wilford 1990) and Kaspin's experiences in Kenya deconstructing the "primitive" (1995). See also Desai's discussion of the "internationalist dangers" of calling other people's traditions invented, or what he claims is "a new form of denial" (1993: 136), Brettell's collection, *When They Read What We Write: The Politics of Ethnography* (1993), and Briggs's thought-provoking article, "The Politics of Discursive Authority in Research on the 'Invention of Tradition.' "(1996). In each case, it is clear that the champions of hybridity are from the newest cultures exporting it.

10.   Translations of all quotations and interviews are by the author unless otherwise noted.

11.   In Venezuela the debate over this terminology has been particularly rancorous. Much of it has focused on the government-supported institutes that work in the area of popular culture and folklore. Until 1986 this included the National Institute of Folklore, the National Museum of Folklore, and the Inter-American Institute for Ethnomusicology and Folklore (INIDEF). After much discussion, the three institutes were consolidated in that year into the Center for the Study of Traditional and Popular Cultures (CCPYT), eliminating the use of the word "folklore." With Carlos Andrés Pérez's reelection in 1989, Isabel Aretz, the former head of INIDEF, was renamed director, and the umbrella institute's title was changed to the Foundation for Ethnomusicology and Folklore (FUNDEF). See Castillo (1987) for a history of this process, along with its ideological significance.

12.   The festival's official slogan, which appeared on the program and all accompanying literature was:

THERE IS NO NATIONALITY WITHOUT TRADITION
FOLKLORE IS POPULAR TRADITION

13.   Liscano also noted the powerful effect that seeing Caracas had upon these performers, who until then had rarely left their communities: "Besides its cultural function, the festival fulfilled another, unexpected, human purpose in giving most of the people who took part in it—drawn from all parts of the country—their first opportunity to see the capital. Their reactions were noteworthy. A sort of daze constantly hung over the campesinos. Old dreams were at last coming true" (1949: 35). In October 1998, a fifty-year anniversary of the Festival of Tradition was held in Caracas. In addition to an academic conference, two concerts were presented, the second of which was entitled "Celebrating Juan Liscano." Among the various tributes to him was Alfredo Chacón's statement that he was "The father and son of the mother of all festivals" (Liscano 1998: 67). FUNDEF republished the materials devoted to the festival that originally appeared in Lis-

cano's 1950 *Folklore y cultura,* along with a selection of articles revisiting the event (Liscano 1998).

14.   Organized as part of Student Week by what became known as the "Generation of '28," these events were scheduled to coincide with Caracas's Carnival preparation. This scheduling, along with the carnivalesque quality of the events, permitted the students to both gather and march through the streets, something rarely done during Juan Vicente Gómez's long dictatorship (1908–1935). A number of the participants were jailed and later forced into exile. Several of these, including Rómulo Betancourt, had been high school students of Gallegos and were to eventually form the core of the Acción Democrática Party. See Skurski (1993) for a detailed description of these events. For earlier examples of the way the Caracas Carnival responded to dramatic political and economic changes in the final quarter of the nineteenth century, see Lavenda (1980).

15.   In his detailed study of Venezuela's struggle to identify as a modern state, Coronil focuses less on popular movements and more on the government orchestration of massive public works. Rather than discuss the Festival of Tradition and the inauguration of Rómulo Gallegos, he concentrates on the dictatorships of Juan Vicente Gómez and Marcos Pérez Jiménez. He argues that their governments (1908–1935 and 1950–1958, respectively), as well as those of Carlos Andrés Pérez (1974–1979 and 1989–1993), used the enormous expenditures on public projects as a form of spectacle, a modern bread and circus so effective that it transformed the state into a magical power capable of the superhuman act of modernization. Here is a different type of performance, with invisible actors behind a massive curtain of material objects. Or, as Coronil writes,

> In their [political actors'] public battles as much as in their private fantasies, the state became a powerful site for the performance of illusions and the illusion of performance, a magical theater where the symbols of civilized life—metropolitan history, commodities, institutions, steel mills, freeways, constitutions—were transformed into potent tokens that could be purchased or copied. As a magical theater, the state became a place possessed with the alchemic power to transmute liquid wealth [oil] into civilized life. (1997: 229–230)

CHAPTER 2

1.   For more on the growing body of literature regarding the manner in which competing social interests help to generate new and varying versions of the past, see Boyarin (1994), Brow (1990), Crain (1990), Gillis (1994), Hall (1981), Handler (1988), Handler and Gable (1997), Handler and Linnekin (1984), Hobsbawm and Ranger (1983), Lincoln (1989), Watson (1994), and Williams (1977).

2.   As Sir James Frazer noted in *The Golden Bough,* "A faint tinge of Christianity has been given by naming Midsummer Day after St. John the Baptist, but we

cannot doubt that the celebration dates from a time long before the beginning of our era" (1953 [1922]: 720). Tracing its spread throughout Europe and even Muslim North Africa, Frazer cited three elements he believed to be common to all: "bonfires, the procession with torches round the fields, and the custom of rolling a wheel" (1953 [1922]: 720–721). These dominant features led him to classify San Juan as a fire festival.

3.   Crespi makes the interesting observation that as distinctions between Indian and non-Indian groups have diminished, so has the significance of this festival in the Cayambe-Imbabura area (1981: 497). For a view somewhat different from Crespi's, see Crain (1989), who believes the festival has actually increased in importance with both the elimination of other celebrations and the new inequities of a more market-oriented economy.

4.   The 1985 census listed the population of Barlovento's four districts as 133,000, or 58.5 percent of the state of Miranda (Monasterio Vásquez 1989: 8–9). For more on the geopolitical formation of this area, see Acosta Saignes (1959), Castillo Lara (1981a, 1981b, 1983), Estado Miranda (1981), and Ponce (1987).

5.   All direct quotations for which no source is given are oral statements made directly to the author.

6.   *Malembe* is a special song played on the final afternoon of the festival. The sadness commonly associated with it is claimed to derive from its role as a farewell song to the saint. García has even suggested that this final stage of the festival, known as the *encierro*, is analogous to a wake: "This is a drumbeat performed with round drums known as culo e' puya. The bearers would make the saint dance very gently, as is suggested by the word malembe, which, in Bantu-Lingala, means 'less fast' or 'slowly,' and so they would proceed all the way to the small chapel where the wake was to be held" (1985: 5).

Sojo also attaches special importance to the word *malembe*, claiming that it is derived from the name for an African deity and actually means "All Powerful." In discussing its role in the San Juan celebration, he explains that it "represented a cult of liberation through death. Death by one's own hand before the slave-owner's henchmen could lay on their fatal lashes once again" (1986: 172).

7.   Bastide points out that, in Brazil and Trinidad, Shango, the God of Thunder, is explicitly identified with San Juan and that the connection of each to fire may well explain their union. He also suggests that the common belief that San Juan must sleep through his own holiday, rather than come down to earth and destroy it, is derived from stories about Shango (Bastide 1972: 156–159; 1978: 274). This tradition is also to be found in Venezuela, where Sanjuaneros sing:

> Si San Juan supiera
> cuando es su día
> del cielo bajará, caramba,
> con gran alegría.

If San Juan knew
it was his day, oh boy,
he'd come down from heaven
with such great joy.
(Adam 1981: 28)

8.   It is difficult to ascertain the origin of the term *culo e' puya*. However, it may derive from the drums' hourglass-shaped interiors. For detailed descriptions of these drum traditions, see Brandt (1978), García (1990), Liscano (1970), and Ramón y Rivera (1971).

9.   The special velorio for dead children not yet baptized is the *mampulorio*. As the Lipners claim, this velorio is considered a happy occasion, "for people strongly believe that the child has gone to heaven to pray for its parents, and no sorrow should be shown" (Lipner and Lipner 1958: 4).

10.   Bastide refers to this phenomenon as "Catholic-fetishist syncretism" (1978: 142).

11.   The poet Andrés Eloy Blanco, writing about the Festival of Tradition, quipped, "Columbus may have discovered America, but Liscano just discovered Venezuela" (cited in Machado 1987: 49). For a detailed account of the preparation, execution, and response to this festival, held on February 17–21, 1948, see Liscano (1950).

12.   In discussing the political dimensions of Trinidad's Carnival and the various interests it arbitrates, John Stewart makes a useful distinction between visitors who are "returnees" and those who are "tourists." He also claims that because they are detached from any community "encumbrances," it is the visitors in both categories who actually enjoy the event most (1986: 314). For more on the concept of the "heritage spectacle," see Acciaioli (1985), Crain (1992), Karp and Lavine (1991), and Kirshenblatt-Gimblett (1991, 1998).

13.   Ruíz subsequently retired from the air force and served as a district councilman for the opposition COPEI party. COPEI, which was founded in January 1946, stands for Comité de Organización Política Electoral Independiente.

14.   The issue of patronage or, as Benito Yrady describes it, "negative interventions" (personal communication 1990), in local festivals was not limited to Curiepe. Begun by the Instituto Nacional de Cultura y Bellas Artes (INCIBA) and continued by its successor, CONAC, these small stipends tie performers to whatever political party is in power. Hence, when parties lose elections, musicians sometimes refuse to play at festivals because their payments are discontinued by those now in office.

15.   A song popular in Barlovento at the time, credited to a farmer named Aureliano Huice, effectively captured this feeling of being overrun by tourists. In its principal refrain one fish sings to another:

Lebranche le dijó a Guabina,
"Vámonos para pozo hondo.
Allá vienen los turistas
Con su destrucción en el hombro."

Lebranche said to Guabina,
"Let's get deep down in the water.
Here come the tourists
With destruction on their shoulders."

16.   In addition to working for the Ministry of Justice, Blanco was a professional drummer with Yolanda Moreno's Danzas Venezuela, a group that has been adapting traditional dance forms for stage and television since the early 1950s. It was through this dance troupe that Blanco became familiar with Curiepe's unique drum tradition and thus interested in returning to the village in 1975 with the ministry's new program.

17.   The publication of Alfredo Chacón's *Curiepe: Ensayo sobre la realización del sentido en la actividad mágicoreligiosa de un pueblo venezolano* (1979) was celebrated in Curiepe during the Culture Week of 1979.

18.   Azpúrua's film was part of a national campaign seeking both to redefine government policy toward indigenous peoples and to evict the North American–backed New Tribes Missions (Guss 1989: 19–20; Luzardo 1988; Mosonyi 1981).

19.   For an indication of how radical this shift in self-perception was, consider the findings of Max Brandt, who, while doing research in this area only several years before, noted that most Curieperos defined themselves as well as their drum traditions as "Indian" rather than African (1978: 5).

20.   Historical instances of the repression of drums are to be found throughout the Americas, from the response to the Stono Rebellion in South Carolina in 1739 (Wood 1974) to Rafael Trujillo's more recent attempt to prohibit their inclusion in Dominican merengue bands. And even though drums were not outlawed in the United States during the 1950s, congas and bongos served as the symbol of resistance for an entire generation of beats. As Dick Hebdige observed in writing about reggae and Rastafarianism:

> The voice of Africa in the West Indies has traditionally been identified with insurrection and silenced wherever possible. In particular, the preservation of African traditions, like drumming, has in the past been construed by the authorities (the Church, the colonial and even some "post-colonial" governments) as being intrinsically subversive, posing a symbolic threat to law and order. These outlawed traditions were not only considered anti-social and unchristian, they were positively, triumphantly pagan. They suggested unspeakable alien rites, they made possible illicit and rancorous allegiances which smacked of future discord. They hinted at that darkest of rebellions: a celebration of Negritude. They restored "deported Africa," that "drifting continent" to a privileged place within the black mythology. And the very existence of that mythology was enough to inspire an immense dread in the hearts of some white slave owners. (1979: 31–32)

21.   *Cumbe, quilombo,* and *palenque* were the terms used for cimarrón communities in Venezuela, Brazil, and Colombia, respectively. The term *cimarrón* (from
cima, or "mountaintop") was originally used for domesticated cattle that had
returned to the wild. As Richard Price observed, "by the early 1500s, it had come
to be used in plantation colonies throughout the Americas to designate slaves
who successfully escaped from captivity" (1983: 1).

22.   Elsewhere I discuss a recent open-air performance about the life of one of
Barlovento's greatest cimarrón heroes, Guillermo Rivas (Guss 1996b).

23.   A similar process to the way in which San Juan has been absorbed into the
cimarrón experience is to be found in Brazil, where black practitioners of Um-
banda have placed the leaders of former quilombos at the head of a hierarchy
of spirits. As John Burdick writes:

> The most well-known version of Umbanda situates the slave at the bottom, beneath
> the Indian and white in the hierarchy of spirits. But this version is adhered to mainly
> by whites and mulattos. Blacks in Umbanda worship a spirit unrecognized by either
> whites or mulattos: Zumbi, one of the chiefs of Palmares, the great maroon society
> that survived for almost a century in the backlands of Alagoas, until finally de-
> stroyed by the Portuguese in 1697. (1992a: 27)

24.   Saints may be owned by individuals, the church, or collective societies.
The possibility that a saint will be manipulated for particular political ends always exists, but ownership by a society or *cofradía* reduces the likelihood of such
behavior.

25.   Although the events of 1979 and earlier reflect a great deal of dissatisfaction
with the tourists, actual sentiment was quite ambivalent. People enjoyed the
attention and national celebrity, as well as the increase in movement and activity.
The reinstitution of the San Juan Congo velorio permitted Curieperos to experience the best of both worlds—a public, tourist celebration and a private, village
one. For some interesting comparisons with tourism's effects on other local festivals, see Stanley Brandes's *Power and Persuasion: Fiestas and Social Control in
Rural Mexico* (1988), in which he traces the transformation of the Night of the
Dead celebration on the 1st and 2nd of November from a small family celebration
to a large tourist one. Despite busloads of tourists and a series of pageants, plays,
and fairs, all orchestrated by the government, Brandes claims, the Tzintzuntzan
remain delighted: "For the most part, villagers appreciate the changes that have
come to the Night of the Dead. They like the liveliness, the outside attention, the
influx of money, the government support and exposure. Not once, and despite
some discreet probes on my part, did I ever encounter a complaint about noise,
impoliteness, or sacrilege as a result of tourism. . . . Most discussions about the
fiesta concern changes needed to accommodate even more tourists" (1988: 108).

26.   The extraordinary price of this image is underscored by the fact that the

most expensive slave at the time was estimated to cost 400 pesos (Sojo 1986: 171). It should also be remembered that much of the power attributed to the new saint derived from its phallus, thus connecting it not only to the Bantu Nkisi tradition but also to one of San Juan's most essential functions, that of fertility.

27.   The details of Curiepe's founding came to light only in the early 1980s, when the historian Guillermo Castillo Lara gained access to a collection of un-archived colonial documents in the Casa Simón Bolívar in Caracas. They proved that a mixed company of free black soldiers and *luangos,* or escaped slaves from the Antilles, led by Captain Juan del Rosario Blanco, founded Curiepe on what Castillo Lara claims was the day of San Juan, 1721 (1981b: 57; also see Monasterio Vásquez 1989: 17).

28.   Walker describes how, in a fascinating Brazilian parallel to the celebration of San Juan, religious societies in the Bahian community of Cachoeira were or-ganized with the express purpose of providing funds for the purchase of "free papers." Although her example explains how the groups that were organized to celebrate the Festa da Boa Morte, or Feast of Good Death, secretly conspired to liberate those still enslaved, she emphasizes that this was by no means unique: "The Brotherhoods and Sisterhoods were organizational structures within which Africans and later Afro-Brazilians could organize under the aegis of the Catholic church to oppose the system of slavery, and in which free Blacks could collab-orate with their still enslaved brothers and sisters to increase the ranks of the free" (1986: 30).

29.   The "myth of *mestizaje,*" or "the myth of racial democracy," is not unique to Venezuela but is found throughout the Caribbean and South America. As Whitten and Torres emphasize, *"Mestizaje,* the ideology of racial intermingling, is an explicit master symbol of the nation in all Latin American countries" (1992: 18). It is also, they point out, "a powerful force of exclusion of both black and indigenous communities in the Americas today. As a consequence, black and indigenous awareness of exclusion and continuous struggle for ethnic power will remain constant" (1992: 21). For further discussions of what Arthur Corwin refers to as "the great national illusion" (1974: 389) and its effects on all of Latin America, see Toplin (1974) and Burdick (1992b). Like Whitten and Torres, Bur-dick makes the point that "whitening," as opposed to *négritude,* or the celebration of blackness, "meant eliminating the racial heritage of Africa by overwhelming it with miscegenation, the importation of Europeans, and restrictions on the im-migration of blacks." He goes on to say that "if 'racial democracy' has any mean-ing at all, it refers to the fact that Latin American societies make some provision for better treatment of people of visibly mixed ancestry" (1992b: 41).

30.   Perhaps no institution demonstrates the way in which this purportedly color-blind ideology confounded the issues of race and class as did the *"gracias al sacar."* Translatable as "thanks for the exclusion," these papers permitted mes-

tizos and blacks who could afford them the right to be classified as white (Wright 1990: 24). While Wright notes that the ruling class in colonial Venezuela expressed opposition to this institution, "certificates of whiteness" were nevertheless common in many parts of the Americas (Burdick 1992b: 42).

31.   Numerous other examples support this position that race is simply not an issue in Venezuelan society. For many people, such as Guillermo Morón, president of the prestigious Academia Nacional de la Historia, the transcendence of race is a symbol of pride, attesting to Venezuela's enlightened, if not superior, state:

> It is true that there exists no negro problem in any Spanish-speaking country today, because the negro has been assimilated into society without any trouble. In Venezuela this phenomenon of complete assimilation, social, political, and economic, is of the greatest importance. Venezuela has a tradition of liberty and equality for all which in some other nations has still to be evolved. The negro of colonial days, a slave, and therefore inferior, has given way to the educated man, the "creole" negro, who is one of the unifying links of the Venezuelan people. (1964: 54)

And many others, such as the celebrated author and philosopher Arturo Uslar Pietri, believe that to speak of race is to be "un-Venezuelan": "Whoever speaks of blacks or whites, whoever invokes racial hatred or privileges, is denying Venezuela. In Venezuela, in political and social matters, there are neither whites nor blacks, neither *mestizos* nor Indians. There are only Venezuelans" (cited in Wright 1990: 122).

Until recently, among the few who had tried to expose the inconsistencies within these racial views were Juan Pablo Sojo and Miguel Acosta Saignes. While Sojo's influence as a folklorist and writer was felt primarily in the communities of Barlovento, where he lived, Acosta Saignes is often credited with being the founder of Venezuelan anthropology. In work after work (1961, 1962, 1967), he documented the history and legacy of Venezuela's African-descended peoples, inspiring a whole new generation of what Gramsci might have called "organic intellectuals" (1971). Like the Sanjuaneros of Curiepe, these young Afro-Venezuelan scholars and activists are also challenging the ideology of invisibility that has dominated all discussions of race up to the present. As Jesús García, one of the most prominent figures among them, recently wrote:

> The study of the African presence in Venezuela has hardly existed up till now for investigators. In fact, one sometimes has the impression that they would like to erase the past and opt for the cliché that we are all mestizos, without recognizing, in a profound way, that to arrive at this "mestizaje," or rather what could be called our "Venezuelan-ness," we had to pass through a long struggle between dominant and dominated groups, between Europeans, Amerindians, and Africans, a process within which the African presence was a catalyzing factor in these conflicts waged for five centuries. (1990: 72)

CHAPTER 3

1.   Several other authors have also addressed the way in which the ideology of mestizaje in Ecuador has functioned as a mechanism of exclusion, both dominating and eradicating indigenous culture and history (Muratorio 1993; Stutzman 1981; Weiss 1991). Muratorio summarizes this well when she writes:

> As part of an *ideology* of domination, *mestizaje* hides dialogue by turning it into a monologue—the monologue of the Self who has incorporated the Other or is in the process of doing so. It creates the illusion that the Other, as forged by the dominator, can be brought into the "imagined community"—the useful term by which Benedict Anderson (1983) refers to national social identities—through the doorway of "natural" ties . . .
>   Like other master fictions, *mestizaje* was invented by the dominant turn-of-the-century elites for the subordinate peoples in order to hide and maintain the asymmetrical relations of power between whites and Indians that they had inherited from the colonial administration. (1993: 23–24)

2.   Soon after this event, Kayapo leaders reciprocated the insult by refusing to allow a group of government officials into their village unless they donned "proper" Kayapo attire.

3.   Such campaigns as that of the Kayapo are not unique. Today in the Brazilian Amazon alone there are more than fifty indigenous federations. In Ecuador the Federación de Centros Shuar, organized in 1964, has not only gained title to its lands but also runs a successful radio station, publishing house, and bilingual education and health programs. Similar developments have also occurred among the Arahuaco of Colombia and the Mapuche of Chile. And among the Amuesha of Peru, the Yanesha cooperative has been developing alternative strategies for harvesting wood products. Although these are only a few of the many projects that indigenous communities have launched over the last three decades, they signal what must be seen as the vanguard of a true cultural diversity movement throughout the continent, a movement that is not simply asking for greater representation but also presents an economic and cultural alternative to the Eurocentric paradigm of development that has dominated the Americas since the arrival of Columbus 500 years ago.

4.   The staging of the Altamira meeting was comprehensively planned with a view to its appearance on film and video. The daily sessions were in effect choreographed, with gorgeous mass ritual performances that framed their beginnings, ends, and major high points. The encampment of the Kayapo participants was created as a model Kayapo village, complete with families, traditional shelters, and artifact production, all on display for the edification of the hundreds of photojournalists, television and film camera crews, and video cameras. The Kayapo leaders saw Altamira as a major opportunity to represent them-

selves, their society, and their cause to the world, and they believed that the impact it would have on Brazilian and world public opinion, via the media, would be more important than the actual dialogue with Brazilian representatives that transpired at the meeting itself (Turner 1991: 307–308).

5.   Stutzman also witnessed this shift from ethnic victim to ethnic resister among indigenous peoples of Ecuador, claiming: "Ethnicity as a cultural system stands in implicit judgement of the expansionist state. . . . Ethnicity protests against the larger national situation, not by struggling to take over or overthrow the state apparatus, but by refusing to be deceived by the definitions of contemporary realities that the controllers of the state are promoting in the name of national development" (1981: 47, 73). Urban and Sherzer (1991) also present various examples of this rapidly changing national-indigenous discourse from throughout Latin America. And finally, it is important to note Cohen's observations that it is a shift in political theory itself that has transformed our notions of ethnicity:

> Democratic theory and ideology has shifted to include both individual and group rights. In this sense, ethnicity has been legitimized in political theory, making it a means not only of anti-alienative, diffuse identity but also a means of asserting one's rights in a political community in which ethnicity is a recognized element. This being so, ethnicity is not just a conceptual tool. It also reflects an ideological position claiming recognition for ethnicity as a major sector of complex societies and points the way to a more just and equitable society. (1978: 402)

6.   Caicareños are equally divided over the origin of the name Caicara. Some claim that it derives from an Indian chief named Caicuara, while others say it comes from an indigenous, yuca-like plant called "caracara." The British botanist Robert Schomburgk wrote that "Kaikara" was a native term for the three stars in Orion's belt (cited in Ramírez 1972: 11). The most thorough study of the term was conducted by Juan José Ramírez, who concluded that, although it is impossible to ever be certain, Caicara is probably a Carib-derived word meaning "Ceiba creek," from *cai*, or ceiba (*Bombax* sp.), and *cuara*, "creek" or "brook" (1972: 9–11).

7.   Most Caicareños seem capable of recounting at least some version of this story. For the most fanciful written account, see Ramírez (1972: 71–73), in which he not only identifies the Indians as Pariagotos but names various chiefs. The following version was told to me by María Maita de Guevara in 1990:

> That was when Caicara was founded, after all of that. There was a church put up by the Spaniards and the bells were in front in a huge tree. One day they said the Indians were about to attack the village. And then the people were frightened and went into the church. And the people all gathered together praying to God and in the night on the 3rd of August when Santo Domingo appeared, there in the gully they call Santo Domingo. And when the warriors came in the night they saw a man mounted on a horse and a dog at the feet of the horse and a huge army and they saw

how the gold and silver from his buckles and buttons glowed. And when the Indians saw that they became frightened and ran away. And they told the other chiefs: "There was an enormous army there at the edge of the village guarding it and we couldn't get by." Then the other Indians crept up very slowly. But they didn't find anything. They were frightened by what the others had told them. They didn't go any further but stayed where they were till dawn. And you know the Indians are very brave so a group of the brave Indians dared to enter the village to see what exactly had happened. They came in little by little, and among them were some of the ones who had seen Santo Domingo when he was riding his horse. They saw the people who were in the plaza and the bells were ringing and so they went into the church and what was their surprise, their terror when they went in and saw the man who had danced upon his horse on a pedestal in the center of the altar. And they all ran out terrified. And it was from that moment on, from the apparition of Santo Domingo, that the Indians became more religious. Ever since then, every August 4th, the Indians come with their parrandas and things, dancing, to make offerings and pay homage to the church.

It should be noted that while Caicareños claim that August 4 was the date of Santo Domingo's miracle and thus the reason for their holiday, it is also the Catholic Church's official day for this saint. Known in English as Saint Dominic, Santo Domingo de Guzmán was a twelfth-century monk who founded the Dominicans, or Order of Friars Preachers. Born in Calaruega, Spain, he rose to prominence for his success in combating the Albergensians in southern France. The events described in Caicara resemble not so much Santo Domingo, however, as Santiago. Patron saint of both the Reconquest of the Moors and the Conquest of the Indians, Santiago frequently appeared in battle to rally Spanish troops from imminent defeat. The description by Garcilaso de la Vega of Santiago's appearance in Peru—"seated on top of a white horse grasping his leather shield in one hand and his sword in the other and many Indians, wounded and dead, thrown down head long at his feet"—is remarkably similar to the accounts of Santo Domingo in Caicara (Silverblatt 1988: 176).

8.   The shift in crops can be attributed to a number of causes, including access to markets and changing settlement patterns. Nevertheless, one important factor has been the agrarian reform movement begun in 1959, which sought the redistribution of arable land into smaller holdings. The most detailed analysis of this area's economic and agricultural history is in Arzolay and others (1984).

9.   Caicara and the surrounding communities form an administrative entity called the Municipio of Caicara, which joins two other municipios to create the Distrito Cedeño. Although the population for the Municipio of Caicara did not increase substantially between 1961 and 1971 (from 9,384 to 10,804), the proportion living within the village of Caicara itself nearly doubled, to between 7,000 and 8,000. Unfortunately, it becomes more difficult after this date to obtain specific data for the village of Caicara, as subsequent censuses report only the populations for the municipio and the distrito. This may be an indication of how

much the municipio is now identified as the town. In any case, the 1981 population for the Municipio of Caicara was 13,638 and for the Distrito Cedeño, 21,909
(Arzolay and others 1984: 313; Ramírez 1972: 7). A reasonable estimate is that
the present population of Caicara is between 9,000 and 10,000. No statistics exist
for the indigenous population of either Caicara or the municipio. However, in
1981 the indigenous population in the state of Monagas was 2,142, up from 515
in 1950 but less than half that first reported in 1783, when it was 5,451. The 1981
population for all of Monagas was 390,071 (Arzolay and others 1984: 104, 313).

10.   The *liquiliqui* is a white linen or cotton suit with a high, upturned collar.
Although various theories exist as to its origins, it is generally assumed to have
come from the southern llanos, or plains, and is considered by many to be the
traje típico, or "typical dress," of Venezuela. Another important aspect of the
Mayordoma's costume is a large straw hat decorated with flowers and fruit.

11.   Although improvisation is most often based on both the people and the
locale immediately surrounding the singer, some popular verses are commonly
repeated each year. The one presented here is among the most famous.

12.   Gavilán is the area in Caicara from which the Rojas group comes. However,
they are also known as the Negros de Chilo Rojas because the group marches
with their entire bodies and faces blackened. It is Rojas's contention that the use
of blue indigo is a recent innovation and that formerly all celebrants were covered in black.

13.   For the last several years, festival organizers have held a large dance on
the evening of December 28th in order to raise funds for the celebration. These
dances, with salsa or merengue bands brought in from either the capital or
Puerto Ordaz, are held in a large hall where an admission fee is charged. Because
of this event, the Monkey Dance usually winds to a close between six and seven
o'clock.

14.   For more on this slow, liturgical music sung in quatrains and most commonly identified with the Kariña or Carib Indians of Venezuela's eastern plains,
see Acosta Saignes (1952), Carreño and Vallmitjana (1967), Corradini (1976), and
Domínguez and Salazar Quijada (1969).

15.   The narrator is speaking metaphorically, or at least referring to fictive historical texts, either indigenous or colonial, when she claims that "this is what we
know from what we've been able to read." Nevertheless, since the publication
of Ramírez's *Remembranzas caicareñas* in 1972, many authors (including Abreu
1984; Guevara Febres 1974; Méndez 1978; Pérez and Bermúdez 1978; Salazar
n.d.; and Zuloaga 1990) have subscribed to the view that the Day of the Monkey
"has to do with ancient rites staged to increase the growth of corn, cotton, and
other garden harvests. For this reason we can detect a magical base, which is
even more undeniable when we remember that these dances were also characteristic of the Cumanagoto who lived from gathering fruit and fishing" (Ramírez

1972: 59). At the same time, it should be noted that Hernández and Fuentes (1992), Ontiveros (1960), and Pollak-Eltz and Fitl (1985), all of whom are from Caracas, have written that the festival is not of indigenous but European origin.

16.   A simple chordophone played with sticks and an inflated pig bladder filled with seeds, the ciriaco is found in various parts of Venezuela and is also known as a marimba, tarimba, guarumba, guasdua, and carángano. While Ramírez claims that *carángano* is a Mandingo word (1986: 60), Aretz cautions against ruling out an indigenous origin for this instrument as well (1967: 117).

17.   As described by Bakhtin:

> Such were the "feasts of fools" *(festa stultorum, fatuorum, follorum)* which were celebrated by schoolmen and lower clerics on the feast of St. Stephen, on New Year's Day, on the feast of the Holy Innocents, of the Epiphany, and of St. John. These celebrations were originally held in the churches and bore a fully legitimate character. Later they became only semilegal, and at the end of the Middle Ages were completely banned from the churches but continued to exist in the streets and taverns, where they were absorbed into carnival merriment and amusements. The feast of fools showed a particular obstinacy and force of survival in France. This feast was actually a parody and travesty of the official cult, with masquerades and improper dances. (1984: 74)

18.   For more on the Day of the Holy Innocents tradition in Venezuela, often referred to by its Andean variation of Locos or Locainas, see the sources from which the examples included here are derived: González (1991), Hernández and Fuentes (1992), Pollak-Eltz and Fitl (1985), Salas de Lecuna (1985), and Salazar (n.d.).

19.   Rojas was born in 1920 and so must have been a good deal younger if this was the late 1920s.

20.   In another statement concerning the recent invention of the Monkey Dance, Rojas was even more candid in his disdain. This statement also explains Rojas's belief that formerly all participants painted themselves black, hence the alternative name for both his group (the Negros de Chilo Rojas) and the festival (Día de los Negros, or "Day of the Blacks"):

> The 28th of December? The Day of the Holy Innocents, and that's that! Day of the Blacks. It was later that . . . my thing is black. Simple. That, that's not indigo. They never used that here. Here they used kettles from the store or grills. . . . Here it is [referring to the soot].
>   Día de los Negros, Día de los Santos Inocentes. They didn't talk about monkeys. That stuff about monkeys they invented. Like now, if I grab that drum and we say, "Shit, let's invent the dance of the rooster, the dance of such and such." And we go out dancing some thing, hopping around.

Because of Rojas's belief that the current Day of the Monkey celebration is a corruption of the earlier holiday, he has refused to take his turn performing onstage, as all other groups do when they enter the plaza.

21.   In 1981 Monagas was responsible for 7.8 percent of the total oil produced in Venezuela, a tremendous amount for a nation in which 80 percent of foreign exports are oil dependent. Almost all of the remaining oil comes from the Lake Maracaibo area of Zulia (Arzolay and others 1984: 249–277).

22.   The main part of this irresistibility was the fact that in the 1920s, when Standard Oil first arrived, farmworkers could increase their salaries from 30 cents a day to $2.50 or more (Guevara Febres 1974: 5). See Arzolay and others for a well-documented analysis of the shift in Monagas's population from rural to urban. In 1950, the population was 42.5 percent urban and 57.5 rural. By 1981 this ratio had shifted to 66.4 percent urban and 33.6 rural. Their estimate is that by 2001 the ratio will be 85.1 to 14.9 (1984: 73).

23.   A more probable explanation for why Caicara is referred to as Caicara de Maturín is to distinguish it from Venezuela's other Caicara, located in the state of Bolívar and known as Caicara del Orinoco. Maturín is currently the site of almost all manufacturing in Monagas and, in 1981, was the home of 58 percent of the state's 390,000 inhabitants (Arzolay and others 1984: 313).

24.   It is worth noting Bentley's (1987) discussion on the difficulties of categorizing ethnicity as either instrumental or primordial, and particularly his warning against interpreting the motives of individuals' actions based on their results: "In ethnicity studies this meant that if ethnic groups act in ways that appear strategically advantageous, then strategic advantage must be the raison d'être of those groups; if ethnicity increases in visibility during times of disorienting change, then it must be because people seek in ethnicity an emotional refuge from change. The theory of practice avoids this fallacious reasoning because it does not identify the systemic consequences of collective action with individuals' intentions" (1987: 48). In a similar fashion, it should be noted that there are other interests, political and economic, which are also achieving strategic advantage through the promotion of the purportedly unique indigenous status of the Day of the Monkey. As the event gains more national attention, tourism increases, as do government grants and stipends for those promoting the festival. Along with such financial support can come an important power base. And indeed, both major political parties, COPEI and Acción Democrática, have their own culture centers with their own parrandas.

25.   In this sense ethnicity may be seen as a modern response to the loss of distinction formerly provided by regional identities as defined by local or "vernacular" economies. With the absorption of these communities into national and even transnational realities, a host of creative cultural responses have arisen, of which ethnicity is one of the primary examples. Sollors articulates this idea well when he writes: "Ethnicity is not so much an ancient and deep-seated force surviving from the historical past, but rather the modern and modernizing feature of a contrasting strategy that may be shared far beyond the boundaries within which it is claimed" (1989: xiv).

26.   The representation of Indians by non-Indians is to be found in numerous other celebrations, not only in Venezuela but throughout the Americas. In nearby Ipure, for example, mestizos regularly perform a dance known as the *Culebra* (Serpent), which is said to derive directly from Chaima mythology. And in Tostos, in the Andean state of Trujillo, the appearance of the Virgin of Coromoto is celebrated by a pageant in which local residents dress up as natives and parade through the streets playing flutes and other indigenous instruments. Mestizos are not the only people to take on this Indian identity, however. In the Día de los Inocentes celebrations of Barlovento, an Indian figure known as the "messenger" or "runner" acts as the mediator between opposing groups of black women and men. Blacks also take on the identity of Indians during the Corpus Christi celebrations in Barbacoas, Colombia, where, as Friedmann explains:

> Since the group has been pushed back to the headwaters of the rivers, the Indians no longer come to Barbacoas. However, in recent years the blacks in the river port have been symbolically representing the Indians who formerly participated in this celebration. (1976: 293)

An even more elaborate example of blacks assuming Indian identities is in New Orleans, where, during Mardi Gras and Saint Joseph's Day, "tribes" of local African-Americans parade through the streets in sequined and feathered costumes that have taken all year to prepare (Lipsitz 1990).

Such ethnic cross-dressing may also go the other way, as Bricker demonstrated among various Mayan groups in Chiapas, Mexico. Here, during carnival and Holy Week, dancers regularly impersonate blacks, Jews, whites, and even monkeys (1981). Indians also dress as whites in various Ecuadorian San Juan celebrations; and in Peru, during Qoyllur Rit'i, highland groups take on the identity of Amazonian tribes who are called *"ch'unchos,"* or "savages" (Sallnow 1987). What is clear from this small sampling of examples is that in the festive language of inversion and conflict, ethnicity is as important an expression as any other.

27.   See Abreu (1984) for a discussion of what he claims "divides the parrandas into two types, the country and the town parrandas." While stating that each has "its own sense of the monkey (*sentimiento monero*)," he still insists that "the purest expression of this ritual dance is to be found in the country parrandas" (1984: 132–133).

28.   The earliest written record I discovered of the celebration of the Day of the Monkey in Caicara was the 1960 article by Benigno Ontiveros. In Ontiveros's description of the event, which he witnessed in 1953, he makes no mention whatsoever of any indigenous connection, stating simply that "it is of genuine Spanish origin" (1960: 302). Only with the publication of Ramírez's *Remembranzas caicareñas* in 1972 did a written tradition linking the Day of the Monkey to an indigenous past begin. However, Ontiveros, like Zuloaga (1990), does mention an

undated colonial document in which Bishop Díaz Madroñero condemns such dances. It is not clear, though, whether the "monkey dances" to which the bishop refers are those associated with Caicara, for he simply denounces "Diabolical dances commonly referred to as fandangos, sarambeques, monkey dances and other such things in whose execution groups or teams of men and women continually offend most gravely Our Lord God" (Ontiveros 1960: 301).

29.   Certain slogans often contain more explicit political messages referring to current issues of national concern. In the late 1980s, for example, when messages like "The hour has come to end the centralization of power" began to appear, the Monkey Dance was being used to comment on the national debate over whether to popularly elect governors and municipal officials.

30.   Hobsbawm claims that, in addition to monuments, public education and public ceremonies are also critical to the invented traditions of the new nation state (1983: 271). It should also be noted that Caicara's Monument to the Dance of the Monkey is not the only one dedicated to a folkloric celebration in Venezuela. In 1993 the town of San Francisco de Yare erected a statue to the Diablos of Yare, famous for the special Devil Dance performed during Corpus Christi. And in 1997 Curiepe constructed its own Monument to the Drum on a small hill overlooking the entrance to the town. Designed by the Cuban sculptor Dagoberto Ramos, it consists of enormous concrete reproductions of the mina and curbata drums, with the three culo e' puya in the background. The plaque announces that the monument is "In homage to Curiepe, founded in June, 1721 by Captain Juan del Rosario Blanco and the Company of Free Blacks of Caracas."

31.   For a discussion of the role of the monkey as a Carib symbol of anticulture par excellence, see Guss (1989), and for an interesting comparative view of the monkey's symbolism in another cultural context, see Ohnuki-Tierney (1987). Consult Abreu (1984: 124) and Guevara Febres (1974: 10) for further evidence of the strong anticlerical sentiments to be found in the Day of the Monkey celebration. Finally, an interesting study of the manner in which inversions are determined by social structure is to be found in DaMatta's comparison of Carnival in Rio de Janeiro and Mardi Gras in New Orleans (1991).

CHAPTER 4

1.   The "Buy American" campaign conceals the fact that so many of the goods meant to benefit from it are actually the products of multinational interests from many nations. An example of this is the current resurgence in "American-made" automobiles, in which imported parts and joint ventures with European and Japanese automakers can often be found. (Note, for instance, the interchangeability of Geo Prisms and Toyota Corollas, both manufactured in the same

factory.) On the other hand, foreign automakers are also attempting to assure American consumers that their products are "American made." Hence Toyota's advertising campaign featuring wooden cutouts of various states surrounding the statement: "Once we started building the Camry in the U.S., all the pieces fell into place" (New York Times Magazine, July 31, 1994: 48). And in an analysis of Honda's efforts to associate its cars with such popular American symbols as hamburgers, cowboy boots, jazz, and baseball, Levin writes:

> For years, the Big Three auto companies and the United Automobile Workers have tried to make patriotism part of the car-buying mentality of Americans. As a marketing pitch, the effect of showroom jingoism has always been debatable—so has its economic logic.
> Still, the idea that driving a Chevy or a Chrysler is a patriotic act, while owning a Honda or a Toyota is not, clearly appealed to some. And in their lobbying efforts and their advertising, Detroit has long argued that buying American-made cars is good for the American economy and that buying imported cars is bad. (1994: 7)

Another common example of "production fetishism" is the manner in which designers appropriate regional or traditional costumes and then attempt to "authenticate" them by photographing the creations interspersed with the peoples who inspired them. One of the most dramatic uses of this technique was Peter Beard's article, "Way Out of Africa" (1993), in which models and natives (in this case Turkana from Kenya) interchanged clothing and body paint with the work of such designers as Armani, Joseph Abboud, and Norma Kamali. The effect was to so confound the viewer that it was impossible to distinguish between what was and was not Turkana. For an interesting comparative analysis of how some of these issues relate to fashion, see Fox-Genovese (1978).

2.   Until 1949 when the revolution forced it to leave, British American Tobacco controlled more than 50 percent of the Chinese market—a full quarter of the company's sales. Today the company is reentering China, which, because of its state monopoly, was in 1993 the only producer of cigarettes greater than BAT. At that time BAT was the world's largest private sector manufacturer of cigarettes. Although the company further increased its market share two years later with the purchase of its old adversary, American Tobacco, in September 1998 it demerged, making it difficult to identify its total assets. Not only did it spin off its financial services from its tobacco interests, but it also changed its name to British American Tobacco P.L.C.

3.   The United States' Public Health Cigarette Smoking Act of 1969 banning all advertising of cigarettes in any broadcast media went into effect on January 1, 1971. Pressure to pass such legislation had been building in the United States since 1953, when the Sloan-Kettering Institute released the first study linking smoking to cancer.

4.   It is impossible to overestimate the importance of the relationship between advertising and tobacco and hence the threat that the advertising industry also

feels when smoking issues are debated. Prior to the 1971 ban on broadcast advertising in the United States, tobacco companies were the largest advertisers on both television and radio. In 1969 a full 80 percent of the advertising budgets of the six major tobacco corporations was spent on television promotion (Miles 1982: 81). In the first three years following the ban the amount spent in advertising declined, but by 1975 these companies had once again reached an all-time high of $350 million, mainly for "printed, outdoor, and point-of-purchase advertising" (Miles 1982: 83). By 1992, Philip Morris's advertising budget alone was $2 billion, the largest of any corporation in the world with the possible exception of Proctor and Gamble (Rosenblatt 1994: 36). Such statistics reveal not only the symbiotic relation of advertising and tobacco but also the undeniable roles of these corporations in cultural apparatuses worldwide.

5.   In Venezuela, the proportion of the population living in cities is much higher than the figure of 60–70 percent reported by García Canclini for all of Latin America. Izcaray and McNelly placed it at 83.3 percent in 1980, predicting that it would rise to 90 percent by the year 2000 (1987: 35–36). In 1950, when these massive demographic shifts began throughout Latin America, the rural population in Venezuela was still over 52 percent (Vilda 1984: 7). For more on the important impact of urbanization on traditional forms of expression in Latin America, see Franco (1982: 8–9), Rowe and Schelling (1991: 97–106), and Yúdice (1992).

6.   Journalist, poet, playwright, and political activist, Aquiles Nazoa (1920–1976) personified for an entire generation the ideal of the working-class artist and intellectual. It is little surprise, therefore, that a movement uniting popular culture with social justice should bear his name. The prose poem from which the line "I believe in the creative powers of the people" is taken is called "The Creed of Aquiles Nazoa" (1979: 199).

7.   For more elaborate discussions of this *Nueva Canción* (New Song) movement, see Carrasco Pirard (1982) and Reyes Matta (1988).

8.   The most notable of these workshops were those of the Plan Sebucan and the Instituto Nacional de Folklore (INAF). The first, sponsored by the Ministry of Culture, was designed to have actual practitioners teaching their art forms in community centers throughout the country. Those organized by INAF were part of a program called the Centro de Formación Técnica (Center for Technical Formation). Dedicated mainly to dance, they took place in the INAF headquarters in Caracas and served a much more restricted audience. A third center of workshop activity was the Centro Vargas organized by the Confederación de Trabajadores de Venezuela (Confederation of Venezuelan Workers, or CTV) for workers and their families. These final workshops are still in operation today.

In commenting on the critical importance of the 1975 Ley de Cultura and the establishment of CONAC, Jesús García, a community activist from Barlovento, stated: "The institutionalization of popular culture really begins with this, because for example before, the Instituto Nacional de Folklore and INCIBA [Instituto Nacional de Cultura y Bellas Artes] were extremely small organizations, and very elitist. But with the passage of the law [Ley de Cultura], people begin to become aware and for the first time start to speak about projection groups."

For more on INCIBA and the history of state support for the arts prior to the establishment of CONAC, see Murzi (1972).

9.   The calendar series was inaugurated in 1983 with the bicentennial celebration of Simón Bolívar's birth. Subsequent editions have focused on such themes as festivals, masks, instruments, textiles, folk artists, and traditional games. The annual books, which began appearing in 1987, covered similar subjects, yet in much greater depth. Agustín Coll described how he initiated the series, along with his motivations for doing so:

> Well, the annual books were an idea which I introduced. I worked for a long time at the Mendoza Foundation, where for many years the company had published a book at the end of the year to be used as a gift for clients and associates, etc. Then when I arrived at Bigott I found that they gave out things you'd buy in the store, so I proposed that in place of them . . . we would give a book, that that would give the company more prestige. So the idea was accepted and the first book was made, which was *Los fabricantes del sonido* (The Makers of Sound).

10.   By comparison, during the same period the John Simon Guggenheim Foundation, one of the United States' most competitive and prestigious, received 3,162 applications, of which 248, or 4.6 percent, were funded.

11.   Bigott's total budget in 1992 was 103,823,305 bolivares, or just over $2 million. Of this, 50 percent was for television and radio, 20 percent for publications, 16 percent for workshops, 6 percent for grants, 4 percent for agricultural assistance, and 4 percent for foundation administration. A major determination of the budget is Venezuela's tax law, which permits corporations to reduce their total tax base by up to 3 percent, depending on the amount of money used for cultural and social projects.

12.   The *cuatro* is a small, four-stringed instrument sometimes referred to as the "little guitar" (Aretz 1967: 122). Though common to a number of Latin American and Caribbean countries, it is perhaps the most widely diffused instrument in Venezuela.

13.   The three founding members of the Clavija, which was officially incorporated as the Instituto Musical "La Clavija," were Enio Escauriza, Cristóbal Soto, and Roberto Antivero. While at the workshops they were fondly known as "the troika."

14.   Personal communication, Enio Escauriza, June 28, 1990.

15.   Soto is also related to an important artist, his father being the internationally acclaimed sculptor Jesús Soto. Raised almost entirely in Paris, Cristóbal returned to Venezuela for only the second time in the mid-1970s. Even in Europe,

however, he was surrounded by Venezuelan music. Although Cristóbal claims that it was the sculptor Cruz Diez who taught him how to play *cuatro*, his father, in addition to being a renowned artist, is a concert musician. Teresa Zapata also spent a number of years in Paris, where she was an executive secretary for Viasa, the Venezuelan national airline.

16.　At a 1989 conference in Cumaná, Escauriza summarized the teaching philosophy of the Clavija as the following: "The greatest emphasis should be on informal education supporting what's learned through everyday life and then in the process developing from it. . . . It's a methodology in which the work continually goes from individual to collective to individual" (1989: 8).

17.　The idea of a "new synthesis," combining traditional Venezuelan styles with urban and imported forms as well as different types of instrumentation, is not the Clavija's alone but is shared by a number of musicians and groups. In many ways it reflects the maturation of the "projection" movement of the 1970s and the realization that to continue to grow and compete with other forms, traditional music must be allowed the same level of dynamism.

18.　For more on the interesting similarities between these two "communities of the arts," see Judith Adler's excellent study of Cal Arts, tracing it from its earliest days as "an institute consisting solely of colleagues" to one of "unambiguously stated professional goals" (1979: 103, 145). Like the Bigott Talleres de Cultura Popular, Cal Arts survived its period of turmoil and, after moving to Valencia, California, became one of the nation's most prestigious art schools.

19.　Hernández addresses this difficulty in his second report, recommending "the establishment of a Temporary Academic Assistance Service," which would aid any teachers who are not academically trained in preparing written programs (1989: 12).

20.　The "de-folklorization" called for by Bigott is the opposite of that referred to by Jesús García and other Venezuelan activists. In fact, it is this same decontextualized standardization of festive forms that various scholars have identified as "folklorization." As Israel and Guerre commented:

> When items produced for personal use become "art," a process which might be considered the folklization of culture has begun. Folklorization of culture refers to a two-sided phenomenon. First, aspects of traditional culture are stereotyped for export. Second, these stereotyped features are internalized by members of the culture in question as markers of their own identity. When indigenous peoples depend entirely upon the commodification of their own culture for export, the process is intensified. (1982: 17)

It is important to note that the new director of the workshops, María Teresa López Arocha, was not a practicing musician like the members of the Clavija but a former museum curator and folk art dealer. While her ideas certainly reflect the viewpoint of someone who has devoted her life to the study, sale, and display of art objects, they also reveal a long and committed struggle for the recognition of folk art as a legitimate aesthetic form, equal in sophistication and beauty to any other. Much of her work was accomplished as the owner of the Callapa Gallery and the founding director of the Petare Museum of Popular Art.

21.   There is an interesting parallel between Ramos's views and the ideas of Adorno and Horkheimer (1977), who also believed that the commodification of a technological "culture industry" would lead to an apathetic public incapable of either authentic experience or critical thought. Yet Ramos's vision is ultimately optimistic, for she believes that popular culture can both liberate and energize the masses once again.

22.   Antonio López Ortega, the present director of the Bigott Foundation, claimed in 1993 that more than 10,000 students had already studied at the workshops. It was also estimated that between 30 and 40 percent of all musicians performing in groups throughout Caracas were trained at Bigott (personal communication). And indeed, while at a San Juan celebration in June 1994 in Caracas's Parroquia San Juan (Plaza Capuchinos), I was surprised to see many of the culo e' puya drummers dressed in Fundación Bigott T-shirts. While I wondered if this attire had become associated with authentic folkloric expression, the musicians confirmed that they had all been trained at the Bigott workshops. None was from an Afro-Venezuelan background, and none had learned how to drum outside a classroom situation.

23.   Bigott had begun broadcasting over radio the previous year. The program, called *Encuentro con . . . Las Expresiones Musicales de Venezuela* (An Encounter with Venezuela's Musical Expressions), is still played once a week on Caracas's cultural station, though to a somewhat limited audience.

24.   The 1987 programs were dedicated primarily to musical groups such as Madera, Malembe, Vera, Gente Nueva, Playa Grande, Odilia, Cabure, the Golperos del Tocuyo, and the Tambores de San Milán. In 1988 the emphasis was on specific genres of both dance and music and included specials on Tamunangue, San Juan, *joropo, gaitas, décimas,* velorios, and work songs. In addition to these half-hour programs, Bigott also produced several longer specials, entitled *Lo Mejor de Encuentro con . . . Nuestras Expresiones Musicales* (The Best of Encounters with . . . Our Musical Expressions).

25.   For many of course, the pairing of Bigott with popular culture remained both strange and contradictory. Yet even Enio Escauriza, echoing García Canclini's notion of "double enrollment" (1993: 45), conceded that there might also be some benefit:

> The fact that popular culture, which is a somewhat irreverent term for a private corporation, and here we're speaking of an economically important corporation like Bigott, the fact that popular culture is being associated with Bigott just sounds a little odd. But we can't tell how much Bigott in adding to its own image through this

work has also contributed to the image of popular culture. In the sense that other private corporations might say, "Hey, look, Bigott did something with popular culture and it worked. Maybe it's not as subversive as we thought." And if the State's not going to take on this work and private industry is, then we'll work with private industry. And maybe if this keeps on growing, the State will finally do something too.

26.   Tulio Hernández described the rationale behind this decision to change formats as the following:

> They decided not to make any more half-hour videos because no one was watching them and instead make two-minute micros and put them on Sunday nights. It was Corpa who recommended it. They told them, "If you want to be heard in this country and get your stuff out, it's better to put the popular music into micros and put them on Sunday evenings at eight. Spend 2 million bolivares on that one night, because 16 million Venezuelans are going to see them and not a half-hour on Saturday morning on Channel 8 or Channel 5."

27.   The Popular Culture Workshops have always had their own site, while the rest of the foundation was located in the same Caracas building in which Bigott manufactures its cigarettes. In 1994 these offices were moved to separate headquarters. As already noted, the relatively small agricultural program has its offices in Valencia.

28.   The Colombian scholar Jesús Martín-Barbero wrote at length about the way in which new forms of mass communication serve as "mediations." In place of characterizing them as the expression of a single hegemonic view, he prefers to see them as confluences of competing forces, both dominant and subaltern: "Because communication is the meeting point of so many new conflicting and integrating forces, the centre of the debate has shifted from media to mediations. Here, mediations refer especially to the articulations between communication practices and social movements and the articulation of different tempos of development with the plurality of cultural matrices" (1993a: 187).

29.   The earlier half-hour series was never taken off the air entirely but went into permanent reruns, showing as early as 7:00 every morning in various parts of the country. The subjects of the ten micros, all of whom obviously participated in the workshops as well, were María Rodríguez and the Joropo Estribillao, Juan Esteban García and the Bandola Guariqueña, Anselmo López and the Bandola Llanera, Epifanio Rodríguez and the Bandola Oriental, Asunción Figueroa and the Cuatro, Pedro Castro and the Arpa Llanera, Cleotilde Billings and the Calypso of El Callao, Juan Gregorio Malavé and the Panflutes of Guaribe, Máximo Teppa and the Venezuelan Maracas, and Fulgencio Aquino and the Arpa Tuyera.

30.   When asked about Bigott's original decision to work in the area of popular culture, López Ortega responded in a manner nearly identical to that of Agustín Coll, with one important addition. He claimed that a new constituency was now the government and that the foundation's work would also have to become "a

strategic weapon" in discouraging legislation harmful to the tobacco industry. In interviews with the corporate heads of Philip Morris, Roger Rosenblatt elicited very similar responses. As an executive vice president of its international division stated:

> We have the best partners in the world: the governments. In a lot of countries, it's incredibly important to the whole welfare state that we sell our products to collect taxes. When you sit with a finance minister or deputy of any government to discuss taxation, he's much cruder about the financial analysis of that taxing than we are. He asks, "How much can I put up the tax, to make sure that the demand is not going to go down so much that my net intake goes down?" Amazing. So no matter how you look at the cigarette business, it's incredibly predictable, it's extremely secure as an investment vehicle and, therefore, it's a great business to be in—if you can deal with the fact that some people are not going to like you." (1994: 41)

Bigott's current position with the government is stronger than ever, and President Chávez has increased Bigott's role in official cultural policies. However, the recent appointment of foundation head López Ortega to a position in the Ministry of Culture has aroused complaints of conflict of interest, hence the title of a recent newspaper article, "I Want an Identity Without Tobacco and Without Cigarettes" (Yolanda Salas, pers. com., 5/15/00).

31.   Although Bigott uses the land as a key symbol to unite a range of different significata (for example, nation and property, agricultural product and tobacco, countryside and folkloric production, nature and the cyclical passage of time), advertisements for Belmont, its principal brand, use water. Unlike the folkloric-related themes of the foundation, these advertisements are both Eurocentric and upper middle class. They focus on three well-bronzed, scantily clad couples cavorting in the Caribbean surf. The fact that these carefree, sexy, and very Caucasian youths are also smoking cigarettes is meant to encourage the consumer to associate tobacco with the same qualities of health, attractiveness, and pleasure (all condensed in the symbol of the ocean). These nearly ubiquitous advertisements, which have been in existence for years, appear on such things as billboards, bus stops, menus, movie houses, kiosks, napkin dispensers, and clocks. The strategy of using nature, particularly water, to promote a healthy and vibrant image for an otherwise toxic and addictive product is not uncommon. In the United States such displacement has been particularly common with mentholated brands like Newport and Salem, which wish to promote their "freshness."

In order to test the effectiveness of its campaign, the Bigott Foundation conducts public opinion polls every several months. Of primary importance is the foundation's level of recognition, along with perceptions of what it does. In the March 1993 poll, the level of recognition was 69.4 percent, second only to the Polar Foundation of the country's largest brewery (73.4 percent). Just as significant was the response to the question of what the foundation produces: 38.5 percent claimed that the Bigott Foundation "promotes culture"; 31.5 percent claimed that it "produces cigarettes" (Servicio Omnibus 1993). This nearly even breakdown is the type of confusion Bigott wishes to cultivate, ensuring that the social responsibility it produces in its cultural product will be consumed in its commercial one. Or, as Lopez Ortega stated, "People are associating the Bigott Corporation with the Bigott Foundation, which is exactly what we want, because we don't want the foundation's work to be seen as something isolated."

CHAPTER 5

1.   For a discussion of this view, wherein any media use of popular culture is seen as a homogenizing and exploitative commodification of subaltern values, see Mattelart (1979), who argues that "The media attempts to deprive the people of its memory. While giving the illusion of relying upon and assuming a patrimony of myths, this culture actually standardizes, serializes and appropriates history, which it mutilates and reduces to a series of miscellaneous news items. . . . [It is] the bourgeoisie's daily appropriation of the life experiences of other classes in information-merchandise, out of context and out of history" (1979: 45). Also, see Tatum (1994) for a survey of the development of popular culture theory in relation to Latin America. Tatum refers to Mattelart's position, in particular, as "the thesis of cultural imperialism, a corollary of the dependency theory of economic development in vogue among social scientists and economists fifteen to twenty years ago" (1994: 200). Hannerz refers to this model elsewhere as "radical diffusionism," a process in which all cultural difference is subsumed by a technologically dominant center (1989a: 206).

2.   Handler makes clear that one of the three principal elements in what he refers to as "cultural objectification" is the selection process, the decision about what is to be consecrated as part of an official body of national tradition (1984: 62). The other two elements in this objectifying process are the formation of new contexts and the new significations or meanings through which audiences will appreciate these reconfigured forms.

3.   For a good discussion of the implications of the move toward a "multilocale ethnography" and its relation to issues of political economy, see Marcus and Fischer (1986: 93–95). One should also consider the implications of "deterritorialization," as discussed by such authors as Appadurai (1990, 1996), Gupta and Ferguson (1997), and MacCannell (1989), as well as Hannerz's argument concerning the relation between center and periphery (1989a, 1989b, 1991).

4.   Cohen refers to this same process as "the ideology of the aesthetic" (1993: 133), and Bauman and Sawin call it the "politics of representation" (1991: 312).

5.   The English name for this saint, who was born in Lisbon, Portugal, and lived from 1195 to 1231, is Saint Anthony of Padua.

6.   A promesa may be inherited, as when a father promises that his children and grandchildren will continue to honor it. Promises may also vary, including anything from a single son or dance to multiple Tamunangues and all-night velorios. What all Tamunangueros agree on is that "San Antonio is a real collector. He charges a lot." It is believed that a person who fails to pay a promesa will start to hear drums, causing such headaches that the debtor is eventually forced to relent. A promesa may be deemed too great, however, and the terms of the annual commitment renegotiated.

7.   As already noted, the way in which Tamunangues are performed varies somewhat from one community to the next. An important part of this variation is the order of the sections, particularly that of the Salve and the first three dances. For example, in Curarigua the Salve is performed at the beginning, in El Tocuyo, at the end, and in Sanare, at both start and finish. The order and terms used in this chapter follow those of the community of Sanare. For a comparison of the dance orders found in other communities, see Aretz (1970 [1956]: 52). A number of sources also note the many variations in the denomination of each of the dance's parts.

8.   For the most complete transcriptions of versions of the Batalla and other Tamunangue songs, see Aretz (1970 [1956]) and González Viloria (1991).

9.   The Ayiyivamos has been recorded in a variety of ways, including "Chichivamos," "Yeyevamos," "Yiyevamos," and "Ayiyevamos."

10.   For more on the various forms of the Galerón and their relation to the *joropo*, which is often referred to as Venezuela's national dance, see Aretz (1970 [1956]: 140) and Ramón y Rivera (1953: 24).

11.   This son is known by a variety of names, including *Seis Corrío, Seis Figuriao, Seis por Ocho, Seis Florido,* and even just *Figuriao.* The "six" found in almost every title no doubt refers to the number of dancers, while other aspects of the names are probably related to the number of "figures" the performers execute. There is little agreement as to how many figures actually exist, although González Viloria (1991: 122) claims to have seen thirty of the thirty-six that performers in Sanare report knowing. In Bigott's *Encuentro con . . .* documentary on Tamunangue, a dancer states that there were originally forty-eight figures but that many have been forgotten, and today it is rare that more than thirty-two are performed (Fundación Bigott 1988). The figure of thirty-two is also reported by Soto (1987: 16).

12.   The first known recordings of Tamunangue were made in 1940 by Juan Liscano on visits to Curarigua, El Tocuyo, and an agricultural fair in Barquisimeto. He returned soon afterward to make a film in El Tocuyo. These Tamunangue recordings are the first archived materials at the Instituto Nacional de Folklore.

13.   In a more recent collection of essays, Liscano referred to a "choreographic mestizoness" (*mestizajes coreográficos*) (1990: 163), from which I also take the title of this section.

14.   Yaracuy, which borders Lara to the east, is one of Venezuela's smallest states. It is also home to some of Venezuela's oldest black communities.

15.   Kurath (1949: 95) and Poole (1990: 110) both note that the Seises performed in Seville incorporated elements of stick fighting. The literature on sword or stick dancing is quite extensive, especially in relation to its migration across the Atlantic to the New World. For more on this subject, consult Caro Baroja (1984), Champe (1983), Kurath (1949), Poole (1990), and Rodríguez (1996). González Viloria also suggests that the Batalla may derive from a similar form found among the Guanches in the Canary Islands (1991: 38). The relation of this tradition and Tamunangue to that of Moors and Christians dances is discussed at length below.

16.   In discussing Tamunangue's mestizo character, Aretz downplays any indigenous contribution. In fact, she states rather pointedly that "Today the dances of blacks and whites are mixed in the Tamunangue just as the people are mixed, acquiring the same hue and cast the performers have" (Aretz 1970 [1956]: 156).

17.   Although born and trained in Argentina, Aretz is one of the most important figures in the history of Venezuelan folklore. She arrived in the country in 1947 at the invitation of Juan Liscano to direct the music section of his newly created National Folklore Investigations Service. An ethnomusicologist and folklorist, as well as a composer trained in Brazil by Hector Villa-Lobos, Aretz went on to found the Inter-American Institute of Ethnomusicology and Folklore (INIDEF). This institute, which has trained numerous students from throughout Latin America, was eventually merged with the National Folklore Institute (INAF) and the National Folklore Museum to form the Ethnomusicology and Folklore Foundation (FUNDEF). She directed FUNDEF from 1990 until her retirement in 1995. Working in close collaboration with her husband, Luis Felipe Ramón y Rivera, Aretz published a monumental number of articles and books. Ironically, *El Tamunangue*, her first major Venezuelan study, was originally published in Peru, due to what she claims was a lack of national interest in such works at the time. A Venezuelan edition only appeared in 1970 as part of the 425-year celebration of the founding of Barquisimeto, Lara's capital.

18.   The original Spanish of this popularly quoted statement is "Mezcla de nuestra raza, hecha a grito y tambor." Linárez refers to its author, José Rafael Colmenárez Peraza, as "the first impresario of Tamunangue" (1987: 7). And indeed, it was Colmenárez Peraza who was one of the leaders of the Tamunangue group that performed at the 1948 Festival of Tradition (see Liscano 1950: 212). Such statements underline how quickly local performers adopted the official interpretation of Tamunangue as a dance celebrating Venezuela's racial democracy.

19.   Linárez also claims there are lyrics suggesting that the African participants were aware of the dangers in performing such a thinly veiled pagan rite. As one quatrain states:

> Anyone who dances the Galerón
> will never see the face of God.
> An old lady danced it
> and the devil took her away.
> (Linárez 1990: 11)

20.   Though mainly Berbers, the invaders were referred to as "Moors," a variation on "Maurus," the Roman term for the inhabitants of the African outpost of Mauritania. The Reconquest celebrated in this dance is also known as the War of Granada. For more on the Moors and Christians tradition, which is still performed throughout the Americas, the Philippines, Spain, and Portugal, see Carrasco (1976), Driessen (1985), Harris (1994), Kurath (1949), and Warman Gryj (1972).

21.   Rodríguez focuses primarily on the Matachines dance found in the American Southwest. However, numerous other variants of the Moors and Christians dance exist, some of which are more easily related to their European ancestor than others. Among them are Moriscas, Morismas, Seises, Santiaguitos, Tastoanes, Rayados, Concheros, Negritos, Paloteos, Sword Dances, Montezuma Dances, Morris Dancing, and Dances of the Conquest.

22.   Although Rodríguez refers to the Matachines as "the beautiful dance of subjugation," she, like Bricker, concludes that "today the dance is not merely an archaic survival but an ongoing way of coping with and commenting on the historical structures of ethnic domination as they continue to unfold for Pueblo and Mexicano communities in the upper Río Grande valley" (1996: 157).

23.   San Antonio's ability to control the rain is clearly related to his association with agriculture and harvests. In Venezuela he is called the patron saint of *conuqueros* (small farmers). In other places he is the patron saint of miners and masons, and he is commonly called on to find lost objects and heal the sick. He is also important to women, who often call upon him to find husbands and lovers. But it is for his oratorical skills that he remains best known, as the following story in *The Catholic Encyclopedia* attests:

> The inhabitants of [Padua] erected to his memory a magnificent temple, whither his precious relics were transferred in 1263, in the presence of St. Bonaventure, Minister General at the time. When the vault in which for 30 years his sacred body had reposed was opened, the flesh was found reduced to dust, but the tongue uninjured, fresh, and of a lively red colour. St. Bonaventure, beholding this wonder, took the tongue affectionately in his hands and kissed it, exclaiming: "Oh Blessed Tongue that always praised the Lord, and made others bless Him, now it is evident what great merit thou hast before God." The fame of St. Anthony's miracles has never diminished, and even at the present day, he is acknowledged as the greatest thaumaturgist of the times. (Herbermann and others, 1913: 558)

24. The tale of how San Antonio brought Tamunangue into the world is also frequently recounted as a décima, a fragment of which is reproduced at the beginning of this chapter. A popular oral poetry form found throughout Venezuela, décimas are organized into units of ten octosyllabic lines with varying rhyme schemes. The verses on page 129 were sung to Isabel Aretz by Fidel Flores in 1947 (1970 [1956]: 18–19) and are almost identical to a version recorded by Norma González Viloria in Sanare thirty-five years later (1983: 43). In the Sanareño version, however, the singer identifies San Antonio's reply to the question of what he was singing as "Pangüé," rather than "Estangüé." It is possible that "Estangüé" is a contraction of *"está"* and *"Tamunangue,"* or "it's Tamunangue."

25. The Batalla also indicates a direct relation to the Moors and Christians tradition and the sword fighting it often includes.

26. The indistinguishability of these two groups is revealed in the following description by an older performer in the village of Sanare: "These are Indians, we should say, from the Indians from Africa, when they had problems and stuff. That's when they began that Tamunangue." Manuel Guédez made the same point to Aretz, stating that "the San Antonio festival comes from the time of the Conquest. San Antonio called the Indians and the conquistadores with his drum. Some of them were already tame, and they brought the others, and San Antonio baptized them. That was around this area" (1970 [1956]: 17).

27. González Viloria, who is arguably the finest scholar of this dance, notes that San Antonio is above all a mediator between worlds—old and new, Christian and pagan, white and black, heaven and earth—and as such becomes the mestizo par excellence. She also makes the observation that, "From a theater of conquest and evangelization, Tamunangue is transformed into a theater of transculturation" (1991: 134–135). Another example of such mestizaje standing for the nation is the cult of María Lionza. Followers and sites abound throughout Venezuela, but the most important center is in the mountain of Sorte in the state of Yaracuy. Despite numerous myths about María Lionza's indigenous origins, Taussig reports several claims that she is actually a mestiza and that this identity is essential to understanding her power:

> That the spirit queen was not an Indian but a *mestiza*, hybrid child of an Indian woman and a *conquistador* (sixteenth century) and that she had had to seek refuge in the mountain until saved by the Liberator (born late eighteenth century) who sent *el Negro Felipe* to care for her.
>
> But to the lanky dark-skinned man who walked all day back and forth along the sand by the far-off ocean selling oysters beyond the capital city, the spirit queen had no particular "racial" identity. No! She was not Black, not White, nor any mixture thereof. Instead, he paused, she was the nation. It was that simple. (1997: 31–32)

But María Lionza's mestizaje may be found less in her own body than in the company she keeps. For in most iconography she is flanked by an indigenous rebel, Guaicaipuro, and a black revolutionary, Negro Felipe. Together they form an outlaw trinity known as the *Tres Potencias,* a different image of mestizaje, in which the European is replaced by an ambiguous, green-eyed queen. It is this combination, like that attributed to Tamunangue, which has rendered the cult so powerful in the popular imagination. For more on this important Venezuelan movement, see Barreto (1987), Pollak-Eltz (1985), and Taussig (1997).

28.   For good examples of how this transformation has occurred in different places, see Acciaioli (1985), Flores (1995), Kirshenblatt-Gimblett (1998), Mendoza (1998), Ness (1992), Schechner (1985, 1988), and Wilcken (1992).

29.   For more on this costume, see Aretz (1977, esp. pp. 194–200) and her discussion of the woman's long dress known as a *fustán.*

30.   The shortest Tamunangue on record may be that performed at the Teresa Carreño Opera House in Caracas to celebrate the 1990 Southern Hemisphere Economic Summit. Several of the twenty-eight countries participating also brought groups, including the National Dance Troupe of Nigeria and Sonal Mansingh of India. Venezuela had two representatives: Soledad Bravo, an internationally known folksinger, and a dance troupe from Bigott's Talleres de Cultura Popular. The latter gave a ten-minute Tamunangue performance that had been completely rechoreographed by the event's organizers. Instead of a single couple dancing alone, as is normal, the entire group performed simultaneously. The organizer insisted that this was necessary in order "to fill the entire space and make it more lively and colorful."

Tamunangue has been adapted to numerous other contexts as well, including television, art museums, and various international festivals, among them the Festival of Youth in the former Soviet Union, the World Festival of Traditional Arts in France, the Festival of Fruits and Flowers in Ecuador, and the Sugar Festival in Colombia.

31.   The demands of the proscenium arch have been critical in the transformation of a number of modern forms. An interesting example of this is the way in which contemporary ballet's most important movements were determined by the introduction of staged dance in late-seventeenth-century France. Kraus and Chapman document this process in what they call "the professionalization of ballet":

> Since the dancer had only to be concerned with how he would look from one direction, it became necessary to think of the audience, *in front,* as a focus. When moving from side to side across the stage, the best way to do this while facing the audience was to turn the hip and knee out, so the feet pointed to the side instead of straight forward. Gradually, the turnout became more and more pronounced, and became the basis of the five positions of the foot in classic ballet which Beauchamps recorded about 1700 and which are essential to all ballet technique even today. (1981: 72)

32.   Stewart makes the interesting observation that in Trinidad, it is the visitors who enjoy carnival most, as they are unaware of the various backstage conflicts and struggles underlying the event's realization: "Those who most enjoy Car-

nival in Trinidad these days are the visitors (returnees and tourists), who by their very journeying have already assumed a status of license and who have no knowledge of the burdening encumbrances carried by local traditionalists and innovators. Their approach to the festival is singularly individual. . . . They are not affronted by anything in the Carnival, where they have no interest in the politics of the event" (1986: 314).

33.   Local residents have also been overwhelmed by the tremendous influx of culture tourists wishing to see Tamunangue in situ. Although many in Lara are apt to criticize the negative effects of such tourism, they also encourage it and ultimately judge the success of the annual festival by the number of outsiders who attend. For Sanare, this has meant up to 10,000 visitors, or nearly half the number of permanent residents. In Curarigua, on the other hand, observance of the festival has been moved to the Saturday closest to June 13, when the celebration traditionally took place. In each instance, tourists are now encouraged to come to the event rather than simply have the event come to them.

34.   As traditional forms are converted into staged events and the visual becomes privileged over all other elements, the women's role often becomes more prominent. This is usually combined with a more seductive and sensual self-presentation, as symbolized by the relentless, even painful smile that most female participants are forced to maintain. It was this feature that critics immediately attacked as soon as Tamunangue was adapted to the stage. Silva Uzcátegui, in particular, complained that women not only "smiled incessantly" but "spun around, laughing happily, jumping about, leaning their bodies from side to side just like the *joropo*" (1990 [1954]: 2).

The importance of the smile is also found in descriptions of a number of other public celebrations, particularly carnival. In her detailed instructions on the proper way to perform samba, for example, Guillermoprieto reserves a special place for the smile and how to effect it:

> Smile: the key rule is, don't make it sexy. You will look arch, coy, or, if you are working really hard, terribly American. Your smile should be the full-tilt cheer of someone watching her favorite team hit a home run. Or it should imitate the serene curve of a Hindu deity's. The other key rule: There is no point to samba if it doesn't make you smile. (1990: 38)

Abner Cohen makes a similar observation about London's Carnival, where "thousands of costumed members . . . are instructed by the rules of samba to smile throughout" (1993: 137).

The hegemony of the smile in staged folkloric events throughout the world has an interesting parallel to Schneider's observations about the smile's relationship to globalization and capitalism:

> One of the great unsolved mysteries of American culture is the devotion Americans have for their teeth. . . . They don't see anything strange about an old man's smile being as polished and glamorous as the grille of a new Cadillac. Some people even

invest the value of a Cadillac in their teeth, if only to show that they are biters. Having perfect teeth proves that we are affluent and influential, the fittest. We see a globalization of the American smile, that bright consumerist smile. (1997: 45)

35.   In his *Enciclopedia Larense,* Silva Uzcátegui elaborates further on the distortions being perpetrated by female dancers:

Whoever has seen Tamunangue performed in a village by dancers who really know how to perform it well has noted the seriousness and circumspection with which they do it, the serenity with which they carry out each movement, because they give the act the *solemnity of a religious ritual.* And that's where the aristocratic elegance that characterizes this dance comes from, as well as the total absence of any sensuality. . . .

In Caracas a group of musicians and dancers recently presented Tamunangue as a theatrical spectacle, but they only danced a few parts and not even in the traditional order. Besides that, they willfully exaggerated various movements and against all custom, the women smiled incessantly, and according to them, they did it because "they'd been told to do it that way." (1981 [1941]: 167)

36.   Berarducci Fernández (1987) proposes a similar argument, wherein Tamunangue provides a metanarrative of the history of male-female relations. In her analysis the Batalla is a male mating ritual; La Bella, the first shy overture; the Ayiyivamos, the eruption of full flirting and suggestiveness; the Juruminga, the establishment of the relationship and the acting out of domestic roles; the Poco a Poco, the developing relationship in crisis; the Perrendenga and Galerón, when the couple is mature and each has a turn to dominate; and, finally, the Seis Corrido, in which the full community celebrates and "various partners share in a festive reunion" (1987: 116).

37.   The Festival Folklórico del Estado Lara was held annually in Barquisimeto from 1966 to 1977 and then, after a ten-year lapse, was reinstituted in 1987.

38.   Schechner equates the terms "ritual" and "theater" with "efficacy" and "entertainment," claiming that "no performance is pure efficacy or pure entertainment:

Efficacy and entertainment are not so much opposed to each other; rather they form the poles of a continuum. The basic polarity is between efficacy and entertainment, not between ritual and theater. Whether one calls a specific performance "ritual" or "theater" depends mostly on context and function. A performance is called ritual or theater because of where it is performed, by whom, and under what circumstances. (1988: 120)

Bibliography

Abrahams, Roger D. 1982. "The Language of Festivals: Celebrating the Economy." *In* Celebration: Studies in Festivity and Ritual. Victor Turner, ed. Washington, D.C.: Smithsonian Institution Press.

———. 1987. "An American Vocabulary of Celebrations." *In* Time Out of Time: Essays on the Festival. Alessandro Falassi, ed. Albuquerque: University of New Mexico Press.

———. 1993. "Phantoms of Romantic Nationalism in Folkloristics." Journal of American Folklore 106(419): 3–37.

Abreu, Leobardo. 1984. Tarabacoa: Ensayos etnográficos sobre el Estado Monagas. Maturín: Ediciones Gobernación del Estado Monagas.

Acciaioli, Greg. 1985. "Culture as Art: From Practice to Spectacle in Indonesia." Canberra Anthropology 8(1): 148–172.

Acosta Saignes, Miguel. 1952. "El Maremare: Baile del jaguar y la luna." Archivos Venezolanos de Folklore 2: 3–19.

———. 1959. "La población del Estado Miranda." *In* El Estado Miranda: Su tierra y sus hombres. Caracas: Editorial Sucre.

———. 1961. La trata de esclavos en Venezuela. Caracas: Centro de Estudios Históricos.

————. 1962. Estudios de folklore venezolano. Caracas: Universidad Central de Venezuela.

————. 1967. Vida de los esclavos negros en Venezuela. Caracas: Hesperides Ediciones.

————. 1983. "Clase magistral." *In* La tradición oral y la vigencia del Tamunangue: Memorias de un seminario. Heufifi Carrasco and Enrique González Ordosgoitti, eds. Caracas: Instituto Nacional de Folklore.

Adam, Henriette. 1981. Barlovento: Cacao y tambores: La historia de Panaquire. Caracas: Biblioteca de Trabajo Venezolana.

Adler, Judith E. 1979. Artists in Offices: An Ethnography of an Academic Art Scene. New Brunswick, N.J.: Transaction Books.

Adorno, Theodor W., and M. Horkheimer. 1977. "The Culture Industry: Enlightenment as Mass Deception." *In* Mass Communication and Society. James Curran, Michael Gurevitch, and Janet Woollacott, eds. London: Edward Arnold.

Allen, Catherine J. 1988. The Hold Life Has: Coca and Cultural Identity in an Andean Community. Washington, D.C.: Smithsonian Institution Press.

Almeida, Bira. 1986. Capoeira: A Brazilian Art Form. Berkeley, Calif.: North Atlantic Books.

Anderson, Benedict. 1983. Imagined Communities: Reflections on the Origins and Spread of Nationalism. London: Verso.

Appadurai, Arjun. 1981. "The Past as a Scarce Resource." Man (n.s.) 16: 201–219.

————. 1990. "Disjuncture and Difference in the Global Economy." Public Culture 2(2): 1–24.

————. 1991. "Global Ethnoscapes: Notes and Queries for a Transnational Anthropology." *In* Recapturing Anthropology. Richard G. Fox, ed. Santa Fe, N.Mex.: School of American Research Press.

————. 1996. Modernity at Large: Cultural Dimensions of Globalization. Minneapolis: University of Minnesota Press.

Appadurai, Arjun, and Carol A. Breckenridge. 1988. "Why Public Culture?" Public Culture 1(1): 5–9.

————. 1992. "Museums Are Good to Think: Heritage on View in India." *In* Museums and Communities: The Politics of Public Culture. Ivan Karp, Christine Mullen Kreamer, and Steven D. Lavine, eds. Washington, D.C.: Smithsonian Institution Press.

Aretz, Isabel. 1953. "Expresiones negras en el folklore musical." Boletín del Instituto de Folklore (Caracas) 1(3).

————. 1955. "La fiesta de San Juan en Cúpira." Boletín del Instituto de Folklore 11(2): 57–61.

————. 1956. El Tamunangue. Lima, Peru: Folklore Americano.

———. 1967. Instrumentos musicales de Venezuela. Cumaná: Universidad de Oriente.

———. 1970 [1956]. El Tamunangue. Barquisimeto: Universidad Centro Occidental.

———. 1977. El Traje del Venezolano. Caracas: Monte Avila Editores.

Arzolay, Cosme, Carlos Loreto, Estervina Marcano, and Omar Morales. 1984. Geografía del Estado Monagas. Maturín: Ediciones Gobernación del Estado Monagas.

Bakhtin, Mikhail. 1984. Rabelais and His World. Bloomington: Indiana University Press.

Barnouw, Victor. 1954. "The Changing Character of a Hindu Festival." American Anthropologist 56: 74–86.

Barreto, Daisy. 1987. María Lionza: Mito e historia. Caracas: Universidad Central de Venezuela.

Bastide, Roger. 1971. African Civilizations in the New World. P. Green, trans. New York: Harper and Row.

———. 1978. The African Religions of Brazil: Toward a Sociology of the Interpenetration of Civilizations. H. Sebba, trans. Baltimore, Md.: Johns Hopkins University Press.

Bauman, Richard. 1986. "Performance and Honor in 13th-Century Iceland." Journal of American Folklore 99: 131–150.

———. 1992. "Performance." In Folklore, Cultural Performances, and Popular Entertainments: A Communications-Centered Handbook. Richard Bauman, ed. New York: Oxford University Press.

Bauman, Richard, and Patricia Sawin. 1991. "The Politics of Participation in Folklife Festivals." In Exhibiting Cultures: The Poetics and Politics of Museum Display. Ivan Karp and Steven D. Lavine, eds. Washington, D.C.: Smithsonian Institution Press.

Baumann, Roland. 1988. " 'Moors, Demons, and Arabs': The Changing Significance of 'Moros y Cristianos' Performances in the Alpujarra (Spain)." Paper presented at the 12th International Congress of Anthropological and Ethnological Sciences, Zagreb.

Beard, Peter. 1993. "Way Out of Africa." Esquire, Fall (1, 2): 166–181.

Beeman, William O. 1993. "The Anthropology of Theater and Spectacle." Annual Review of Anthropology 22: 369–393.

Beezley, William H., Cheryl English Martin, and William E. French, eds. 1994. "Introduction: Constructing Consent, Inciting Conflict." In Rituals of Rule, Rituals of Resistance: Public Celebrations and Popular Culture in Mexico. Wilmington, Del.: Scholarly Resources.

Bentley, G. Carter. 1987. "Ethnicity and Practice." Comparative Studies in Society and History 29(1): 24–55.

Berarducci Fernández, Anna Griselda. 1987. Una aproximación al estudio de presencia de eroticismo y sensualidad en el Tamunangue a través de sus participantes. Thesis, Universidad Central de Venezuela, Caracas.

Bettelheim, Judith. 1991. "Negotiations of Power in Carnaval Culture in Santiago de Cuba." African Arts 24(2): 66–75.

———. 1993. "Carnival in Santiago Cuba." In Cuban Festivals: An Illustrated Anthology. Judith Bettelheim, ed. New York: Garland Publishing.

———. 1994. "Ethnicity, Gender, and Power: Carnaval in Santiago de Cuba." In Negotiating Performance: Gender, Sexuality and Theatricality in Latin/o America. Diana Taylor and Juan Villegas, eds. Durham, N.C.: Duke University Press.

Boissevain, Jeremy, ed. 1992. "Introduction." In Revitalizing European Rituals. London: Routledge.

Boyarin, Jonathan, ed. 1994. Remapping Memory: The Politics of TimeSpace. Minneapolis: University of Minnesota Press.

Brandes, Stanley. 1988. Power and Persuasion: Fiestas and Social Control in Rural Mexico. Philadelphia: University of Pennsylvania Press.

Brandt, Max Hans. 1978. An Ethnomusicological Study of Three Afro-Venezuelan Drum Ensembles of Barlovento. Ph.D. diss., Queen's University of Belfast, Northern Ireland.

———. 1994. "African Drumming from Rural Communities around Caracas and Its Impact on Venezuelan Music and Ethnic Identity." In Music and Black Ethnicity: The Caribbean and South America. Gerard Béhague, ed. New Brunswick, N.J.: Transaction Books.

Brettell, Caroline B., ed. 1993. When They Read What We Write: The Politics of Ethnography. Westport, Conn.: Bergin and Garvey.

Briceño, Ivonne. 1990a. "Día de San Antonio y del folklore larense." El Informador (Barquisimeto), June 13: 6B.

———. 1990b. "El pueblo le cumplió a San Antonio." El Informador (Barquisimeto), June 14: 6B.

Bricker, Victoria Reifler. 1981. The Indian Christ, the Indian King: The Historical Substrate of Maya Myth and Ritual. Austin: University of Texas Press.

Briggs, Charles. 1996. "The Politics of Discursive Authority in Research on the 'Invention of Tradition.' " Cultural Anthropology 11(4): 435–469.

Brito Figueroa, Federico. 1985. El problema tierra y esclavos en la historia de Venezuela. Caracas: Universidad Central de Venezuela.

Brow, James. 1990. "Notes on Community, Hegemony, and the Uses of the Past." Anthropological Quarterly 63(1): 1–6.

Browning, Barbara. 1995. Samba: Resistance in Motion. Bloomington: Indiana University Press.

Burdick, John. 1992a. "Brazil's Black Consciousness Movement." NACLA, Report on the Americas 25(4): 23–27.

———. 1992b. "The Myth of Racial Democracy." NACLA, Report on the Americas 25(4): 40–43.

———. 1998. Blessed Anastácia: Women, Race and Popular Christianity in Brazil. New York: Routledge.

Burke, Peter. 1978. Popular Culture in Early Modern Europe. New York: Harper and Row.

Cahill, David. 1996. "Popular Religion and Appropriation: The Example of Corpus Christi in Eighteenth-Century Cuzco." Latin American Research Review 31(2): 67–110.

Caillois, Roger. 1959. Man and the Sacred. Glencoe, Ill.: Free Press.

Cantwell, Robert. 1993. Ethnomimesis: Folklife and the Representation of Culture. Chapel Hill: University of North Carolina Press.

Caro Baroja, Julio. 1965. El Carnaval: Análisis histórico-cultural. Madrid: Taurus Ediciones.

———. 1979. La estación de amor: Fiestas populares de mayo a San Juan. Madrid: Taurus Ediciones.

———. 1984. El estío festivo: Fiestas populares del verano. Madrid: Taurus Ediciones.

Carrasco, Heufifi, and Enrique González Ordosgoitti, eds. 1983. La tradición oral y la vigencia del Tamunangue: Memorias de un seminario. Caracas: Instituto Nacional de Folklore.

Carrasco, María Soledad. 1976. "Christians and Moors in Spain: History, Religion, Theatre." Cultures 3(1): 87–116.

Carrasco Pirard, Eduardo. 1982. "The Nueva Canción in Latin America." International Social Science Journal 34(4): 599–623.

Carreño, Francisco, and Abel Vallmitjana. 1967. Comentarios sobre el origen indígena del Mare Mare criollo. Archivos Venezolanos de Folklore 8: 327–335.

Castillo, Ocarina. 1987. "Un centro de investigación cultural: El Instituto Nacional de Folklore." In Instituciones científicas en la historia de la ciencia en Venezuela. Hebe Vessuri, ed. Caracas: Fundación Fondo Editorial Acta Científica Venezolana.

Castillo Escalona, José Anselmo. 1987. Las fiestas en honor a San Antonio: Sanare y el Tamunangue. Sanare: Consejo Municipal.

Castillo Lara, Lucas Guillermo. 1981a. Apuntes para la historia colonial de Barlovento. Caracas: Biblioteca de la Academia Nacional de la Historia.

———. 1981b. Curiepe: Orígenes históricos. Caracas: Biblioteca de Autores y Temas Mirandinos.

———. 1983. La aventura fundacional de los Isleños. Caracas: Biblioteca de la Academia Nacional de la Historia.

Castillo Vásquez, Andrés. 1975. Versiones folklóricos larenses. Barquisimeto: Universidad Centro Occidental.

Centro Cultural y Deportivo de Curiepe. 1979. Programa de la Semana Cultural de Curiepe. Curiepe: Centro Cultural y Deportivo de Curiepe.

Chacón, Alfredo. 1973. Contra la dependencia. Caracas: Síntesis Dosmil.

————. 1979. Curiepe: Ensayo sobre la realización del sentido en la actividad mágicoreligiosa de un pueblo venezolano. Caracas: Universidad Central de Venezuela.

Chai, Alan, Alta Campbell, and Patrick Spain. 1993. Hoover's Handbook of World Business. Austin, Tex.: Reference Press.

Champe, Flavia Waters. 1983. The Matachines Dance of the Upper Rio Grande: History, Music, and Choreography. Lincoln: University of Nebraska Press.

Chaney, David. 1983. "A Symbolic Mirror of Ourselves: Civic Ritual in Mass Society." Media, Culture and Society 5: 119–135.

Chapman, Malcolm, Maryon McDonald, and Elizabeth Tonkin. 1989. "Introduction." In History and Ethnicity. ASA Monographs 27. Elizabeth Tonkin, Maryon McDonald, and Malcolm Chapman, eds. London: Routledge.

Chitty, J. A. de Armas. 1982. Historia de la tierra de Monagas. Maturín: Ediciones Gobernación del Estado Monagas.

Clifford, James. 1987. "Of Other Peoples: Beyond the 'Salvage Paradigm.' " In Discussions in Contemporary Culture. Hal Foster, ed. Seattle, Wash.: Bay Press.

————. 1988. The Predicament of Culture: Twentieth-Century Ethnography, Literature, and Art. Cambridge, Mass.: Harvard University Press.

Cohen, Abner. 1980. "Drama and Politics in the Development of a London Carnival." Man (n.s.) 15: 65–87.

————. 1993. Masquerade Politics: Explorations in the Structure of Urban Cultural Movements. Berkeley and Los Angeles: University of California Press.

Cohen, Ronald. 1978. "Ethnicity: Problem and Focus in Anthropology." Annual Review of Anthropology 7: 379–403.

————. 1993. "Conclusion: Ethnicity, the State, and Moral Order." In Ethnicity and the State. Judith D. Toland, ed. New Brunswick, N.J.: Transaction Publishers.

Cohn, William H. 1976. "A National Celebration: The Fourth of July in American History." Cultures 3(1): 141–156.

Colmenárez, Juan B. 1978. "Tamunangue, danza y folklore." Petroglifo (Carabobo) 2(7): 16–18.

Colmenárez Guédez, Raúl. 1966. "El Tamunangue." La República, Supplement (Barquisimeto), Primer Festival Folklórico del Estado Lara, October 8–14: 8–9.

Coluccio, Felix. 1978. Fiestas y celebraciones de la República Argentina. Buenos Aires: Editorial Plus Ultra.

Comisión Nacional. 1977. "Encuentro por la defensa nacional de la cultura 'Aquiles Nazoa': Pronunciamiento nacional." Caracas: Comisión Nacional.

Corina, Maurice. 1975. Trust in Tobacco: The Anglo-American Struggle for Power. New York: St. Martin's Press.

Coronil, Fernando. 1997. The Magical State: Nature, Money, and Modernity in Venezuela. Chicago: University of Chicago Press.

Corradini, Henry. 1976. "Divulgación de las culturas indígenas: Maremare, cantos sagrados de los indios Kariña." El Luchador (Ciudad Bolívar), December 28, 29, 30: 5.

Corwin, Arthur F. 1974. "Afro-Brazilians: Myths and Realities." In Slavery and Race Relations in Latin America. Robert Brent Toplin, ed. Westport, Conn.: Greenwood Press.

Cowan, Jane K. 1992. "Japanese Ladies and Mexican Hats: Contested Symbols and the Politics of Tradition in a Northern Greek Carnival Celebration." In Revitalizing European Rituals. Jeremy Boissevain, ed. London: Routledge.

Crain, Mary. 1989. Ritual, memoria popular y proceso político en la sierra ecuatoriana. Quito: Abya-Yala.

———. 1990. "The Social Construction of National Identity in Highland Ecuador." Anthropological Quarterly 63(1): 43–59.

———. 1992. "Pilgrims, 'Yuppies,' and Media Men: The Transformation of an Andalusian Pilgrimage." In Revitalizing European Rituals. Jeremy Boissevain, ed. New York: Routledge.

———. 1997. "The Remaking of an Andalusian Pilgrimage Tradition: Debates Regarding Visual (Re)presentation and the Meanings of 'Locality' in a Global Era." In Culture, Power, Place: Explorations in Critical Anthropology. Akhil Gupta and James Ferguson, eds. Durham, N.C.: Duke University Press.

Crespi, Muriel. 1981. "St. John the Baptist: The Ritual Looking Glass of Hacienda Ethnic and Power Relations." In Cultural Transformations and Ethnicity in Modern Ecuador. Norman E. Whitten Jr., ed. Urbana: University of Illinois Press.

Cultural Survival. 1989. Brazil: Who Pays for Development? Cultural Survival Quarterly 13(1).

Curcio-Nagy, Linda A. 1994. "Giants and Gypsies: Corpus Christi in Colonial Mexico City." In Rituals of Rule, Rituals of Resistance: Public Celebrations and Popular Culture in Mexico. William H. Beezley, Cheryl English Martin, and William E. French, eds. Wilmington, Del.: Scholarly Resources.

DaMatta, Roberto. 1991. Carnivals, Rogues, and Heroes: An Interpretation of the Brazilian Dilemma. Notre Dame, Ind.: University of Notre Dame Press.

Daniel, Yvonne. 1995. Rumba: Dance and Social Change in Contemporary Cuba. Bloomington: Indiana University Press.

Davis, Natalie Zemon. 1975. Society and Culture in Early Modern France. Stanford, Calif.: Stanford University Press.

Dean, Caroline S. 1993. "Ethnic Conflict and Corpus Christi in Colonial Cuzco." Colonial Latin American Review 2(1–2): 93–120.

———. 1999. Inka Bodies and the Body of Christ: Corpus Christi in Colonial Cuzco, Peru. Durham, N.C.: Duke University Press.

de Carvalho, Jose Jorge. 1991. "Los dos caras de la tradición: Lo clásico y lo popular en la modernidad Latinoamericana." Anuario FUNDEF 2: 21–41.

de Carvalho-Neto, Paulo. 1978. "Folklore of the Black Struggle in Latin America." Latin American Perspectives 5(2): 53–88.

———. 1990. "Valor de la palabra 'Folklore.' " Revista de Investigaciones Folklóricas 5: 53–56.

de Certeau, Michel. 1980. "On the Oppositional Practices of Everyday Life." Social Text: Theory/Culture/Ideology 3: 3–43.

Desai, Gaurav. 1993. "The Invention of Invention." Cultural Critique 24: 119–142.

Directory of Corporate Affiliations. 1999. "British American Tobacco P.L.C." Directory of Corporate Affiliations, Vol. 5. New Providence, N.J.: National Register Publishing.

Dirks, Nicholas B. 1990. "History as a Sign of the Modern." Public Culture 2(2): 25–32.

———. 1994. "Ritual and Resistance: Subversion as a Social Fact." In Culture/Power/History. Nicholas B. Dirks, Geoff Eley, and Sherry B. Ortner, eds. Princeton, N.J.: Princeton University Press.

Domínguez, Luis Arturo, and Adolfo Salazar Quijada. 1969. Fiestas y danzas folklóricas de Venezuela. Caracas: Monte Avila Editores.

Driessen, Henk. 1985. "Mock Battles between Moors and Christians: Playing the Confrontation of Crescent with Cross in Spain's South." Ethnologia Europaea 15(2): 105–115.

Duvignaud, Jean. 1976. "Festivals: A Sociological Approach." Cultures 3(1): 13–25.

Eliade, Mircea. 1959. Cosmos and History: The Myth of the Eternal Return. New York: Harper and Brothers.

Ellement, John, and Chris Black. 1994. "SJC Says Gays May March in Parade, Veterans Threaten to Cancel Event." Boston Globe, March 12: 1, 25.

Escauriza, Enio. 1989. "Talleres de Cultura Popular de la Fundación Bigott: Balance de una alternativa para el fortalecimiento de la cultura popular." Paper presented at the I Congreso de Universidades Nacionales sobre Tradición y Cultural Popular. Cumaná, Venezuela.

Estado Miranda, Venezuela. 1981. XI censo general de población y vivienda. Caracas: Oficina Central de Estadística e Informática.

Ewell, Judith. 1984. Venezuela: A Century of Change. Stanford, Calif.: Stanford University Press.

Fiske, John. 1994. "Popular Culture in a Multicultural and Post-Fordist World." Paper presented at the Fourth Conference on Latin American Popular Culture, Brown University, Providence, R.I.

Flores, Richard R. 1994. " 'Los Pastores' and the Gifting of Performance." American Ethnologist 21(2): 270–285.

———. 1995. Los Pastores: History and Performance in the Mexican Shepherd's Play of South Texas. Washington, D.C.: Smithsonian Institution Press.

Fox-Genovese, Elizabeth. 1978. "Yves Saint Laurent's Peasant Revolution." Marxist Perspectives 1(4): 58–90.

Franco, Jean. 1982. "What's in a Name? Popular Culture Theories and Their Limitations." Studies in Latin American Popular Culture 1: 5–14.

Frazer, James G. 1953 [1922]. The Golden Bough: A Study in Magic and Religion. New York: Macmillan.

Friedemann, Nina S. de. 1976. "The Fiesta of the Indian in Quibdó, Colombia." In Ethnicity in the Americas. Frances Henry, ed. The Hague: Mouton Publishers.

Fuentes, Cecilia, and Daría Hernández. 1988. "San Juan Bautista." Revista Bigott 12: 2–39.

Fundación Bigott. 1988. Encuentro Con . . . Tamunangue o Son de Negros. Caracas: Fundación Bigott.

Fundación Polar. 1989. "Luis Bigott." In Diccionario de historia de Venezuela. Caracas: Fundación Polar.

Galaskiewicz, Joseph. 1989. "Corporate Contributions to Charity: Nothing More than a Marketing Strategy?" In Philanthropic Giving: Studies in Varieties and Goals. Richard Magat, ed. New York: Oxford University Press.

García, Jesús. 1985. "Saint John the Baptist and Saint John Congo: Reinterpretation and Creation of African-Inspired Religion in Venezuela." In Culturas africanas. N.p.: UNESCO.

———. 1989. Contra el cepo: Barlovento tiempo de cimarrones. Caracas: Editorial Lucas y Trina.

———. 1990. Africa en Venezuela, pieza de Indias. Caracas: Cuadernos Lagoven.

———. 1992. Afroamericano soy. Caracas: Ediciones del Taller de Información y Documentación de la Cultura Afrovenezolana.

García Canclini, Néstor. 1977. Arte popular y sociedad en América Latina. Mexico City: Grijalbo.

————. 1988. "Culture and Power: The State of Research." Media, Culture and Society 10: 467–497.

————. 1990. Culturas híbridas: Estrategias para entrar y salir de la modernidad. Mexico City: García Grijalbo.

————. 1992. "Cultural Reconversion." In On Edge: The Crisis of Contemporary Latin American Culture. George Yúdice, Jean Franco, and Juan Flores, eds. Minneapolis: University of Minnesota Press.

————. 1993. Transforming Modernity: Popular Culture in Mexico. Lidia Lozano, trans. Austin: University of Texas Press.

————. 1995. Hybrid Cultures: Strategies for Entering and Leaving Modernity. Minneapolis: University of Minnesota Press.

Geertz, Clifford. 1973. The Interpretation of Cultures. New York: Basic Books.

————. 1991. "The Year of Living Culturally." New Republic 205: 30–36.

Gennino, Angela, ed. 1990. Amazonia, Voices from the Rainforest: A Resource and Action Guide. San Francisco: Rainforest Action Network.

Gerente Venezuela. 1990. "La guerra del humo." Gerente Venezuela, February: 8–25.

Gillis, John R., ed. 1994. Commemorations: The Politics of National Identity. Princeton, N.J.: Princeton University Press.

Gilmore, David. 1975. "Carnival in Fuenmayor: Class Conflict and Social Cohesion in an Andalusian Town." Journal of Anthropological Research 31(4): 331–349.

Gluckman, Max. 1954. Rituals of Rebellion in South-East Africa. Manchester, England: University of Manchester Press.

Goffman, Erving. 1959. The Presentation of Self in Everyday Life. New York: Doubleday.

————. 1974. Frame Analysis: An Essay on the Organization of Experience. New York: Harper and Row.

Gómez Zuloaga, José. 1990. "Bailemos El Mono en Caicara." El Oriental, Edición Aniversaria (Maturín), August 3: n.p.

González, Enrique Alí. 1989. Ritmos, plegarias y promesas: La música en las festividades populares. Caracas: Fundación Venezolana para la Investigación Antropológica.

————. 1991. La festividad de los Santos Inocentes en Osma. Anuario FUNDEF (Fundación de Etnomusicología y Folklore) 2: 60–65.

González Viloria, Norma. 1983. "El Tamunangue." In La tradición oral y la vigencia del Tamunangue: Memorias de un seminario. Heufifi Carrasco and Enrique González Ordosgoitti, eds. Caracas: Instituto Nacional de Folklore.

————. 1991. El Tamunangue como teatro de imitación y simbólico de la realidad. M.A. thesis, Instituto Pedagógico de Caracas.

Gramsci, Antonio. 1971. Selections from the Prison Notebooks of Antonio

Gramsci. Quintin Hoare and Geoffrey Nowell Smith, eds. and trans. London: Lawrence and Wishart.

Guerra Cedeño, Franklin. 1984. Esclavos negros, cimarroneras y cumbes de Barlovento. Caracas: Cuadernos Lagoven.

Guevara Febres, Jesús Alberto. 1974. Sobre las huellas de El Mono: Caicara de ayer y siempre. Puerto Ordaz: Diego de Ordaz.

Guillermoprieto, Alma. 1990. Samba. New York: Vintage.

Gupta, Akhil. 1992. "The Song of the Nonaligned World: Transnational Identities and the Reinscription of Space in Late Capitalism." Cultural Anthropology 7(1): 63–79.

Gupta, Akhil, and James Ferguson, eds. 1997. Culture, Power, Place: Explorations in Critical Anthropology. Durham, N.C.: Duke University Press.

Guss, David M. 1977. "Parishira." Maratto 3: 49–51.

———. 1984. "San Francisco: A Town the Water Took Away." Daily Journal [Caracas], August 14: 14–15.

———. 1985. "Parishira and the ABC Song." In The Language of the Birds: Tales, Texts, and Poems of Interspecies Communication. David M. Guss, ed. San Francisco: North Point.

———. 1989. To Weave and Sing: Art, Symbol, and Narrative in the South American Rain Forest. Berkeley: University of California Press.

———. 1993. "The Selling of San Juan: The Performance of History in an Afro-Venezuelan Community." American Ethnologist 20(3): 451–473.

———. 1994. "Reimaginando la comunidad imaginada: La política de la diversidad cultural en América Latina y el Caribe." In Teoría y política de la construcción de identidades y diferencias en América Latina y el Caribe. Daniel Mato, ed. Caracas: Editorial Nueva Sociedad.

———. 1996a. "Celebrating Dissent: The St. Patrick's Day Protest of 1995." Unpublished manuscript, files of the author.

———. 1996b. "Cimarrones, Theater, and the State." In History, Power, and Identity: Ethnogenesis in the Americas, 1492–1992. Jonathan D. Hill, ed. Iowa City: University of Iowa Press.

———. 1997. "Hidden Histories: African-American Tales of Resistance and Arrival." Journal of Latin American Lore 20(1): 161–171.

Hale, Lindsey Lauren. 1997. "Preto Velho: Resistance, Redemption, and Engendered Representations of Slavery in a Brazilian Possession-Trance Religion." American Ethnologist 24(2): 392–414.

Hall, Stuart. 1981. "Notes on Deconstructing 'the Popular.' " In People's History and Socialist Theory. Raphael Samuel, ed. Amsterdam: Van Gennep.

———. 1994. "Cultural Studies: Two Paradigms." In Culture/Power/History. Nicholas B. Dirks, Geoff Eley, and Sherry B. Ortner, eds. Princeton, N.J.: Princeton University Press.

Hanchard, Michael, ed. 1999. Racial Politics in Contemporary Brazil. Durham, N.C.: Duke University Press.

Handler, Richard. 1984. "On Sociocultural Discontinuity: Nationalism and Cultural Objectification in Quebec." Current Anthropology 25(1): 55–71.

———. 1988. Nationalism and the Politics of Culture in Quebec. Madison: University of Wisconsin Press.

Handler, Richard, and Eric Gable. 1997. The New History in an Old Museum: Creating the Past at Colonial Williamsburg. Durham, N.C.: Duke University Press.

Handler, Richard, and Joyce Linnekin. 1984. "Tradition, Genuine or Spurious." Journal of American Folklore 97: 273–290.

Hannerz, Ulf. 1989a. "Culture between Center and Periphery: Toward a Macroanthropology." Ethnos 54(3–4): 200–216.

———. 1989b. "Notes on the Global Ecumene." Public Culture 1(2): 66–75.

———. 1991. "Scenarios for Peripheral Cultures." In Culture, Globalization and the World-System: Contemporary Conditions for the Representation of Identity. Anthony D. King, ed. Binghamton: State University of New York.

———. 1992. Cultural Complexity: Studies in the Social Organization of Meaning. New York: Columbia University Press.

Harris, Max. 1994. "Muhammed and the Virgin: Folk Dramatizations of Battles between Moors and Christians in Modern Spain." TDR 38, 1: 45–61.

Hatch, Jane M. 1978. The American Book of Days. New York: H. W. Wilson.

Hebdige, Dick. 1979. Subculture: The Meaning of Style. London: Methuen.

Herbermann, Charles G., Edward A. Pace, Condé B. Pallen, Thomas J. Shahan, and John H. Wynne, eds. 1913. The Catholic Encyclopedia, Vol. 1. New York: Encyclopedia Press.

Hernández, Daría, and Cecilia Fuentes. 1992. Fiestas tradicionales de Venezuela. Caracas: Fundación Bigott.

Hernández, Tulio. 1986. Fundación Bigott: Principios orientadores, diagnóstico y modelos de acción institucional para el desarrollo de las culturas populares venezolanas. Caracas: Fundación Bigott.

———. 1989. Programa de evaluación de los talleres de cultura popular de la Fundación Bigott. Caracas: Fundación Bigott.

Herzfeld, Michael. 1982. Ours Once More: Folklore, Ideology, and the Making of Modern Greece. Austin: University of Texas Press.

Hill, Errol. 1972. The Trinidad Carnival: Mandate for a National Theater. Austin: University of Texas Press.

Hobsbawm, Eric. 1983. "Mass-Producing Traditions: Europe, 1870–1914." In The Invention of Tradition. Eric Hobsbawm and Terence Ranger, eds. Cambridge, England: Cambridge University Press.

Hobsbawm, Eric, and Terence Ranger, eds. 1983. The Invention of Tradition. Cambridge, England: Cambridge University Press.

Huayhuaca Villasante, Luis A. 1988. La festividad del Corpus Christi en el Cusco. Lima: Talleres Gráficos P.-L. Villanueva.

Hymes, Dell. 1975. "Folklore's Nature and the Sun's Myth." Journal of American Folklore 88: 345–369.

———. 1981 [1975]. "Breakthrough into Performance." In "In Vain I Tried To Tell You": Essays in Native American Ethnopoetics. Philadelphia: University of Pennsylvania Press.

Israel, Pamela, and Maurizio Guerre. 1982. "The Amazon in Plexiglas." Cultural Survival Quarterly 6(4): 15–17.

Izcaray, Fausto, and John T. McNelly. 1987. "Selective Media Use by Venezuelans: The Passing of the Passive Audience in a Rapidly Developing Society." Studies in Latin American Popular Culture 6: 27–41.

James, Edwin O. 1963. Seasonal Feasts and Festivals. New York: Barnes and Noble.

Jameson, Fredric. 1981. The Political Unconscious: Narrative as a Socially Symbolic Act. Ithaca, N.Y.: Cornell University Press.

Karp, Ivan, and Steven D. Lavine. 1991. Exhibiting Cultures: The Poetics and Politics of Museum Display. Washington, D.C.: Smithsonian Institution Press.

Karp, Ivan, Christine Mullen Kreamer, and Steven D. Lavine, eds. 1992. Museums and Communities: The Politics of Public Culture. Washington, D.C.: Smithsonian Institution Press.

Kaspin, Deborah. 1995. "On Ethnographic Authority and the Tourist Trade: Anthropology in the House of Mirrors." Paper presented at the 94th Annual Meeting of the American Anthropological Association. Washington, D.C.

Kelly, William. 1990. "Japanese No-Noh: The Crosstalk of Public Culture in a Rural Festivity." Public Culture 2(2): 65–81.

Kirshenblatt-Gimblett, Barbara. 1988. "Mistaken Dichotomies." Journal of American Folklore 101(400): 140–155.

———. 1991. "Objects of Ethnography." In Exhibiting Cultures: The Poetics and Politics of Museum Display. Ivan Karp and Steven D. Lavine, eds. Washington, D.C.: Smithsonian Institution Press.

———. 1998. Destination Culture: Tourism, Museums, and Heritage. Berkeley and Los Angeles: University of California Press.

Kraus, Richard, and Sarah Alberti Chapman. 1981. History of the Dance in Art and Education. Englewood Cliffs, N.J.: Prentice Hall.

Kurath, Gertrude Prokosch. 1949. "Mexican Moriscas: A Problem in Dance Acculturation." Journal of American Folklore 62(244): 87–106.

Lavenda, Robert H. 1980. "From Festival of Progress to Masque of Degradation: Carnival in Caracas as a Changing Metaphor for Social Reality." In Play and Culture: 1978 Proceedings of the Association for the Anthropological Study of Play. Helen B. Schwartzman, ed. West Point, N.Y.: Leisure Press.

Levin, Doron P. 1994. "A Patriotic Pitch: Honda Is American." New York Times, Section 3, November 6: 7.

Ley Orgánica de Educación. 1986. Ley Orgánica de Educación, Gaceta Oficial No. 2.635. Caracas: Ediciones Orley.

Licausi, Raúl. 1981. "La publicidad de licores y cigarillos: O los vicios del estado." ININCO, Revista del Instituto de Investigaciones de la Comunicación (Caracas) 2(3): 10–11.

Limón, José E. 1983. "Western Marxism and Folklore: A Critical Introduction." Journal of American Folklore 96(379): 34–52.

———. 1994. Dancing with the Devil: Society and Cultural Poetics in Mexican-American South Texas. Madison: University of Wisconsin Press.

Linárez, Pedro. 1987. Sones de negros. Caracas: Catedra "Pio Tamayo," Universidad Central de Venezuela.

———. 1990. Los sones de negro: Orígenes y expansión. Superguía Dominical, July 15: 11.

Lincoln, Bruce. 1989. Discourse and the Construction of Society: Comparative Studies of Myth, Ritual, and Classification. New York: Oxford University Press.

Lipner, Ronnie, and Stu Lipner. 1958. Dances of Venezuela. New York: Folkways Records.

Lipsitz, George. 1990. Time Passages: Collective Memory and American Popular Culture. Minneapolis: University of Minnesota Press.

Lira Espejo, Eduardo. 1941. El Tamunangue. El Universal, February 19.

Liscano, Juan. 1947. Las fiestas del solsticio de verano en el folklore de Venezuela. Separada de la Revista Nacional de Cultura 63. Caracas: Ministerio de Educación Nacional.

———. 1949. "Hear the People Sing." Américas 1(5): 12–15, 34–35.

———. 1950. Folklore y cultura. Caracas: Nuestra Tierra.

———. 1951. "Folklore del Estado Lara: 'El Tamunangue.' " Tópicos Shell (Caracas) 146: 18–23.

———. 1970. "Lugar de origen de los tambores redondos Barloventeños de Venezuela." Folklore Americano (Lima) 17/18(16): 134–139.

———. 1973. La fiesta de San Juan el Bautista. Caracas: Monte Avila Editores.

———. 1990. Fuegos sagrados. Caracas: Monte Avila Editores.

———. 1998. La fiesta de la tradición 1948: Cantos y danzas de Venezuela. Edición Conmemorativa. Caracas: Fundación de Etnomusicología y Folklore.

Liscano, Juan, and Charles Seeger. 1947. Folk Music of Venezuela. Washington, D.C.: Division of Music, Library of Congress.

Lombardi, John V. 1974. "The Abolition of Slavery in Venezuela: A Nonevent."

In Slavery and Race Relations in Latin America. Robert Brent Toplin, ed. Westport, Conn.: Greenwood Press.

Lomnitz, Claudio. 1994. "Decadence in Times of Globalization." Cultural Anthropology 9(2): 257–267.

Luzardo, Alexander. 1988. Amazonas: El negocio de este mundo, investigación indigenista. Caracas: Ediciones Centauro.

MacAloon, John J. 1984. Rite, Drama, Festival, Spectacle: Rehearsals toward a Theory of Cultural Performance. Philadelphia: ISHI.

MacCannell, Dean. 1989. The Tourist: A New Theory of the Leisure Class. New York: Schocken.

Machado, Arlette. 1987. El apocalipsis según Juan Liscano. Caracas: Publicaciones Seleven.

Mackenzie, Neil. 1987. "Boy into Bishop, A Festive Role Reversal." History Today 37: 10–16.

Madriz Galindo, Fernando. 1964. Folklore de Barlovento. Cumaná: Ediciones de la Universidad de Oriente.

Manning, Frank E. 1977. "Cup Match and Carnival: Secular Rites of Revitalization in Decolonizing, Tourist-Oriented Societies." *In* Secular Ritual. Sally Falk Moore and Barbara Myerhoff, eds. Amsterdam: Van Gorcum.

Manning, Frank E., ed. 1983. The Celebration of Society: Perspectives on Contemporary Cultural Performance. Bowling Green, Ohio: Bowling Green University Popular Press.

Marcus, George E., and Michael M. J. Fischer. 1986. Anthropology as Cultural Critique: An Experimental Moment in the Human Sciences. Chicago: University of Chicago Press.

Mariátegui, José Carlos. 1970 [1927]. "Heterodoxía de la tradición." *In* Peruanicemos al Peru. Lima: Empresa Editora Amauta.

Martín-Barbero, Jesús. 1993a. Communication, Culture and Hegemony: From the Media to Mediations. Elizabeth Fox and Robert A. White, trans. London: Sage.

———. 1993b. "Latin America: Cultures in the Communications Media." Journal of Communication 43(2): 18–30.

Martínez-Echazábal, Lourdes. 1998. "*Mestizaje* and the Discourse of National/Cultural Identity in Latin America, 1845–1959." Latin American Perspectives 25(3): 21–42.

Mattelart, Armand. 1979. "Introduction: For a *Class Analysis* of Communication." *In* Communication and Class Struggle, Vol. 1. Armand Mattelart and Seth Siegelaub, eds. New York: International General.

———. 1983. Transnationals and the Third World: The Struggle for Culture. David Buxton, trans. South Hadley, Mass.: Bergin and Garvey.

Méndez, Doris Ruíz de. 1978. Trabajo monográfico sobre el Baile de "el Mono" de Caicara de Maturín. Caracas: Instituto Nacional de Folklore, Centro de Formación Técnica.

Mendoza, Zoila S. 1998. "Defining Folklore: Mestizo and Indigenous Identities on the Move." Bulletin of Latin American Research 17(2): 165–183.

Miles, Robert H. 1982. Coffin Nails and Corporate Strategies. Englewood Cliffs, N.J.: Prentice Hall.

Miller, Daniel. 1994. Modernity, an Ethnographic Approach: Dualism and Mass Consumption in Trinidad. Providence, R.I.: Berg.

Monasterio Vásquez, Demetria Casimira. 1989. Curiepe: Teatro y danza en Barlovento. M.A. thesis, Universidad de Havana, Havana, Cuba.

Moore, Sally Falk, and Barbara Myerhoff. 1977. "Secular Ritual: Forms and Meanings." In Secular Ritual. Sally Falk Moore and Barbara Myerhoff, eds. Amsterdam: Van Gorcum.

Morón, Guillermo. 1964. A History of Venezuela. John Street, ed. and trans. London: George Allen and Unwin.

Morote Best, Efraín. 1955. "La Fiesta de San Juan, el Bautista." Archivos Peruanos de Folklore 1(1): 160–200.

Mosonyi, Esteban Emilio. 1982. Identidad nacional y culturas populares. Caracas: Editorial La Enseñanza Viva.

———, ed. 1981. El Caso Nuevas Tribus. Caracas: Editorial Ateneo de Caracas.

Mosse, George L. 1971. "Caesarism, Circuses, and Monuments." Journal of Contemporary History 6(4): 167–182.

Muratorio, Blanca. 1993. "Nationalism and Ethnicity: Images of Ecuadorian Indians and the Imagemakers at the Turn of the Nineteenth Century." In Ethnicity and the State. Judith D. Toland, ed. New Brunswick, N.J.: Transaction Publishers.

Murzi, Alfredo Tarre. 1972. El estado y la cultura. Caracas: Monte Avila.

Myers, Fred R. 1994. "Culture-Making: Performing Aboriginality at the Asia Society Gallery." American Ethnologist 21(4): 679–699.

Nájera-Ramírez, Olga. 1997. La Fiesta de los Tastoanes: Critical Encounters in Mexican Festival Performance. Albuquerque: University of New Mexico Press.

Nazoa, Aquiles. 1979. Obras Completas, Vol. 2. Caracas: Universidad Central de Venezuela.

Nealon, Patricia. 1995. "St. Pat's Parade Can Go without Gays, Judge Says." Boston Globe, January 19: 1, 10.

Ness, Sally Ann. 1992. Body, Movement, and Culture: Kinesthetic and Visual Symbolism in a Philippine Community. Philadelphia: University of Pennsylvania Press.

Ohnuki-Tierney, Emiko. 1987. The Monkey as Mirror: Symbolic Transformations in Japanese History and Ritual. Princeton, N.J.: Princeton University Press.

Olivares Figueroa, R. 1960 [1949]. Diversiones pascuales en Oriente y otros ensayos. Caracas: Ardor.

Oliven, Ruben George. 1986. "State and Culture in Brazil." Studies in Latin American Popular Culture 5: 180–185.

Ontiveros, Benigno. 1960. "Fiesta de los Locos o Baile del Mono en Caicara de Maturín." Boletín del Instituto del Folklore 3(7): 298–303.

Ortiz, Manuel Antonio. 1983. "Vigencia y proyección del Tamunangue." In La tradición oral y la vigencia del Tamunangue: Memorias de un seminario. Heufifi Carrasco and Enrique González Ordosgoitti, eds. Caracas: Instituto Nacional de Folklore.

———. 1998. "Donde la brisa sopla con rima." Revista Bigott 46: 24–41.

Ozouf, Mona. 1988. Festivals and the French Revolution. Cambridge, Mass.: Harvard University Press.

Parkin, David. 1996. "Introduction: The Power of the Bizarre." In The Politics of Cultural Performance. David Parkin, Lionel Caplan, and Humphrey Fisher, eds. Providence, R.I.: Berghahn Books.

Pérez, María Auxiliadora, and Eduardo Bermúdez. 1978. Caicara de Maturín, Estado Monagas, 250 años. Ministerio de Información y Turismo. Boleíta: Escuela Técnica Popular "Don Bosco."

Pollak-Eltz, Angelina. 1972. Vestigios africanos en la cultura del pueblo venezolano. Caracas: Universidad Católica Andrés Bello.

———. 1979. "Migration from Barlovento to Caracas." In The Venezuelan Peasant in Country and City. Luise Margolies, ed. Caracas: Ediciones Venezolanas de Antropología.

———. 1985. María Lionza: Mito y culto venezolano. Caracas: Universidad Católica Andrés Bello.

———. 1994. "The Preservation and Recuperation of Folklore in Venezuela: 'El Rescate de Folklore.'" Paper presented at the Fourth Conference on Latin American Popular Culture. Brown University, Providence, R.I.

Pollak-Eltz, Angelina, and Regina Fitl. 1985. "La locaina en Venezuela y sus antecedentes en el Medio Oriente y en Europa." Montalbán 16: 71–104.

Poole, Deborah A. 1990. "Accommodation and Resistance in Andean Ritual Dance." Drama Review 34(2): 98–126.

Ponce, José Tomás. 1987. "El espacio geo-histórico de Barlovento." Anatema 1(1): 62–80.

Price, Richard. 1983. First-Time: The Historical Vision of an Afro-American People. Baltimore, Md.: Johns Hopkins University Press.

Price, Richard, and Sally Price. 1980. Afro-American Arts of the Surinam Rain Forest. Los Angeles: Museum of Cultural History, University of California, Los Angeles.

Proposiciones aprobadas. 1990. Proposiciones aprobadas en el encuentro de cultures populares: Oralidad, la palabra viva. Yaracuy.

Quintero, Rodolfo. 1976. La cultura nacional y popular. Caracas: Universidad Central de Venezuela.

———. 1985. La cultura del petróleo. Caracas: Universidad Central de Venezuela.

Radcliffe-Brown, A. R. 1965. Structure and Function in Primitive Society. New York: Free Press.

Rahier, Jean Muteba. 1999. Representations of Blackness and the Performance of Identities. Westport, Conn.: Bergin & Garvey.

Ramírez, Juan José. 1972. Remembranzas caicareñas. Caracas: "La Bodoniana."

———. 1985. Monagas y su saber tradicional. Maturín: Ediciones Gobernación del Estado Monagas.

———. 1986. Diccionario folklórico ilustrado. Maturín: Ediciones Gobernación del Estado Monagas.

———. 1988. "El Mono de Caicara: Una tradición monagüense que se pierde en el abismo del tiempo." Folklor Oriental, December: n.p.

Ramón y Rivera, Luis Felipe. 1951. "Tambores de San Juan." Revista del Estado Miranda 1(3): 14–17.

———. 1953. El Joropo, baile nacional de Venezuela. Caracas: Ediciones del Ministerio de Educación.

———. 1963a. "Cantos negros en la fiesta de San Juan." Boletín del Instituto de Folklore (Caracas) 4(3): 109–153.

———. 1963b. Música folkórica y popular en Venezuela. Caracas: Ministerio de Educación.

———. 1971. La música afrovenezolana. Caracas: Universidad Central de Venezuela.

Ramos, Julio. 1936. Los conuqueros. Caracas: Tipografía Americana.

Ramos, Nelly J. 1987. Traducciones de una experiencia. Caracas: Talleres de Cultura Popular de la Fundación Bigott.

Randall, Robert. 1982. "Qoyllur Rit'i: An Inca Fiesta of the Pleiades: Reflections on Time and Space in the Andean World." Bulletin de l'Institut Français Andines 11(1–2): 37–81.

Reyes Matta, Fernando. 1988. "The 'New Song' and Its Confrontation in Latin America." In Marxism and the Interpretation of Culture. Cary Nelson and Lawrence Grossberg, eds. Urbana: University of Illinois Press.

Rodríguez, Miguel A. 1991. "Public Sector Behavior in Venezuela." In The Public Sector and the Latin American Crisis. Felipe Larraín and Marcelo Selowsky, eds. San Francisco: ICS Press.

Rodríguez, Sylvia. 1991. "The Taos Pueblo Matachines: Ritual Symbolism and Interethnic Relations." American Ethnologist 18(2): 234–256.

———. 1996. The Matachines: Ritual Symbolism and Interethnic Relations in the Upper Río Grande Valley. Albuquerque: University of New Mexico Press.

Rodríguez Cárdenas, Manuel. 1966 [1956]. "Transformaciones del Tamunangue." El Nacional, September 30. Reprinted in La República, Supplement (Barquisimeto), Primer Festival Folklórico del Estado Lara, October 8–14, 1966: 13.

Rosenblatt, Roger. 1994. "How Do Tobacco Executives Live with Themselves?" New York Times Magazine, March 20: 34–41, 55, 73–76.

Rowe, William, and Vivian Schelling. 1991. Memory and Modernity: Popular Culture in Latin America. London: Verso.

Salas de Lecuna, Yolanda. 1985. "La inversión simbólica de lo sagrado y secular en las Locainas." Montalbán 16: 47–70.

Salazar, Rafael. N.d. Música y folklore de Venezuela. Caracas: Editorial Lisbona.

Sallnow, Michael J. 1987. Pilgrims of the Andes: National Cults in Cusco. Washington, D.C.: Smithsonian Institution Press.

Sanoja, Eduardo. 1984. Juego de garrote larense: El método venezolano de defensa personal. Caracas: Miguel Angel García e Hijo.

Sanoja, Eduardo, and Irene Zerpa. 1990. El garrote en nuestras letras. Caracas: Miguel Angel García e Hijo.

Schechner, Richard. 1985. Between Theater and Anthropology. Philadelphia: University of Pennsylvania Press.

———. 1988. Performance Theory. New York: Routledge.

———. 1993. The Future of Ritual: Writings on Culture and Performance. New York: Routledge.

Schiller, Herbert I. 1989. Culture Inc.: The Corporate Takeover of Public Expression. New York: Oxford University Press.

Schneider, Peter. 1997. "Whitened: Polished, Straightened, Made Flawless— Perfect Teeth for the Perfect Bite." New York Times Magazine, June 8: 45.

Seneviratne, H. L. 1977. "Politics and Pageantry: Universalisation of Ritual in Sri Lanka." Man (n.s.) 12(1): 65–75.

Servicio Omnibus. 1993. Medición, Marzo de 1993, Resumen de Resultados. Caracas: Fundación Bigott.

Silva Uzcátegui, Rafael Domingo. 1941. "El Tamunangue." El Universal, February 12.

———. 1966 [1956]. "Deformación del folklore nacional." El Universal, November. Reprinted in La República Supplement (Barquisimeto), Primer Festival Folklórico del Estado Lara, October 8–14, 1966: 13.

———. 1981 [1941]. Enciclopedia larense. 3d ed. Caracas: Biblioteca de Autores Larenses.

———. 1990 [1954]. "Raíces hispánicas del Tamunangue." Revista Elite 1.521. Reprinted in El Curarigüeño, June 1990, No. 15: 2.

Silverblatt, Irene. 1988. "Political Memories and Colonizing Symbols: Santiago and the Mountain Gods of Colonial Peru." In Rethinking History and Myth:

Indigenous South American Perspectives on the Past. Jonathan D. Hill, ed. Urbana: University of Illinois Press.

Silverman, Sydel. 1985. "Towards a Political Economy of Italian Competitive Festivals." Ethnologia Europaea 15(2): 95–103.

Singer, Milton. 1959. Traditional India: Structure and Change. Philadelphia: American Folklore Society.

———. 1972. When a Great Tradition Modernizes: An Anthropological Approach to Indian Civilization. New York: Praeger.

Siskind, Janet. 1992. "The Invention of Thanksgiving: A Ritual of American Nationality." Critique of Anthropology 12(2): 167–191.

Skidmore, Thomas E. 1974. White into Black: Race and Nationality in Brazilian Thought. New York: Oxford University Press.

Skurski, Julie. 1993. The Leader and the "People": Representing the Nation in Postcolonial Venezuela. Ph.D. diss., University of Chicago.

Sojo, Juan Pablo. 1943. Temas y apuntes afro-venezolanos. Caracas: Tipografía La Nación.

———. 1959a. "Biografía de la fiesta de San Juan en Venezuela." In El Estado Miranda: Su tierra y sus hombres. Caracas: Editorial Sucre.

———. 1959b. "José Larito: Negro que no quiso ser esclavo." In El Estado Miranda: Su tierra y sus hombres. Caracas: Editorial Sucre.

———. 1976 [1943]. Nochebuena negra. Los Teques: Biblioteca Popular Mirandina.

———. 1986. Estudios del folklore venezolano. Caracas: Biblioteca de Autores y Temas Mirandinos.

Sollors, Werner. 1989. "Introduction: The Invention of Ethnicity." In The Invention of Ethnicity. Werner Sollors, ed. New York: Oxford University Press.

Soto G., Alfredo. 1987. El Tamunangue. Barquisimeto: Fundatamunangue.

Stewart, John. 1986. "Patronage and Control in the Trinidad Carnival." In The Anthropology of Experience. Victor Turner and Edward M. Bruner, eds. Urbana: University of Illinois Press.

Stutzman, Ronald. 1981. "El Mestizaje: An All-Inclusive Ideology of Exclusion." In Cultural Transformations and Ethnicity in Modern Ecuador. Norman Whitten Jr., ed. Urbana: University of Illinois Press.

Sullivan, Lawrence E. 1986. "Sound and Senses: Toward a Hermeneutics of Performance." History of Religions 26(1): 1–33.

Tamayo, Francisco. 1945. Datos sobre el folklore de la región de El Tocuyo. In Monografía de El Tocuyo. Caracas: Central Tocuyo.

Tatum, Chuck. 1994. "From Sandino to Mafalda: Recent Works on Latin American Popular Culture." Latin American Research Review 29(1): 198–214.

Taussig, Michael. 1980. The Devil and Commodity Fetishism in South America. Chapel Hill: University of North Carolina Press.

———. 1987. Shamanism, Colonialism, and the Wild Man: A Study in Terror and Healing. Chicago: University of Chicago Press.

———. 1997. The Magic of the State. New York: Routledge.

Taylor, Julie M. 1982. "The Politics of Aesthetic Debate: The Case of Brazilian Carnival." Ethnology 21(4): 301–311.

———. 1988. "Carnival, Media, and Regional Traditions: Integration and Manipulation in Brazil." Studies in Latin American Popular Culture 7: 101–107.

Thompson, E. P. 1991. Customs in Common. New York: New Press.

Thornton, John K. 1998. The Kongolese Saint Anthony: Dona Beatriz Kimpa Vita and the Antonian Movement, 1684–1706. Cambridge, England: Cambridge University Press.

Thurston, Herbert, and Donald Attwater. 1956. Butler's Lives of the Saints. New York: P. J. Kenedy and Sons.

Toland, Judith D., ed. 1993. Ethnicity and the State. New Brunswick N.J.: Transaction Publishers.

Toplin, Robert Brent, ed. 1974. Slavery and Race Relations in Latin America. Westport, Conn.: Greenwood Press.

Troconis de Veracoechea, Ermila. 1984. Historia de El Tocuyo colonial. Caracas: Universidad Central de Venezuela.

Tucker, David. 1982. Tobacco: An International Perspective. London: Euromintor Publications.

Turner, Terence. 1991. "Representing, Resisting, Rethinking: Historical Transformations of Kayapo Culture and Anthropological Consciousness." In Colonial Situations: Essays on the Contextualization of Ethnographic Knowledge. George Stocking, ed. Madison: University of Wisconsin Press.

———. 1995. "An Indigenous People's Struggle for Socially Equitable and Ecologically Sustainable Production: The Kayapo Revolt against Extractivism." Journal of Latin American Anthropology 1(1): 98–121.

Turner, Victor. 1969. The Ritual Process: Structure and Anti-Structure. Ithaca, N.Y.: Cornell University Press.

———. 1974. Dramas, Fields, and Metaphors: Symbolic Action in Human Society. Ithaca, N.Y.: Cornell University Press.

———. 1975. "Symbolic Studies." Annual Review of Anthropology 4: 145–161.

———. 1982. From Ritual to Theatre: The Human Seriousness of Play. New York: PAJ Publications.

———. 1986. The Anthropology of Performance. New York: PAJ Publications.

Turner, Victor, and Edward M. Bruner, eds. 1986. The Anthropology of Experience. Urbana: University of Illinois Press.

Twine, France Winddance. 1997. Racism in a Racial Democracy: The Maintenance of White Supremacy in Brazil. New Brunswick, N.J.: Rutgers University Press.

Urban, Greg, and Joel Sherzer, eds. 1991. Nation-States and Indians in Latin America. Austin: University of Texas Press.

Urlin, Ethel L. 1971 [1915]. Festivals, Holy Days, and Saint's Days: A Study in Origins and Survivals in Church Ceremonies and Secular Customs. Ann Arbor, Mich.: Gryphon Books.

Uslar Pietri, Arturo. 1975. Baile de tambor. El Vigía: Ateneo "Dr. Alberto Adriani."

Van Young, Eric. 1994. "Conclusion: The State as Vampire—Hegemonic Projects, Public Ritual, and Popular Culture in Mexico, 1600–1990." In Rituals of Rule, Rituals of Resistance: Public Celebrations and Popular Culture in Mexico. William H. Beezley, Cheryl English Martin, and William E. French, eds. Wilmington, Del.: Scholarly Resources.

Vila, Marco Aurelio. 1978. Antecedentes coloniales de centros poblados de Venezuela. Caracas: Universidad Central de Venezuela.

Vilda, Carmelo. 1984. Proceso de la cultura en Venezuela, III (1935–1985). Caracas: Centro Gumilla.

Wade, Peter. 1993. Blackness and Race Mixture: The Dynamics of Racial Identity in Colombia. Baltimore, Md.: Johns Hopkins University Press.

———. 1995. "The Cultural Politics of Blackness in Colombia." American Ethnologist 22(2): 341–357.

Wagner, Roy. 1981. The Invention of Culture. Chicago: University of Chicago Press.

Walker, Sheila S. 1986. "The Feast of Good Death: An Afro-Catholic Emancipation Celebration in Brazil." Sage 3(2): 27–31.

Walkowski, Paul J., and William M. Connolly. 1996. From Trial Court to the United States Supreme Court, Anatomy of a Free Speech Case: The Incredible Inside Story behind the Historic Hurley v. G.L.I.B. First Amendment St. Patrick's Day Parade Case. Boston: Brandon Publishing.

Warman Gryj, Arturo. 1972. La danza de moros y cristianos. Mexico City: Sep/Setentas.

Watanabe, John M. 1990. "From Saints to Shibboleths: Image, Structure, and Identity in Maya Religious Syncretism." American Ethnologist 17(1): 131–150.

Watson, Rubie S., ed. 1994. Memory, History, and Opposition under State Socialism. Santa Fe, N.Mex.: School of American Research.

Weiss, Wendy. 1991. "Mestizaje as Metaphor." Paper presented at the 90th Annual Meeting of the American Anthropological Association, Chicago.

Whitten, Norman E., Jr. 1981. "Introduction." In Cultural Transformations and Ethnicity in Modern Ecuador. Norman E. Whitten Jr., ed. Urbana: University of Illinois Press.

Whitten, Norman E., Jr., and Arlene Torres. 1992. "Blackness in the Americas."
    NACLA, Report on the Americas 25(4): 16–22.
Whitten, Norman E., Jr., and Arlene Torres, eds. 1998. Blackness in Latin
    America and the Caribbean: Social Dynamics and Cultural Transformations,
    Vol. 1. Bloomington: Indiana University Press.
Wilcken, Lois E. 1992. "Staging Folklore in Haiti: Historical Perspectives." Pa-
    per presented at the Haiti in the Global Context Conference, Tufts Univer-
    sity, Medford, Mass.
Wilford, John Noble. 1990. "Anthropology Seen as Father of Maori Lore."
    New York Times, February 20: C1, C12.
Williams, Raymond. 1977. Marxism and Literature. Oxford: Oxford University
    Press.
———. 1980. Problems in Materialism and Culture. London: Verso.
Wilson, William A. 1976. Folklore and Nationalism in Modern Finland. Bloom-
    ington: Indiana University Press.
Wolff, Janet. 1984. The Social Production of Art. New York: New York Univer-
    sity Press.
Wood, Peter H. 1974. Black Majority: Negroes in Colonial South Carolina from
    1670 through the Stono Rebellion. New York: Knopf.
Wright, Winthrop R. 1974. "Elitist Attitudes toward Race in Twentieth-
    Century Venezuela." In Slavery and Race Relations in Latin America. Rob-
    ert Brent Toplin, ed. Westport, Conn.: Greenwood Press.
———. 1990. Café con leche: Race, Class, and National Image in Venezuela.
    Austin: University of Texas Press.
Yúdice, George. 1992. "Postmodernity and Transnational Capitalism in Latin
    America." In On Edge: The Crisis of Contemporary Latin American Cul-
    ture. George Yúdice, Jean Franco, and Juan Flores, eds. Minneapolis: Uni-
    versity of Minnesota Press.

Index

Abrahams, Roger D., 175n5
Acosta Saignes, Miguel, 153, 183n31
Adler, Judith, 195n18
advertising: ban on tobacco, 96, 192n3; of Bigott Foundation, 119 (fig. 18), 198n31; relationship between tobacco and, 192n4
Africa: as Dance of Monkey origin, 70–72, 188n16; as Fiesta de San Juan influence, 30, 32 (fig. 3), 33, 178nn6–7, 179n8; saints as disguised gods of, 151; as Tamunangue influence/origin, 145, 147, 148–53
Afro-Venezuelans: Fiesta de San Juan associated with, 28–33, 36, 46–51, 51 (fig. 6), 180n19; race vs. class as issue for, 58, 183n31; on Tamunangue origin, 147, 150, 152–53. *See also* Barlovento
Alma de Lara, 170, 171 (fig. 28)
American Tobacco, 94, 192n2
Anderson, Benedict, 184n1
Angleró, Roberto, 24
Anthony of Padua, Saint, 200n5. *See also* Antonio de Padua, San

Antigua, state-linked festival in, 13, 49
Antivero, Roberto, 194n13
Antonio de Padua, San, 133, 200n5; image of, and Tamunangue, 135, 142, 162; life of, 156, 202n23; Moors and, 154–55, 156; New World visit by, 160, 203n26; origin of Tamunangue and, 156–60, 157 (fig. 25), 203n24, 203n26; as patron saint of blacks in El Tocuyo, 151; race of, 152, 160
Appadurai, Arjun, 25, 92–93, 174n2
Aquino, Fulgencio, 121, 197n29
Aretz, Isabel, 148, 150; career of, 176n11, 201n17; on ciriaco origin, 188n16; on influences in Tamunangue, 153, 156, 201n16; study of Tamunangue by, 148, 150; term *Tamunangue* introduced by, 147, 148, 153
Argentina, Fiesta de San Juan in, 27
Augustine, Saint, 27, 30
authenticity, broadened definition of, 4
Ayiyivamos dance, in Tamunangue, 135–36, 152, 200n9, 206n36
Azpúrua, Carlos, 46, 180n18

Designer: Ina Clausen
Compositor: Binghamton Valley Composition
Text: 10/14 Palatino
Display: Snell Roundhand Script, Bauer
  Bodoni
Printer: Friesens
Binder: Friesens